sturg.

D1413474

THE ECONOMY OF CANADA

THE ECONOMY OF CANADA

A Study of Ownership and Control

by
Jorge Niosi

Translated by Penelope Williams

with the collaboration of
Hugh Ballem

BLACK ROSE BOOKS   Montréal

BLACK ROSE BOOKS No. H 40

Hardcover — ISBN: 0-919618-49-9
Paperback — ISBN: 0-919618-75-8

French-language edition published by Les Presses de l'Université de Québec, 1978.

Canadian Cataloguing in Publication Data
Nioso, Jorge E., 1945-
    The economy of Canada

Translation of Le contrôle financier du capitalisme canadien.
Bibliography: p
ISBN 0-919618-49-9 bd. ISBN 0-919618-75-8 pa.

1, Corporations — Canada — Finance. 2. Capitalists and financiers — Canada. 3. Canada — Industries.
I. Title.

HD2809.N5613   658.1'5'0971   C78-000050-1

Cover Design: Michael Carter

BLACK ROSE BOOKS LTD.
3981 boulevard Saint-Laurent
Montréal H2W 1Y5, Québec

Printed and bound in Québec, Canada

Contents

Contents

TO GRACIELA

"The banks grow unrelenting in power, and become the founders and finally the masters of industry, whose profits they reap as dividends of finance capital."

Rudolf Hilferding, *Le capital financier*, Paris, 1970, p. 319.

INTRODUCTION

THERE ARE FEW STUDIES of the question of control and concentration in large corporations in Canada. Certainly, the works of G. Rosenbluth,[1] Kari Levitt's *The Silent Surrender*[2] and the Gray Report on foreign direct investment in Canada[3] have thrown light on the extent of foreign control of large corporations in this country and the determination of the level of concentration in the Canadian economy. On the other hand, studies on the control of large Canadian-owned corporations are next to nonexistent. Where traces of interest are to be found, there are three outstanding streams of interpretation. First of all, according to the most popular Marxist interpretation, that of Libbie and Frank Park,[4] the chartered banks and other financial institutions hold control of non-financial Canadian corporations. Second, there is the theory of managerial control, often taught in schools of business administration and university faculties of commerce and finance. This position holds that it is professional managers, without ownership interest, who effectively hold power in joint-stock companies. Third, radical sociologists such as John Porter or Wallace Clement contend that the large Canadian corporations are under the control of an economic or corporate élite formed by the members of their boards of directors.[5]

The main objective of this study is to criticize these three current interpretations, using the most recent data from official and private sources. The data have been collected and are presented with this prime purpose in mind. The numerous official and private sources include the monthly Bulletins of the Ontario Securities Commission and the *Commission des Valeurs Mobilières du Québec*, which reveal the ownership of stock in public companies incorporated in Canada. To the author's knowledge, this present study represents the first thorough investigation of data from the provincial Securities Commission, which yield valuable information on the shares held by the administrators and senior managers of companies quoted on the Canadian stock exchanges. The series of *Directories* of the New York firm Moody's, Toronto's *Financial Post* Surveys and Statistics Canada's *Inter-Corporate Ownership* are sources concerned mainly with institutional inter-corporate ownership. The remainder of the empirical data upon which this study is based has been gathered from financial papers, official publications of Statistics Canada, Royal Commissions and Parliamentary Committees.

The second major goal of this research is to demonstrate the existence of a Canadian big bourgeoisie, to determine its inner composition and to analyze its means of controlling the large corporations. Although the "nationalist" school, in its broadest sense, has contributed to the analysis of foreign control in Canada, it has unfortunately neglected to study the indigenous ruling class. The terms "bourgeoisie" or "ruling class" are taken here to mean the social group that owns the means of production and distribution and employs salaried workers. In the industrialized capitalist countries, however, the means of production and distribution are, for all intents and purposes, owned by public or private joint-stock companies belonging to their various shareholders. Any serious study of the Canadian bourgeoisie must therefore begin by identifying the owners of the joint-stock companies and by determining the legal, social and financial mechanisms that enable them to hold on to the control of these companies and to pass it on from generation to generation.

Joint-stock companies are not, of course, all of equal importance. This study analyzes only the largest Canadian-controlled companies in the various sectors of the economy. In order to obtain a manageable list restricted to firms of an international scale, all companies with assets totalling less than $100 million by the end of 1975 have been excluded from this enquiry. The scope of this study is not that of the bourgeoisie as a whole, but of only one of its parts, its upper stratum, that which owns the biggest Canadian corporations. The term "big bourgeoisie" used to designate this group has been preferred to the concept of "financial oligarchy" dear to certain other students of the question in view of the latter's committment to the theory of finance capital criticized in the pages that follow.[6]

Also examined here are various financial and legal means of controlling companies, such as private or public holding companies. Control is understood basically as the ability to choose the board of directors (or a majority of its members) of a joint-stock company. This power is usually vested in individuals, groups of associates or families whose bloc of shares is big enough to enable them to impose their choice. It is crucial to distinguish *control* from *influence*, the latter meaning the ability to bring about changes in the long-term policy of a company concerning investments, mergers, diversification etc.) without being in a position of control over that company. Influence being naturally more elusive and difficult to measure than actual control, it too lies beyond the scope of this study.

The author believes that the twin objectives outlined above have been fulfilled. Yet, when one surveys the vast expanse that remains to be probed, they appear modest indeed. There is still much too little known about the means and degree of control of Canadian corporations

12

in the past, the successive waves of mergers (particularly the one that led to a complete reorganization of Canadian industry between 1925 and 1930) and Canadian multinationals abroad. Until these problems have been elucidated, it is impossible to understand fully the process of Canadian monopoly capital formation and the attendant production and reproduction of the Canadian ruling class.

Sincere thanks are owed to Philip Ehrensaft and Tom Naylor, who generously read through the whole original manuscript and offered helpful criticism. They in no way, of course, bear any responsibility for this book's eventual errors or omissions.

Montréal
June 1977

NOTES

(1) G. Rosenbuth: *Concentration in Canadian Manufacturing Industries*, Princeton University Press, 1957. "Concentration and Monopoly in the Canadian Economy," in M. Oliver (ed.): *Social Purpose for Canada*, University of Toronto Press, 1961. "The Relation Between Foreign Control and Concentration in Canadian Industry," in *Canadian Journal of Economics*, vol. 3, Feb. 1970, pp. 14-38.

(2) K. Levitt: *The Silent Surrender*, Macmillan of Canada, Toronto, 1970.

(3) "The Gray Report": *Foreign Direct Investment in Canada*, Information Canada, Ottawa, 1972.

(4) F. and L. Park: *Anatomy of Big Business* (1962), J. Lewis & Samuel, Toronto, 1973.

(5) J. Porter: *The Vertical Mosaic*, University of Toronto Press, Toronto, 1973. W. Clement: *The Canadian Corporate Elite*, McClelland & Stewart, Toronto, 1975.

(6) Among others: Lenin, *Imperialism, The Highest Stage of Capitalism*, in *Lenin: Selected Works*, International Publishers, New York, 1967.

J.-M. Chevalier, *La structure financière de l'industrie américaine*, Cujas, Paris, 1970.

CHAPTER I

FINANCE CAPITAL AND
THE CONTROL OF INDUSTRY

IN 1910, THE AUSTRIAN Marxist Rudolf Hilferding expounded his theory that industrial and commercial enterprises were becoming increasingly dependent on the banks. This was the theory of finance capital, and it was later adopted and partially modified by Lenin and other Marxist scholars in several countries who were convinced they had detected the dominance of banking over industry in each national state, no matter how specific that reality might be. Some Marxists however, notably Baran, Sweezy, Magdoff and O'Connor, have criticized the finance-capital theory at least in the context of the United States. More recently still, other Marxists such as Menshikov and J.-M. Chevalier have advanced evidence in support of a new theory of financial control over industry. The first part of this study will be devoted to outlining the major thrusts in the development of the theoretical debate among Marxists on this question in order to establish the appropriate historical framework. The second section will review what little has been written on this subject by Canadian authors as an introduction to the main body of this work: the formulation of our own hypotheses on finance capital in Canada and the presentation of the supporting evidence. Our central thesis is that financial institutions exert very little control over Canadian industry, and that the hold of the banks over productive enterprises is weak. In other words, it is our view that the theory of finance capital is largely inapplicable in any of its forms to Canadian economic realities and that the control of the country's non-financial institutions lies, with few exceptions, outside the financial institutions.

Hilferding and Lenin on the Control of Banks Over Industry

The major argument of Hilferding's famous *Finance Capital* is that banks have an increasing tendency to control joint stock companies due to their dominant role in the capital and money markets. In the first place, it is the banks' financing of company stock and bond issues that enables them to gain control over the corporations. There is no doubt that, as intermediaries in the marketing of stocks, the banks are in a position to retain control of a bloc of voting shares and thereby of the corporations themselves—all the more so since such a company can be controlled, as Hilferding pointed out, with as little as a third, a quarter or even less of the total stock.

This means of gaining control over industry can be implemented either at the time of the foundation or the merger of several enterprises, or when capitalization takes the form of a fresh stock issue. But banks can also act by repeatedly extending commercial credit to a corporation, thus becoming a creditor with an ever-greater stake in the fate of its borrowers and familiarity with their administrative and financial evolution:

> "It is the transferability and negociability of shares that is the very essence of the joint-stock company. This gives the banks the opportunity of 'founding' them, and, through their role as founders, of gaining ultimate control."[1] "But a bank may not only extend more credit to a joint-stock company than to an individual enterprise. It may also invest some of its own capital in shares for a more or less extended period of time. One way or the other, the bank acquires a lasting interest in the stock company, that it must on the one hand control if it wants to see its credit used properly and on the other dominate as much as possible in order to ensure that all possible profit-making financial transactions are made. This explains why the banks go to such pains to carry out constant surveillance on the companies they have interests in through securing representatives on the latters' boards of directors."[2]

The banks provide a powerful impetus toward concentration as they develop an interest in the profits to be reaped in the fresh stock issue that accompanies each merger. The banks secure some of the shares of the newly-merged companies (founder's shares) and thus acquire the right to representation on their boards of directors.

Hilferding describes the growing subordination of commercial to industrial capital and ultimately to banking capital in these terms:

> "The development of commercial capital is altogether different. The rise of industry slowly but surely pushes it out of the dominant position it occupied during the early era of manufacture. This set-back has been decisive, and the development of finance capital has reduced commerce both absolutely and relatively and transformed the once haughty merchant into a mere agent of industry, now monopolized by finance capital."[3]

Hilferding's position, then, is that industrial capital falls prey to finance capital through the financing of stock issues, through commercial loans and through the reorganization (mergers) of industry. He also notes the gradual subordination of commercial to industrial capital.

This is, in essence, the theory of finance capital put forward by Lenin. It is true that his *Notebooks on Imperialism* and his preface to *Imperialism* are critical of Hilferding's theories on money (in particular his quantitative theory of money) and of some of the Austrian Marxist's ideas about imperialism and the partition of the world by the imperialist powers, but he did not question Hilferding's definition of finance capital as such. [4]

> "When a bank discounts a bill for a firm, opens a current account for it, etc., these operations, taken separately, do not in the least diminish its independence, and the bank plays no other part than that of a modest middleman. But when such operations are multiplied and become an established practice, when the bank 'collects' in its own hands enormous amounts of capital, when the running of a current account for a given firm enables the bank—and this is what happens—to obtain fuller and more detailed information about the economic position of its client, the result is that the industrial capitalist becomes more completely dependent on the bank." [5]
>
> "Finance capital, concentrated in a few hands and exercising a virtual monopoly, exacts enormous and ever-increasing profits from the floating of companies, issue of stocks, state loans, etc., thereby strengthening the domination of the financial oligarchy. . ." [6]

In the same work, however, Lenin uses terms that are vaguer and less categorical than those of Hilferding. He thus defines finance capital as the "merger," the "interpenetration" or the "interdependence" of banking and industry, without assigning a dominant role to one or the other.

Within Marxist literature there exist two kinds of definitions of finance capital, one in terms of "bank control" and the other in terms of the merging of banks and industry. They are sometimes clearly distinguished from each other and sometimes used coterminously. This is exemplified by the different treatment given to them in two of the major Marxist works on the United States. Anna Rochester refers to interpenetration and not to bank control when she defines finance capital:

> "Bankers acquire industrial interests. Industrial corporations acquire banking interests. A new type of financier emerges who functions in both fields and represents the 'finance capital' (as distinct from banking capital) which is characteristic of monopoly capitalism and the imperialist era. Such a fusion of banking and industrial capital was first recognized as the dominant feature of American economic life during the crisis and the depression of 1893-97 and the boom years that followed the Spanish-American War of 1898." [7]

On the other hand, we have Victor Perlo who does not make the distinction, and combines both definitions into one:

"Finance capital, the result of the merger of the monopolies with the monopoly bankers and industrialists, gives rise to supermonopolies that dominate even the biggest industrial conglomerates."[8]

It is not necessary to dwell upon the innumerable ways in which the Leninist interpretation of finance capital has been propounded, for they can all be traced back to the ambiguous position Lenin expressed in *Imperialism*.

Baran, Sweezy, Magdoff: Finance Capital as a Transitional Phase

Paul Baran, Paul Sweezy and Harry Magdoff represent a total departure from this tradition. They point to the decline of bank control over industrial companies in the United States. Their first step is to distinguish, within the American financial system, between the commercial banks which extend short-term credit to industry and the investment banks involved in financing stock issues. It would appear the commercial and the investment banks, not legally separated until 1933, had already begun to lose ground in the control of industry at the end of the First World War.

The big corporations succeeded in freeing themselves from the grip of banking capital in the following manner: (a) they developed their own working capital to finance current operations; (b) they restricted stock and bond issues and financed long-term investment from undistributed profits; (c) the big corporations have grown to become several times larger than the investment banks and are now comparable to the largest commercial banks in size; (d) the growth of institutional investors (insurance companies, mutual funds, closed-end and fixed capital investment companies, public pension funds, etc.) which are not interested in controlling corporations, enables the large corporations to market their securities without resorting to investment banks; these institutional investors seem to be more interested in the rate of return on their shares than in using them to control industrial companies, and even when they are big share-holders, they do not insist on having "their man" on the corporate boards.[9] Lastly, these authors agree that the legal separation between commercial and investment banks brought about by the Glass-Seagall Act in 1933 dealt a fatal blow to the reign of the banks over American industry.

Baran, Sweezy and Magdoff go even farther; they claim that the financial alignment of "interest groups," those conglomerate entities made up of several parent companies and one or more subsidiaries, no longer exists in the United States. In his classic 1939 study for the *Temporary National Economic Commission* (T.N.E.C.) of the United

States, Sweezy identified eight major American financial groups: the Rockefeller, Morgan, Mellon, Kuhn, Loeb, Chicago, Cleveland, Boston and Du Pont groups. In 1936, Anna Rochester found the big league to consist of a triumvirate (Rockefeller, Mellon and Morgan), followed by seven juniors (*Kuhn, Loeb, and Co., Lee, Higginson and Co., Kidder Peabody and Co., Brown Bros. Harriman and Co., Hayden Stone and Co., Lehman Bros.* and *Goldman Sachs and Co.*).[10] In 1960, Perlo, who may have been influenced by the T.N.E.C. study, identified the same eight financial groups as Sweezy had done in 1939.[11]

As for Jean-Marie Chevalier, his analysis of the data available in 1965-66 singles out six big American groups—the Rockefellers, Morgan, Mellon, Cleveland, the Manufacturers Hannover Trust and the Chemical Bank.[12] In all of the cases just cited, the delimiting criteria were the interlocking directorships, the ownership of shares and operational integration. These are not entirely satisfactory criteria, given the way common subsidiaries, minority control and the low-value criterion of administrative exchange tend to blur the boundaries between the groups. Baran and Sweezy nevertheless asserted in 1966 that interest groups had all but disappeared:

> "We are not of course maintaining that interest groups have disappeared or are no longer of any importance in the United States economy. We do hold that they are of rapidly diminishing importance and that an appropriate model of the economy no longer needs to take account of them."[13]

Having previously attacked the validity of the "strongest" version of the finance capital theory (namely, bank control over industry), Baran and Sweezy now reject even the "mild" view, that of the interpenetration or fusion of banking and industrial capital.

Chevalier and Menshikov, or Finance Capital Revisited

Jean-Marie Chevalier [14] argues that American financial institutions, with the exception of the commercial banks, play no role in the control of industry. He sees the investment banks, insurance companies, investment companies and brokerage houses as mere investors who by and sell shares solely on the basis of their rate of return and their standing on the stock exchange. If an industrial corporation in which they hold shares is performing badly, they prefer to sell their shares rather than try to influence or control company management. The commercial banks, on the other hand, have trust departments—which serve to administer pension funds—where they accumulate large blocs of corporate shares, so large in fact that they begin having trouble in divesting themselves of them. In 1965 American commercial banks held shares totalling $110 billion, representing 18% of the total value of all shares issued in the United States. This percentage has continued to rise from year to year.[15] By including bank short-term financing of industrial enterprises (which remains considerable) and the directors' network of personal ties, Chevalier musters significant evidence in support of a theory of bank control that is no longer that of Hilferding. Instead of the power base of the banks coming from stock issues or the founding of companies, it now comes from the accumulation of stocks in trust departments, especially pension-fund trusts. This accumulation is such that it prevents the banks from behaving as mere investors and practically forces them to try first to influence and then to control the companies in which they hold shares. According to Chevalier, this phenomenon can be traced back to the post-World War II period, after which it grew to such an extent that the banks regained their dominant position in the American economy.

The Russian economist Menshikov[16] suggests that the growth of self-financing (and the consequent wane of external financing) prevailed for only a few years between the First and Second World Wars, and that corporations are once again as dependent on credit from banks as they were before. He does admit, however, that absolute majority control (whether it be by families or by financial institutions) has given way to widespread minority control. At the same time, the financial groups no longer have the well-defined boundaries they had at the turn of the century. Joint control of corporations by several groups has become common, and the accumulation of shares by commercial banks gives them latent power:

> "Superficially it looks as though there is no outside control or that control is exerted by a group of top executives. Most of the arguments of the 'managerial revolution' theory are based on the latter illusion. . . But if the banks own or administer a considerable block of stock, the machinery of voting by proxy remains an effective means of control by top executives only in alliance with the banks or if the latter maintain a favorable neutrality. In such cases joint control by top managers and the bankers is in evidence, with the latter frequently having decisive say. . . Since the blocks of stock concentrated in their trust departments are sufficiently large, they are always a threat to the top management of corporations."[17]

Menshikov therefore agrees in several respects with Chevalier, but qualifies the theory of finance capital by clarifying the mechanisms of bank control and by arguing that it is possible that at least part of corporate control has passed into the hands of senior management.

Whereas Chevalier and Menshikov simply state that the spectacular growth of pension funds converted into stock could eventually produce a new form of bank control, R. Fitch and M. Oppenheimer[18] content that this has already begun to happen. They conclude, on the basis of the *Putnam Report* on the share-holdings of American commercial banks, that the come-back of finance capital is already a fact in the United States. From this assumption, they draw some rather imaginative conclusions about the consequences of this control over big corporations: slowing of the growth of companies subordinated to finance capital, bad management of the new comglomerates, which are seen as financial dinosaurs bound to serve the short-term profit motive of the banks. In other words, they foresee a new wave of speculative mergers similar to those of 1896 to 1905 and 1925 to 1930, this time led by the commercial banks and to their advantage (rather than, as before, the investment banks). Sweezy and O'Connor[19] easily dispose of this argument by demonstrating that the big corporations, supposedly subservient to finance capital, are growing faster than the others, that their profit-orientation is basically the same no matter what the size, and that the new conglomerates are apparently doing quite well for themselves. Sweezy and O'Connor do not attach any particular importance to the accumulation of shares in the trust departments of American commercial banks, since in their view share-holding is not a proof of control; in fact, they go so far as to argue that big corporations act independently of such control, their market performance remaining a matter of capitalist logic regardless of who holds formal control. An argument of this sort obviously makes the question of corporate control trivial from the scientific point of view, and Fitch exploits this when he counters that Sweezy and O'Connor are too quick to believe in the rationality of the big corporations and conglomerates and to place all the anomalies of capitalism at the level of the system as a whole, i.e. in the realm of macro-economics.[20] Yet Fitch and Oppenheimer do not succeed in proving that finance capital does control American industry, any more than Sweezy and O'Connor succeed in demonstrating the contrary.

Finally, in his critique of the new theory of bank control, Edward S. Herman gives a series of reasons why the trust departments of the commercial banks cannot be used by bankers to seize control of companies:

"One negative factor has to do with bank organization: in the larger banks, trust departments are separate bureaucracies whose function is managing and servicing trust accounts and other investor clients. These bureaucracies are competing with other professional investing groups (like investment counselling firms), and they are under strong competitive and moral pressure to adhere to professional performance standards" (. . .) "This bureaucratic factor is closely related to a second major constraint on bank investment for control: the pressures from clients who have placed their funds with the bank to be managed. (. . .) Any bank whose investment policy was dominated by a desire for control would probably do badly as an investment performer, and would soon lose trust department (and other) business in consequence. (. . .)"
"A third major constraint on bank use of trust department resources for purposes of control is the law. Bank control over corporate customers by means of stock ownership would probably be barred under the antitrust laws as an illegal form of vertical integration." (. . .)
"A fourth constraint on bank quest for control is the fact, mentioned earlier, that the management groups controlling corporations would not relish being displaced, or even sharing control, with the external interests."[21]

Herman points out that the proponents of the bank control theory have been unable to supply evidence of the displacement of already established boards of directors by bankers, and that the percentages of shares held by the banks plus one or two administrators is a sign of bank-management co-operation rather than bank control.

The Marxist Theory in Historical Perspective

In the preceding section we briefly reviewed some of the major contributions to the Marxist theory of finance capital and indicated a number of points under debate. We shall now attempt to explain the differences that have arisen in the light of the national and historical conditions to which the various theories refer. The pioneer in this area was Jean Bouvier, a French historian of banking.[22] Bouvier distinguishes two models: on the one hand, "the continental model of bank-industry relationship", which he ascribes to Germany, Austria, Belgium, Czarist Russia, Italy and most European countries, centered around large multi-functional banks acting simultaneously as investment banks, commercial banks, investment houses, etc.; and, on the other, the highly specialized banking and financial system that prevailed in Britain. Bouvier sees the French banking system as an intermediate form, with its savings (or commercial) banks and business (or industrial) banks.

> "Hilferding's analytical model corresponds remarkably well to the structures of German and Austrian capitalism in his time and more generally with the 'continental' model of bank-industry relationships as they can be ascertained in Belgium. Italy, Russia and elsewhere. . . This is less true for the English and French systems in which finance capital remains much less centralized."[23]

Seen in this light, the theory of Hilferding and Lenin acquires a historical perspective that is well worthy of further investigation. Bouvier's insight also renders explicit some of the problems inherent in the classical model of finance capital: the difficulties encountered in the measurement of both the extent of control and the boundaries of the financial groups, the vagueness of the notion of "fusion," the often-noted phenomenon of large industrial firms that are independent of such groups, and the take-over of banks and other financial institutions by industrial concerns.

Unfortunately, Bouvier's contribution goes no further than opening the door to a critical review of the Marxist theory of finance capital. As a specialist of the French banking system, he does not deal at all with the British and American financial systems, and these are crucial to the understanding of "finance capital" in Canada. Moreover, Bouvier analyses only the classic Hilferding-Lenin version of the Marxist theory of finance capital. This remains, of course, a necessary step before the question of Canadian "finance capital" can be meaningfully discussed.

It is not hard to believe that Hilferding and Lenin based their theory on their understanding of the "continental model" of bank-industry relationships, since nearly all of their examples are taken from German, Austrian and Russian sources. Industry, born late in these countries, found itself in a weak and dependent position in respect to the already imposing multi-functional banks that had risen to prominence through the financing of public expenditures, credit operations related to foreign trade and currency exchange at a time when industrialization was barely underway. It should be pointed out that neither Hilferding nor Lenin consider different types of banks and that they hold investment transactions just as responsible for industry's dependence on the banks as commercial credit. This is a clear indication that they were unfamiliar with the situation in Britain, France or the United States where several different types of banks were active. It was not uncommon in Germany to find the big banks behind both the founding of new industrial concerns and the merger of previously independent firms. Their combined status of savings and business banks offered numerous means of influencing companies and gaining control of them.[24] In fact, the German Credit banks epitomize the kind of bank that controls industry through commercial credit, the founding of new firms and the fusion of existing ones, the long-term accumulation of portfolio shares, and so on.

The "continental model" was also in evidence in Belgium with the foundation in 1822 of a mixed savings and investment bank—the *Société Générale de Belgique*—that was very active in industry and trade. In France, the *Crédits mobiliers* of the Péreire brothers (from 1852 to 1867) and the business banks from the 1860's on were strikingly close to the Hilferding-Lenin finance capital model. As for Russia and Italy, the establishment of the "continental" banking system was largely a result of the penetration of French and German business banks: in 1914, the largest mixed chartered banks in Russia were controlled either by French (the Russian-Asiatic, Union Moscow, St. Petersburg Private and Russo-French banks) or German (Russian Foreign Trade, International, Warsaw Commercial and St. Petersburg Loan and Discount) interests. In Italy, German banks set up two big business banks—the *Banca Commerciale Italiana* and the *Credito Italiano*—during the 1896-1914 wave of industrialization. In both countries, the leaders in industrial promotion and credit were "imported" business banks. It is worth mentioning that an equally high degree of fusion of banking and industry took place in Japan after the Meiji Restoration, although the Japanese banks did not acquire as dominant a position as in the other cases.[25]

In studying the kind of country that gave rise to a "continental" type of banking system, it is tempting to agree at least in part with Gerschenkron,[26] who argues that late industrialization, coupled with an inadequate capital market and the forced adoption of large-scale techniques, led in all likelihood to a high degree of coordination between the banks and industry, so high in some cases that it would be more accurate to speak of outright bank control. *The "continental" model appears to have been a characteristic of late capitalist industrialization.*

In contrast to the "continental" model, the British financial system is extremely diversified with many types of banks, none of which is particularly interested in the control of industry. "Joint-stock banks" (or commercial banks such as Lloyd's Bank) or investment banks such as Baring Bros., were more interested in colonial and world finance than in the development of British industry; they were even less concerned with industrial control. The "country banks" or local banks, which had contributed to the financing of industry in the 18th and 19th centuries, were not big enough to take part in the control of manufacturing organizations. According to two authorities on the subject:

> "British banking consists in banking alone. It considers its duty to be finance only and does not care to enter into industry itself. An English banker would consider it absolutely unsound for him to take part in the development of a country or business, except as the financier. He believes that a banker should never be a partner and that when once the money has been supplied to a borrower, it is up to him to make his own use of it. [27] "The German banking system has been held up as an example of what complete cooperation between investment houses and industry will accomplish, but British banks have not followed suit. They are more conservative and prefer to exercise their banking functions in as narrow a field as possible. . . Their interests are financial and will probably remain so."[28]
>
> "Another characteristic is the complete absence of anything that can be described as industrial banking. Industry and the banks are independent of each other and in this way they differ from most other countries. The banks are merely lending institutions; they do not participate in business or exercise any control over it, except when their loans are threatened."[29]

For Nash and Grant, the reason for the disinterest of British banks in industry was their highly attractive position at the center of world trade and finance. This non-involvement of the commercial banks and investment houses in industrial credit and the securities of industrial companies, is the ultimate explanation of the separation of banking and industry in Great Britain and the absence of anything that could be termed finance capital at least up until the Second World War.

Hilferding and Lenin elaborated their theory as observers of continental European capitalism at the turn of the century. Baran and Sweezy, on the other hand, were students of the evolution of *American* capitalism over a much longer period of time. As in France, so too in the United States there was a progressive differentiation of two kinds of banks throughout the second half of the 19th century: (a) American commercial banks, organized as stock companies and far removed from the control of industry, took in public savings deposits and specialized in short-term credit; (b) the investment banks, organized as partnerships, operated with their own capital and that of a few large accounts of wealthy individuals or companies and specialized in industrial reorganization and government and company bond and stock issues. *J.P. Morgan and Co.* was the biggest and most characteristic of the latter type.[30] These private investment banks played a key role in the reorganization of the American railway system as well as in the two big waves of industrial mergers that took place from 1896 to 1905 and from 1923 to 1930. At the beginning of the First World War investment bankers headed up a large number of financial groups in transportation, public utilities, manufacturing and mining. The Morgan group, for example, reigned in large part over the American steel industry (*U.S. Steel Corp.*), the production of electricity (the *United Corp.* was a holding company founded by Morgan along with two other investment banks, *Bonbright and Co.* and *Drexel*, in 1929) and the railways system (Morgan controlled the *New York Central Systen*).[31] The decline of the investment banks, and with them of finance control over American industry, was a phenomenon of the 1930's resulting from a whole series of autonomous developments within American capitalism. With the growth in the 1920's of institutional investors, in particular investment trusts and insurance companies, corporations were often able to avoid resorting to the investment banks in order to market their securities. There was also the enactment of the *Glass-Seagall Act* in 1933, the outcome of a campaign by various sectors of business against the overbearing power of the investment bankers, which forced the separation of the savings banks and the investment banks. The struggle had been a protracted one, starting with the Pujo Inquiry for the House of Representatives (1913) in which the "money trusts" were denounced, and continuing with various State laws regulating stock issues, the Senate Gray-Pecora Inquiry (1932-34) that disclosed many of the practices of the investment bankers, the *Securities Act* (1933) and the *Securities Exchange Act* (1934) that made the registration of securities and public announcements by the issuing companies mandatory. As a result of all of these legal measures and the other inquiries and laws that followed in the 1930's and '40's, many bankers were forced to give up the positions they had held in the administrations of industrial companies.[32]

Chevalier and Menshikov, however, are concerned with an even more recent era of American capitalism. In studying the phenomena that have been gradually emerging since the Fifties but have only taken on significant proportions over the last ten years, they are positing a form of financial control held by the commercial banks rather than by the investment banks. They're talking about *potential* control, not *actual* control, and use the more subtle term of *influence* to describe the present situation. Both consider that the tendency for shares to accumulate in commercial banks' trust departments can only result in an increasing control by these banks over industrial firms in some far-distant future, an opinion long shared by some non-Marxist experts. D.J. Baum and N.B. Stiles[33] also foresee a growing influence of the commercial banks over industrial firms in the long term, and add that investment companies and life insurance companies will be involved. In their response to Berle and Means, for whom institutional investors do not use the voting power they possess and remain aloof from the procuration race, Baum and Stiles argue that blocks of shares of the size held by the commercial banks cannot be easily resold. Moreover, institutional investors deal in the best shares, the ones that are the most difficult to find on the market. In this way, the commercial banks, investment companies and insurance companies are forced to get involved in the management of the corporations in which they hold shares, and can no longer behave as simple investors.

Whatever the case may be in the United States, it is clear that the Marxist theory of finance capital has suffered from quick generalizations, which have disregarded international differences and the changes of bank-industry relationships over time. No study of financial control of a country's industry can be seriously carried out without a prior, thorough investigation of the existing banking and financial systems. Nor may one overlook other possible forms of control, such as family control, control by groups of capitalists or, finally, internal control by the firm's own senior management. In this sense, the studies of Chevalier on the United States and F. Morin on France[34] are useful models for any analysis of the control of large corporations in Canada. Finally, as both J. O'Connor[35] and Bouvier[36] have cautioned, the Marxist theory of finance capital is plagued with too many ambiguities to be used uncritically as an analytical tool.

Finance Capital in Studies on Canada

The scarcity of Canadian studies on the financial control of industry has perhaps one meager advantage: discussing them is largely a matter of running through the list of authors who have addressed this question.

Libbie and Frank Park[37] support the classic Hilferding-Lenin conception of finance capital, adding however the other major financial institutions to their explanation of the mechanisms of corporate control:

> "It is through the control of financial institutions that the financial groups maintain their control of the wealth-producing companies. . . At the center of this financial and industrial corporate structure lie the chartered banks. . . Linked to the banks are trust companies, the life insurance companies, the loan and mortgage companies, the investments trusts, all in control of vast assets and contributing to the ability of the financial oligarchy to control the economy of the country."[38]

Park and Park are clearly leading up to a theory of finance control over industry exerted by several kinds of financial institutions, as is evidenced in the following quotations:

25

"The holdings of the banks in securities are large and are growing."[39]
"The large amounts of common stocks among the securities held under administration by the trust companies have of course voting rights and these rights are exercised by the trust companies"[40] "The life insurance companies receive in premiums billions of dollars to be invested on the decisions of their directors (as limited by law) in stocks and bonds and mortgages. . .; their stock holdings give them influence on the policy of the corporations."[41] "In theory the investment trust has nothing to do with control of the enterprises in which it invests its money. . . The distinction between the investment trust and the holding company is one of degree; the influence of the investment trust is less direct than that of the holding company but it is also vital to the question of control."[42]

This is nothing less than a broadened but essentially orthodox version of Hilferding's original finance capital model. Nevertheless, even though they contend that it is the ownership of stock in industrial companies and the appointment of directors to their boards that give financial institutions their power of control, the Parks argue that:

"The point is not of course whether the banks dominate industry or industry the banks; it is that the same group of finance capitalists control both."[43]

This latter statement brings us right back to the "fusion of banking and industry" view. If Park and Park hesitate over the type of finance control they find in Canadian capitalism, it is because they have not examined the stock distribution of the large corporations nor the securities portfolios of the banks and financial institutions. Their study came out in 1962, before the most systematic sources of the federal or provincial governments on stock ownership (*Inter-Corporate Ownership*, the *Bulletins* of the Ontario Securities Commission and the *Commission des valeurs mobilières du Québec*, respectively) began to be published. It would have been possible, albeit extremely tedious and consuming, to obtain the appropriate information on stock ownership from newspapers, financial directories, book reviews and monographes on the financial institutions and big industrial corporations. In the absence of such data, the only apparent uniting factor in the financial groupings that the Parks discovered was interlocking directorships, rather weak evidence when it is impossible to match the directorates with actual corporate ownership. Furthermore, it is not surprising that the Parks' only convincing example, complete with details on stock ownership, is that of *Argus Corp.* (see chapter V); *Argus* is a holding company, one of the few cases of direct control over industrial firms by a financial institutions in Canada. Had Park and Park looked into the stock distribution of non-financial firms, they would have discovered, in fact, that chartered banks hold little stock, that they have always made a policy of abstaining from long-term investment in corporate stock, and that in Canada investment and insurance companies operate, with a few exceptions (like *Argus Corp.* and *Power Corp.*), as simple investors that do not delegate directors to the boards of the companies in which they hold shares. Park and Park are wrong to conclude that there is financial control over industry from their observation of a group of directors common to institutions in both sectors: in fact, the Canadian directors of Canadian banks can be found as much on the boards of local industrial firms as on those of American subsidiaries. We shall also see further on that there are not infrequent cases of companies controlled more than 50% by other companies which have only one or two directors in common. Moreover, the Parks' failure to analyse the pertinent legislation has led them to neglect certain forms of control and to formulate erroneous hypotheses, since both interlocking directorships and shareholding on the part of financial institutions are subject to laws and regulations that have a certain effect on the contours of the "financial groups" identified by one or the other criterion, or both. Even so, Park and Park are not completely wrong in claiming that the same group of finance capitalists control both industry and finance. The fact is that Canadian capitalists control (and have always controlled) a part of both sectors, although American penetration is slowly but surely cutting into their share.

It is to Tom Naylor [44] that we owe the historical background crucial to any understanding of the role of Canadian financial institutions in the control of industry or, more precisely, their inactivity as finance capitalists in the established sense. Naylor shows how and why the Canadian chartered banks followed the example of the British joint-stock banks in dealing exclusively in commercial credit. He recalls the colonial and mercantile nature of the Canadian Dominion and its bourgeoisie, the latter being mainly involved in financing the extraction, transport and exchange of raw materials and staples on behalf of first Great Britain and then the United States. This is why Canadian chartered banks did not participate in the financing of industry, were not involved in the founding of companies nor their fusion or reorganization, and do not carry out long-term investment in industrial firms. Canadian banks are therefore specialized in a way similar to the French savings banks, but the Canadian financial system has never had its French-style business banks (like the *Banque de Paris et des Pays-Bas*) nor the business banks such as *J.P. Morgan and Co.* that can be found in the United States. Naylor also shows that the insurance companies, mortgage and loan companies and other financial institutions, second in importance to the chartered banks at the time, did not make up for the chronic shortage of industrial credit resulting from the purely commercial orientation of the chartered banks. [45]

Naylor's work has, of course, its limitations. It deals only with the period extending from Confederation to 1914, to the exclusion of those financial institutions—the fixed-capital investment companies (the holding companies in particular), the brokerage houses, the trust companies and the newcomers to the insurance sector—that developed in the 20th century. Nor was Naylor interested in the debate over the financial control of industry to study the question in any depth. Still, the gist of his analysis is that the industrial dependence of Canada is linked to the commercial orientation of the chartered banks, from which we can reasonably conclude that the disinterest of Canadian financial institutions in national industry also prevented them from playing a major role in industrial control, both before and after the First World War.

Is there a Finance Control of Canadian Industry?

The Canadian financial system has undergone considerable changes over the last 60 years. The chartered banks were the dominant institutions from Confederation up until the First World War, holding three-quarters of all assets of all Canadian financial intermediaries in 1870 and no less than 56% in 1914.[46] In second place behind the chartered banks were the mortgage and loan companies and the insurance companies, with 9.6% and 2.4% of all Canadian financial assets in 1870 and 10.6% and 14.0% in 1914, respectively.[47] None of these institutions, as Naylor has shown, were particularly interested in industrial credit, thereby disqualifying themselves from the race for the control of industry. The turn of the century was to usher in important changes for the financial configuration that had accompanied Confederation. The trust companies, many of which had formed during the last two decades of the 19th century, progressed to 2.6% of Canadian financial intermediary assets in 1914, to 4.4% in 1930, and to 5.0% in 1970. Stock-market speculation and growing Canadian public interest in stocks thrust the fixed-capital investment companies in less than 10 years up to a heady 3.2% in 1929; after the Depression the open-ended investment companies accounted for most of the growth of this sector that held more than 4.0% of the assets of the Canadian financial system in 1970. As these new intermediaries were growing, the chartered banks were continuing to lose ground. In 1929 they represented no more than 49% of the financial system's assets, a figure that had shrunk to only 28% by 1970. While the mortgage and loan companies also slid from 5% in 1929 to 3% in 1970, the life insurance companies succeeded in staying in second place just behind the chartered banks, in spite of their share of assets shrinking from 23% in 1929 to 14% in 1970.

For the purposes of this study of financial control in Canadian industry, we have selected those institutions that have at least the *potential* of playing an important role in this regard by investing massively and regularly in corporate shares. This means chartered banks, trust companies, investment companies, life insurance companies and investment banks.

Our thesis is that the theory of bank or finance control is inapplicable to the Canadian context, for two inter-related reasons. The first is the almost exclusive and highly conservative orientation of the Canadian financial system toward commerce, as opposed to industrial credit and industrial control. This characteristic, to which Naylor rightly ascribed British ancestry, is also true of the new institutions that have appeared since the end of the 19th century, with the sole exception of the investment companies of the holding type, directly borrowed from the American financial system. The second reason is the high level of foreign, above all American, control of manufacturing and mining. In this respect Canada's case is not unique. Canada follows the rule of all of those countries that entered the industrial stage of capitalism late and saw their manufacturing industries developed by foreign investment, with industrial subsidiaries being controlled from outside and the local bourgeoisie confined to the most traditional spheres of capitalist activity. This is the case of countries like Argentina and Brazil, where the strongholds of the local bourgeoisie—agriculture, stock breeding, commerce and finance—are sectors it already controlled before direct foreign investment started pouring into manufacturing. The local industrial bourgeoisie is almost always weak and limited to the most traditional branches, like the manufacturing of clothing and footwear, food, textiles, etc. This is also the general situation in Canada, a few industrial branches such as farm machinery and steel notwithstanding. It is not, however, our intention with this book to add to the already impressive body of literature on foreign control of Canadian industry.[48]

The Chartered Banks

In spite of the fact that they have never played a role in industrial credit or sought control of industry, and that there is a general tendency toward a decline of their relative importance, these banks remain, by their size and economic concentration, in the forefront of Canadian finance.

The percentage of corporate shares, which has never been significant in Canadian bank portfolios, is continuing to diminish. From the very outset the overwhelming majority of bank assets has been made up of commercial loans and call loans. Industrial and railway shares only reached their all-time high of 5% between 1900 and 1915 because of the expansion of bank holdings in railway stock.[49]

When the Canadian Northern and the Grand Trunk declared bankruptcy, the banks rid themselves of railway stock once and for all. Likewise, as the analysis of the statements of the big chartered banks shows, the proportion of total assets in the form of securities other than federal and provincial bonds by the four largest banks has declined over the last fifteen years, although the absolute value of the securities held has gone up slightly. The following table indicates that company shares and bonds, plus Canadian municipal and foreign bonds, make up no more than 2% to 3% of the present total assets of the same four largest banks.

Finally, the most complete source of information on shareholding by companies, *Inter-corporate Ownership*, published by Statis-

TABLE 1

SECURITY HOLDINGS OF THE FOUR LARGEST CANADIAN CHARTERED BANKS

(Selected years, figures in current Cdn. $)

Royal Bank	1960		1970		1974	
Gvt. of Canada bonds	537		1,430		2,052	
Provincial bonds	92		48		59	
Foreign & Cdn. municipal bonds & stocks	524	(12%)	398	(3%)	702	(3%)
Total assets	4,296	(100%)	11,369	(100%)	21,670	(100%)
Canadian Imperial Bank of Commerce[1]						
Gvt. of Canada bonds	771		1,942		1,911	
Provincial bonds	62		60		64	
Foreign, & Cdn. municipal bonds & stocks	392	(9%)	513	(4%)	636	(3%)
Total assets	4,213	(100%)	11,050	(100%)	18,947	(100%)
Bank of Montréal						
Gvt. of Canada bonds	706		1,287		1,652	
Provincial bonds	60		78		101	
Foreign, and Cdn. municipal, bonds & stocks	218	(6%)	208	(2%)	490	(2%)
Total assets	3,485	(100%)	8,730	(100%)	17,651	(100%)
Bank of Nova Scotia						
Gvt. of Canada bonds	294		621		902	
Provincial bonds	19		39		53	
Foreign & Cdn. municipal, bonds & stocks	151	(7%)	189	(2%)	415	(3%)
Total assets	2,125	(100%)	6,369	(100%)	13,462	(100%)

Source: *Yearly Statements,* Financial Post Corporation Service
(1) The 1960 figures combine the securities and assets of both the Canadian Bank of Commerce and the Imperial Bank of Canada, which merged in 1961.

tics Canada in 1965, 1967, 1969 and 1972 confirms the assertion that the chartered banks have little interest in industrial shares and company control. The chartered banks claimed almost without exception to control no other companies than those that manage the real estate housing their main operations. The Bank of Montréal, for example, has a 30% interest in Doreal Investments and owns Bankmont Realty outright; the Bank of Nova Scotia controls 100% of the voting stock of Empire Realty and the Imperial Bank of Commerce 100% of Dominion Realty stock. Beyond this, a few banks have ventured timidly into other sectors of finance in recent years. In 1962, the Royal Bank, the Canadian National

Bank, the Montréal Trust, the Canada Trust and the General Trust set up an investment company specialized in industrial development named Roynat Ltd. The Royal Bank and the Canadian National Bank held 41.5% and 34% of Roynat stock respectively. The Royal Bank also entered the field of mutual funds with Royfund Ltd., where the Toronto Dominion-owned Corporate Investors was also active. As for mortgage lending, the Royal Bank founded Roynor Ltd. In 1968 in association with the Winnipeg-based Interior Trust, itself 40%—controlled by the Royal Bank. None of these developments are significant enought to alter the Canadian chartered bank tradition of holding shares solely as liquid assets or in order to control a few profit-making companies in sectors related to finance.

The testimony of bankers appearing before the Royal Commissions and Parliamentary Committees on banking also supports this view. In 1928, Mr. Henry T. Ross, secretary of the Canadian Bankers' Association, testified before the subcommittee formed by the House of Commons Select Standing Committee on Banking and Finance. He made the following revealing statement in response to criticisms by J.S. Woodsworth that Canadian banks invested too little in industry:

> ". . . It is not a banker's function to take the hazards of the commencement of a manufacturing business. It must be established, and have its margin of surplus. A banker should know that is against all principles of banking in any country. I think the German banks risk more than any other banks; certainly the English banks do not."[50]

Statements made by several other bankers before the same Standing Committee in 1934 are equally conclusive. Bank of Montréal General Manager Jackson Dodds, Bank of Montréal President Sir Charles B. Gordon, Royal Bank General Manager M. W. Wilson, Royal Bank President Sir Herbert Holt and Canadian Bank of Commerce General Manager S.H. Logan all testified, figures in hand, that the only companies controlled by their banks were a few real estate companies that administered the buildings housing the banks themselves. Asked to explain the interlocking of directors between the chartered banks and the large industrial and financial firms, all replied that bank directors are chosen by the existing board from among the major share-holders and clients of the bank and outstanding figures in the business milieu.[51] The Royal Commission on Banking and Finance reached identical conclusions in 1964.[52]

It can therefore be said that very close relationships of a personal nature between chartered banks and commercial, financial or industrial firms are by no means synonymous with ownership, contrary to what Park and Park contend and John Porter implies. They are more likely indicative of the interaction between a commercial-credit lender and his client or of the fact the many of the major share-holders of Canadian bank stock are simultaneously major share-holders in the larger Canadian industrial, commercial or transportation firms.

31

It is worth noting that the laws that regulate banking and finance have never prevented chartered banks from playing a role in the control of industry. Article 91 [15] of the British North America Act, adopted in 1867, placed legislation on banking under federal jurisdiction and inaugurated a series of Bank Acts starting in 1871. Given that there was full government-bank collaboration in the drafting of these laws, it is not surprising that they placed no restrictions whatsoever on the purchase, sale or holding of shares by banks. There is unanimity on this point among all the experts: both legally and financially, bankers have always enjoyed complete freedom of investment. [53] It is only since the passage of the Bank Act of 1967, Section 76, that restrictions on share-holding by chartered banks have been introduced, prohibiting the latter from owning more than 50% of the voting stock issued by a firm if the purchase value of the stock is less than $5 million. Beyond $5 million, a bank cannot hold more than 10% of the voting stock of a company, this restriction also applying to indirect control since the banks are not allowed to hold stock in a foreign firm that owns a block of shares in a Canadian company larger than that which the law permits the banks themselves. The same law also prevents the banks from holding more than 10% of the voting stock issued by a Canadian trust or loan company, and while it is legal for banks to own stock in foreign companies, the ceiling is again 10% in the case of foreign companies owning more than 10% of the voting stock of a Canadian trust or loan company. It should be pointed out that only those trust and loan companies under federal jurisdiction and open to public savings deposits are subject to these rules, and that it is possible to get around all of the above-mentioned restrictions provided the irregular situation does not last more than two years.

Significantly enough, the initial draft of the 1967 Bank Act would have prevented the founding and control of finance companies by chartered banks that has now begun to occur. Fortunately for the banks, the bill was amended in such a way that the 10% ceiling applied only to financial institutions open to public savings deposits, thus allowing the Royal Bank and the Canadian National Bank to continue controlling *Roy Nat Ltd.*, and the Dominion Bank to hold onto *U.N.A.S. Investment* (acquired in 1963 with the aid of the *Canada Permanent Mortgage Corp.*). Here again it is clear that the banks' investment strategy was in no way affected by government legislation, and that the few new developments that have taken place over the last fifteen years do not mean a radical change in the behaviour of the banks, which are no more tempted by industrial control than before.

As a final note on this point, we should mention the recent founding of the eleventh Canadian chartered bank, the Canadian Bank of Industry and Commerce. Established as a business rather than savings bank (a first in Canada) the CBIC started with a share-capital of $22 million, of which 10% is held by the *Banque de Paris et des Pays-Bas*, 10% by the London business bank *S.G. Warburg and Co.* and the rest by various Canadian and American companies and financiers.[54] It seems highly unlikely that the CBIC will bring any striking changes to the panorama that we have presented above.

The Trust Companies

The trust company is a financial institution imported from the United States during the last two decades of the 19th century, to offer trustee and estate-executor services. There were already about fifty trust companies south of the border by 1850 and their growth and functional convergence with the commercial banks was such that the 1913 Federal Reserve Law placed the banks and the trust companies under a single jurisdiction. In Canada, however, the trust companies have remained legally separate from the chartered banks and are alone entitled to act as fiduciaries. As we have already indicated, the trust companies play a secondary role to the banks, but are continuously increasing their share of the total assets of the Canadian financial system.

The civil and property rights handled by the trust companies are under provincial jurisdiction, and most of the companies are incorporated under provincial law, in Québec for the Royal Trust and the Montréal Trust (1892 and 1889 respectively) and in Ontario for the General Trust and the National Trust (in 1894 and 1898 respectively), amongst others. However, since they could be established by an act of Parliament up until 1970 and by thereafter federal authorization, the legislation (that is to say, the powers and constraints set down by the appropriate authority) vary from one level of government to another. There are, of course, certain common denominators: all trust companies are empowered to receive, administer or liquidate personal or corporate property, to carry out the provisions of wills, and to register company stocks and to invest sums of money entrusted to them. These powers have given rise to three categories of funds administered by trust companies: (a) the funds of the company itself (share-capital plus undistributed dividends); (b) funds deposited in trust by clients and guaranteed by company funds; (c) E.T.A. (executors, trustees and agents) accounts, or inheritance, pension and other funds deposited by individuals or companies in trust. In Ontario this latter category was eleven times larger than the first two combined ($2.8 billion compared to $242 million) in 1945, while in 1969 it was four times larger than the agency and trusteed funds ($20.3 billion compared to $5.2 billion) combined.[55]

The holding of shares in Canadian companies by trust companies varies according to whether it involves agency or guaranteed funds or E.T.A. funds. In the first case, shares comprise only a small proportion of assets. As can be seen in the following table on the proportion of guaranteed funds in seventeen trust companies registered either federally or provincially in Canada and representing 94% of the assets of all trusts, the percentage of shares in the assets of these companies is in constant decline.

33

TABLE 2

TRUST COMPANIES (CANADA)
COMPANY AND GUARANTEED FUND ASSETS

(Selected Years, in millions of Cdn. $) [1]

Year	Canadian Shares		Total Assets	
1947	15	(5%)	300	(100%)
1952	16	(3.7%)	429	(100%)
1958	29	(3.2%)	897	(100%)
1964	67	(2.3%)	2,860	(100%)
1969	107	(1.9%)	5,771	(100%)
1974	227	(1.8%)	12,443	(100%)

Source: Review of the Bank of Canada: Statistical Summary
(1) The 1947, 1952 and 1958 figures are based on the 17 largest companies representing no less than 94% of the assets of all of the trust companies registered in Canada. The 1964, 1969 and 1974 figures include all of the trust companies registered in Canada, both federally and provincially.

At the same time, the proportion of shares in E.T.A. fund assets has undergone precisely the opposite trend. In Ontario registered companies, it went from 12.7% to 45.3% ($980 million to $9.17 billion) between 1961 and 1969.[56] The trust companies have been particularly successful in attracting pension funds, with a consequent ballooning of E.T.A. funds, as can be seen from the following table.

TABLE 3

CANADA—TRUSTEED PENSION PLANS—BOOK VALUE OF ASSETS

(Selected Years; in millions of Cdn. $)

Type of Fiduciary	1960	1966	1974
a) Trust company	25.7%	33.5%	32.2%
b) Private trusteeship	62.4%	54.4%	54.9%
c) a) and b) combined	—	2.3%	6.9%
d) Pension fund company	11.9%	9.8%	6.1%
Total (%)	100.0%	100.0%	100.0%
Total (Cnd. $)	(3,583)	(7,250)	(18,284)

Source: Trusteed Pension Plans Financial Statistics, Statistics Canada, 1961 and 1976.

And as the table on the next page shows, the proportion of shares in the pension funds administered by trust companies has also grown regularly.

The decrease of bonds and the increase of shares and mortgages in pension-fund assets can be attributed to a preference for equities in an attempt to compensate for the inflation of the last decade. This is parti-

34

cularly evident in the efforts of private pension funds to slow down their purchasing of bonds. As a result of this preference, pension funds, and especially the trust companies, have acquired a potential power of control over the companies in which they hold stock. To the question—do the trusts actually use this power to control companies?—the 1964 Royal Commission on Banking and Finance answered *no*:

"Concern has been expressed at the concentration of equity holdings in the trust companies' own portfolios and administered accounts. As already indicated, these appear to represent well under 20% of all Canadian common stocks and are spread between a fairly sizable number of companies, many of whose E.T. and A clients vote their shares independently. Moreover, the trust companies' normal policy is to support existing management except in very unusual circumstances or unless they have very large stock holdings in one or a number of accounts, in which case they normally have an officer on the board to keep a watching brief in the interests of their clients. Where conflicts arise, as between common and preferred share-holders, they must vote each account in its own interests, and have told us that they do so. This essentially passive role as shareholders does not mean that they take no interest in how competently the companies in which they or their clients have invested are being managed. In fact, many trust companies follow the corporate affairs of such companies very closely, and if they do not like developments, they sell out or take steps to intervene. As long as this continues to be the practice, we see no danger of shareholder control being abdicated. Nor do we foresee any possibility in the near future that trust company influence on corporate life will become so pervasive as to constitute a danger to the interests of the public."[57]

There is no public source providing names which would enable any estimation of the control or the influence of the major trust companies on the corporations of which they are shareholders. It is a known fact, however, that neither federal nor provincial legislation sets any formal obstacle to the takeover of a company by a trust company using pension fund monies. A few restrictions do exist regarding the type and amount of pension funds that may be invested in shares, particularly for guaranteed funds. An example of this is the Ontario Loan and Trust Corporation Act of 1960 which prohibits trust companies from holding more than 20% of the stock of a company that pays regular dividends, and when such investment takes places, allows no more than 15% of the trust's own share-capital and reserves to be used.[58] The federal law of 1970 also places restrictions on the nationality of the shares that federally chartered companies may buy with their own and guaranteed funds, these being investable only in the stock of companies incorporated in Canada or with the purpose of establishing Canadian companies outside of Canada.

The very high level of economic concentration among these institutions increases the potential for trust companies to exercise control over the companies in which they are shareholders. In 1969, four

TABLE 4

CANADA—PENSION FUNDS ADMINISTERED BY TRUST COMPANIES

(Value of assets in 1960 and 1974 in millions of current Cdn. $)

	1960		1974		
	a) Individually administered funds	b) Common funds	a) Individually administered funds	b) Common funds	c) a and b combined
1) Investments in common or mutual funds	—	66.2%	0.6%	96.1%	11.9%
2) Bonds	76.2%	23.8%	33.9%	—	27.6%
3) Stock in Canadian companies	13.2%	2.9%	37.0%	—	37.6%
4) Stock in non-Canadian companies	0.8%	0.2%	5.3%	—	3.2%
5) Mortgages	5.8%	1.7%	8.9%	—	8.3%
6) Miscellaneous	3.7%	5.2%	14.3%	3.9%	11.0%
Total (%)	100.0%	100.0%	100.0%	100.0%	100.0%
Total ($)	(799)	(119)	(2,366)	(614)	(2,900)

Source: Pension Funds in Trust, Financial Statistics, Statistics Canada, 1961 aud 1976

trust companies (the Royal Trust, the Montreal Trust, the National Trust and the Canada Permanent Trust) concentrated 75% of the assets of E.T.A. funds and 50% of corporation funds and guaranteed funds. In 1926, the Royal Trust, the Montreal Trust, the National Trust and the Toronto General Trust—the latter merged with the Canada Permanent in 1961— held 95% and 43% respectively of these funds. The very high degree of centralization of these funds has not changed in 50 years.[59]

The question then arises as to whether control by the banks, previously discounted, may not in fact exist in an indirect form through chartered-bank control of the trust companies. A number of authors have indeed emphasized the extensive sharing of directors that goes on between the chartered banks and the trust companies. Park and Park have found in these interlocking directorships proof of banker control of trust companies, pointing out that in 1958, there were 14 directors of the Bank of Montreal on the Board of the Royal Trust, 15 from the Royal Bank on the Board of the Montreal Trust, 9 from the Canadian Bank of Commerce on the Board of the National Trust, 7 from the Toronto Dominion Bank on the Board of the Toronto General Trust and as many on the Board of the Canada Permanent Trust.[60] In fact, at least as far as the big trust companies such as the Royal Trust, the Montreal Trust and the National Trust are concerned, their association with the banks (those cited by Park and Park) date back to their very foundation. The Toronto General Trust is in a somewhat different situation, having been connected with the Canadian Bank of Commerce[61] when founded in 1882 but sliding gradually into the orbit of the Bank of Nova Scotia, the Dominion Bank, the Toronto Bank and the Bank of Commerce. Also, the banks declared for a long time they were not exerting any control over the trust companies even when the exchange of directorships was particularly strong.[62] During the 1960's, however, the links between the chartered banks and the trust companies became closer and closer. Here is how the Porter Commission on Banking and Finance (1964) saw this development:

"Despite this recent tendency for banks to acquire interests in other financial concerns, however, it is the relations between banks and trust companies where the clearest pattern emerges. Moreover, these relations are becoming both closer and more widespread. Each of the banks has a close association with at least one trust company, some of them loose working relations of long standing and others ownership affiliations of very recent origin. The form of these bank-trust company relations thus varies a good deal: in some cases there are as many as 15 common directors, while in others there are few. Five banks have an equity investment in at least one affiliate, varying from relatively small holdings to effective control, while the others have no equity investments."[63]

The Commission not having deemed it appropriate to disclose any figures on the holding of shares in trust companies by the banks, the first detailed information on trust company control came out in 1965 in Statistic Canada's *Intercorporate Ownership*. It was then found that Montréal Trust was controlled by Power Corporation via the 24% of Montréal Trust stock held by the Power subsidiary Investor Group; National Trust's main shareholder was Canada Life Insurance (19.5%); no mention was made of Royal Trust, but *Moody's Bank and Finance Directory* revealed that Canada Permanent Trust, also left out, is controlled by Canada Permanent Mortgage Corp. in which the Bank of Nova Scotia and the Toronto Dominion Bank have interests. Meanwhile, in a attempt to stimulate competition, the 1967 Bank Act (resulting from the Porter Commission recommendations) banned the exchange of directors between the chartered banks and the trust companies, as well as bank ownership of more than 10% of trust company voting stock after July 1971. The institutions concerned complied with these measures.

It seems clear that for three-quarters of a century, each of the big chartered banks did indeed control at least one large trust company. The ties, however, now appear to have been broken. It remains an open question whether the banks intended to profit from their control by using the immense financial resources of the trusts to take over non-financial companies (as the Parks, following Lenin, would say), or whether they saw it simply as a means of getting involved in trust operations that were otherwise legally closed to them. This author agrees with the Porter Commission's preference for the second hypothesis.[64] After all, the chartered banks have always called the shots in Canadian financial legislation, and if they had had serious objections to their forced divorce from the trusts, the government would have run into heavy resistance to those restrictions. No one has been able to prove that the trust companies have been anything more than ordinary investors as far as the shares they administer are concerned, although information on this score is admittedly scarce. Last but not least, the 1967 Bank act came into effect when the Trust companies' E.T.A. funds were surging ahead, in other words, at the very moment when the trusts had more available financial resources than ever before. Had the banks really wanted to direct the investment policy of their affiliates, they would surely not have surrendered their control over the trust companies without a fight. For all of these reasons, it is our opinion that the hypothesis of indirect bank control via the trust companies should be rejected, and that it is next to impossible to prove that the trust companies exercise any direct control over the firms in which they hold shares.[65]

The Life Insurance Companies

The life insurance companies rose to second place among Canadian financial institutions (just behind the chartered banks,) at the turn of the century, and have held their ground ever since. The following table shows that this sector has been highly concentrated since its inception.

TABLE 5

FEDERALLY—REGISTERED LIFE INSURANCE COMPANIES IN CANADA

(Assets in percentage, Selected years)

	1900	1930	1969
Canada Life	38.1%	12.5%	8.1%
Confederation Life	13.1%	5.4%	4.9%
Great West Life	1.6%	8.5%	9.2%
Manufacturers Life	3.8%	7.2%	12.6%
Mutual Life of Canada	8.7%	7.7%	7.7%
Sun Life	17.6%	39.0%	23.1%
London Life	1.7%	4.3%	10.1%
Other companies	15.4%	15.4%	20.5%
Number of companies	10	19	27

Source: E. Neufeld The Financial System of Canada, 1972, Toronto, p. 247.

All of the life insurance companies were Canadian until 1929, the year of the first foreign take-over. The second took place in 1954 and was followed by several others between 1954 and 1961. The Canadian bourgeoisie reacted to the potential threat of foreign domination of what had previously been its undisputed private reserve by having the British and Canadian Insurance Company Act amended in 1965 so as to prevent foreign ownership of more than 25% of the stock of a Canadian life insurance company and any one non-Canadian shareholder from owning more than 10%. The life insurance companies also received federal authorization to become mutuals, and since 1971, Ontario companies may be double-licensed as both insurance companies and mutual funds. As well, federally-chartered life insurance companies were required by federal law to have a majority of resident Canadian citizens on their boards and empowered to put a ban on the sale of their shares outside of Canada.

The transformation of the big life insurance companies into mutuals, already underway in the 1950's, was largely sparked by senior-management concern about possible absorption by American financial groups. Four of the six big Canadian companies became mutuals: Confederation Life and Manufacturers Life in 1958 and Canada Life and Sun Life in 1959. Mutual Life had always been a mutual, and Great West Life, as already mentioned, is controlled by the Power Corporation subsidiary Investors Group. [66]

Yet it is highly unlikely that the conversion of the life insurance companies into mutuals had anything to do with economic nationalism. The undistributed dividends of these highly profitable companies had been accumulating for three-quarters of a century, and had they been used to pay high dividends, personal revenue taxes would have taken a sizeable chunk. "Normal" dividends were therefore used to avoid an underisable rise on the stock market and thus enable the companies to continue to rake in the profits without attracting undue public attention. To gain access to the undistributed benefits, shareholders had only to form mutuals that would buy back the shares and then turn over to the holders the full value of their holdings: these holdings would then be taxed at the minimal rate as capital gains. The fact is, the big Canadian shareholders in life insurance companies almost missed this particular fall of manna from heaven, for many American financiers with their eye on the stock-market quotations were preparing to make the move themselves.[67]

Canadian life insurance companies have been wary of any risky industrial investment, and therefore of controlling non-financial institutions. Their assets show that their two major fields of investment are bonds (mainly bonds of the various Canadian and foreign governments) and mortgages. Canadian corporate stock has never accounted for more than 6% of their assets,[68] a high reached at the turn of the century, but hardly because provincial or federal legislation has been a deterrent to control of non-financial concerns. Previous to 1899, there were no legal provisions for any sort of restrictions on investments by life insurance companies, and the federal legislation of that year continued to leave them free rein in this area. Yet with the exception of a few investments that were particularly advantageous to the directors, the companies showed very little inclination to purchase stock.[69] The findings of the 1907 Royal Commission on Life Insurance in Canada resulted in more restrictive legislation being passed in 1910. Life insurance companies could no longer buy more than 30% of the stock of another company, and only then if the latter had paid regular dividends during the seven previous years. No ceiling on the percentage of life insurance company assets investable in shares was fixed. In spite of the fact that the 1920's witnessed a watering-down of the legislation pertaining to stock investments, none of the life insurance companies except Sun Life took advantage of the changes. Sun Life liked to buy stock in the safer and more profitable American companies, yet never went beyond a self-imposed ceiling of 10% per company nor became involved in the management of companies in which it held shares.[70]

In 1932, partially as a response to Sun Life's financial difficulties, the federal government established a ceiling of 25% on the portion of their assets which life insurance companies could invest in shares. In a gesture that smacks distinctly of highly-conservative financiers of the British mould and not at all of Hilferding's "finance capitalists," the industry itself successfully requested that this ceiling be lowered to 15%.[71] The ceiling was raised again to 25% in 1965, but once again, the change was at the behest of the industry. Their motive was to protect themselves against inflation by investing in equities; their interest in control was no greater than before. The clauses concerning the maximum amount to be invested in a company's stock and the minimum yield of shares are still in effect. This review of federal legislation can be considered valid for the whole industry, given not only that the overwhelming majority of life insurance companies are federally incorporated, but also that provincial legislation is largely dependent on the federal laws.

There remains a final point to be made. Life insurance companies in the last ten years have become interested in the establishment and operation of real-estate companies. The 1965 legislation therefore abolished the 30% maximum limit with respect to these development companies, and the major life insurance companies have since set up or expanded subsidiaries in this highly speculative field. This did not, however, bring about any change in their traditional attitude of indifference toward development and control in industrial corporations.

Investment Companies

Investment companies developed in Canada after 1920 in two definite stages: from 1920 to 1930, closed-end investment companies appeared on the scene; from 1932, mutual fund companies have been preeminent. Within the former type, a further distinction must be drawn between investment trusts and holding companies. The investment trusts, which form the large majority, are yet another feature borrowed by the Canadian financial system from the British model. They are financed through periodic stock issues and they invest the funds thus obtained in a diversified portfolio of stocks in corporations which they do not seek to control.

These investment companies were primarily an offspring of Canadian investment bankers: three, for example, were created by the firm Nesbitt Thomson during the 1920's, four were incorporated by Wood Gundy, and four others by Arthur Meighen, financier and Prime Minister of Canada. Towards the end of 1929, there were about fifty investment companies in Canada, all with fixed capitalization, or closed-ended, and of these only four or five were holding companies.[72]

The growth of investment companies was sparked by the development of a Canadian market for government securities during the First World War. Canadian investment bankers revived public interest in securities after the War in order to keep up demand for the increased numbers of company stocks and shares arising from the wave of mergers that took place between 1924 and 1930. The investment bankers often promoted these mergers, since they were on the look-out for securities to handle and the investment companies they set up afforded handsome outlets for their activities.[73] Control of industrial corporations was not sought by investment companies of the pure type. During the 1930's the fixed-capital investment companies lost their popularity because the public discovered that much of the stock held in portfolio by the companies was worthless, and that they, the public, were therefore to rid themselves of their own investment company stock. Again, Canadian

41

financiers followed the British example and moved into mutual funds, or, open-end investment companies. The first mutual fund, the Canadian Investment Fund, was formed in 1932 by a group of men involved both in finance and politics, and brought together for the occasion by Calvin Bullock. They were: former prime minister of Canada Robert L. Borden, premier of Québec Louis A. Taschereau, Senator C.C. Ballantyne, the Right Honorable Arthur B. Purwis (President of Canadian Industries), the Honorable Charles A. Dunning (former Minister of Finance), along with Sir Edward Beatty (President of the CPR), Sir Charles Gordon (President of the Bank of Montréal), and other business men.[74] Mutual funds gained momentum from that time on. Mutual funds were under the legal obligation to buy back, at their market value, any investment company stocks that a fund share-holder should chose to sell and at any time he should chose to do so.

Mutual funds have shown no more interest in controlling industrial concerns of which they are share-holders than have most fixed-capital investment companies. Both diversify their purchases and only rarely place directors on corporation boards. This hypothesis was difficult to prove during the 1920's, when investment companies did not disclose their holdings. It has however become obvious since 1962, when the Financial Post Survey of Investment Funds began publishing data showing both the invariably high diversification of their portfolios and the near nonexistence of interlocking directorships between both the open-end and closed end (non-holding) investment companies, and the companies in which they hold shares.

This can be illustrated by showing the percentage of the voting stock of 31 companies listed by the Financial Post as being among the biggest in Canada (including chartered banks, industrial, commercial and service corporations) which are controlled by Investor Group and its mutual fund subsidiaries. The latter are eight in number: Investors Mutual of Canada, Investors Growth Fund, Investors Retirement Mutual Fund, Provident Mutual Fund, Provident Stock Fund and Investors Mortgage Fund. In 1969 this Power Corporation-controlled group of mutual funds was the largest in Canada, with 31% of all mutual-fund assets. The following table shows both the voting stock percentages and the directors common to the mutual funds and these Canadian-controlled companies.

As for the second kind of closed-end investment company—the holding company—a preliminary distinction should be made between the pure holding company, one which issues shares and debentures in the public market in order to acquire the stocks of a limited and fixed number of corporations which they seek to control, and the mixed holding company which also holds stock in other firms and industrial, commercial and transportation companies. Only the first type is of interest here, since all non-financial companies with subsidiaries fall into the second category.

TABLE 6

PROPORTION OF VOTING STOCK OF 31 CANADIAN COMPANIES HELD BY INVESTOR GROUP AND ITS SUBSIDIARIES AS OF DECEMBER 31, 1974

Company	Voting Stock Number	(%)	Directors in Common with: The Mutual Funds	Power Corp.
Abitibi P & P	180,640	(1%)	1	1
Alcan Aluminium	158,000	(0.4%)	—	—
Algoma Steel	155,170	(1.3%)	—	1
Bank of Montréal	569,365	(1.7%)	—	—
Bank of Nova Scotia	516,630	(2.8%)	—	—
Can. Imp. Bank of Commerce	1,311,825	(3.8%)	—	2
C.P. Ltd	1,750,000	(2.4%)	1	1
Consumers'Gas	793,576	(4.5%)	1	—
Dofasco	726,070	(4.6%)	—	—
Dominion Stores	398,400	(4.8%)	—	—
Domtar	137,000	(0.9%)	—	—
Falconbridge	148,375	(3.0%)	—	—
Hudson Bay	215,500	(1.5%)	—	—
I.N.C.O.	1,054,237	(1%)	—	—
McMillan-Bloedell	694,620	(3.3%)	—	—
Massey Ferguson	481,910	(9.6%)	—	—
Molson Ind.	521,867	(4.2%)	—	—
Moore Corp.	549,425	(1.9%)	—	—
Noranda Mines	519,439	(2.2%)	—	—
Northern & Central Gas	345,200	(2.6%)	1	—
Price Co.	62,000	(0.6%)	—	—
Seagram Co.	568,650	(1.6%)	—	—
Stelco	665,971	(2.8%)	—	—
Thomson Newspapers	953,750	(1.9%)	—	—
Toronto-Dominion Bank	681,498	(4.0%)	—	—
Trans-Canada Pipelines	1,310,544	(4.2%)	—	1
Union Gas	572,826	(3.8%)	—	—
Hiram Walker	235,260	(1.5%)	—	—
Royal Bank	969,990	(2.9%)	—	2
Bell Canada	120,076	(0.3%)	—	1
Dominion Textile	—	—	1	—

Sources: F. Post Survey of Investment Funds, 1975
Moody's Bank & Finance, 1975
Moody's Transportation, 1975
Moody's Industrials, 1975
F. Post Directory of Directors, 1975

The table indicates that the Power Corp's & the Investors group's distribution of their directors is unrelated to the distribution of its investments. The highest percentages of stock are in companies where there are no common directorships. Even the cases of very high percentage are not in themselves proof that the mutual funds are anything other than mere investors.

The pure holding company is a financial institution that actually controls, by owning stock and designating directors, both financial and non-financial companies. It is for that legally authorized purpose that these companies are formed. Given the unanimity with which each and every Canadian author points to Argus Corp. and Power Corp. as examples, it almost seems as if we have at last come across our very own Canadian finance capitalist.

Before jumping to such a conclusion, though, it is worth looking into the development of this kind of company in Canada. Its growth parallelled that of the straight-forward type of investment company: its concentration took place largely in the 1920's though others have been formed more recently. The first major holding company was the Brazilian Traction, Heat and Light Co., formed in 1912 by Sir William MacKenzie (of Canadian Northern), Sir Henry Pellat, (an investment banker with the Toronto firm Pellatt and Osler), Sir William Van Horne (of the CPR), the corporate lawyer Z.A. Lash, and various other capitalists from London, New York and Toronto. Brazilian Traction held almost all of the stock of three tramway, electricity and telephone companies in Rio de Janiero and in Saõ Paulo in Brazil. After fifty years of acquiring numerous Brazilian utilities, Brazilian Traction has, in the last ten years, diversified into food products, banking, hotels and mining, and bought control of several Canadian industrial and service corporations such as John Labatt's (in May 1967), Western Minerals and the Great Lakes Power Corporation (in 1973).

Power Corporation was set up by the Nesbitt Thomson and Co. investment bank in 1925 in order to take over the Canada Northern Power Corp., the Ottawa-Montréal Power Corp., the Ottawa and Hull Power Corp., and other Canadian hydro-electric companies, as well as to manage minority participation in the East Kootenay Power Co. (Alberta and British Columbia), the Southern Canada Power Co. (Quebec), the Winnipeg Electric Co., the Dominion Power and Transmission Co., and the Manitoba Power Co. These assets commanded the generation of 300,000 HP and a potential capacity of 600,000 HP. In each case, Power Corp. named its principal associates, such as A.J. Nesbitt and P.A. Thomson, to the boards of the companies it controlled. For thirty years, Power stuck to hydro-electricity without any real change in its investment policy, notwithstanding its 1944 decision to sell its shares in Canada Northern power to Hydro Ontario. The real strategical reorientation, which completely changed the composition of its holdings, occurred in 1957 when Power sold its subsidiary, Southern Canada, to Shawinigan Water and Power in exchange for Shawinigan stock and began buying shares in companies in a variety of sectors: Bathurst Power and Paper, the Royal Bank, Trans Canada Pipelines, etc. In 1963, Power sold its shares in Shawinigan Water and Power but held on to the latter's industrial subsidiaries grouped together as Shawinigan Industries. By 1964, Power Corp. had been dropped from the *Moody's Public Utility* list only to reappear in

Moody's Bank and Finance. Power was no longer a holding company in hydro-electricity, as the following break-down of its investments for that year clearly show:

TABLE 7 [75]

Sector	% of securities in portfolio
1) Public hydro-electric utilities	4.25%
2) Oil, gas, pipelines	11.10%
3) Finance	9.00%
4) Chemicals	17.06%
5) Pulp and paper	15.07%
6) Transportation	14.09%
7) Mining	8.15%
8) Real Estate	5.19%
9) Miscellaneous	3.87%
10) Short-term notes............................	12.22%

Since 1964, Power Corp. has focused its holdings around a few big corporations (including Consolidated Bathurst, Investors Group, Laurentide Finance and Canada Steamships Ltd.) and sold its participation in others.

Alcan Aluminium Ltd. offers an example of a holding company involved in manufacturing. Formed in 1928 to hold the stock of the Aluminium Company of Canada (a former subsidiary of Alcoa) and many other Alcoa subsidiaries in Canada and elsewhere, Alcan is now at the head of an international conglomerate, although the core of its board of directors remains American.[76] Its preferred spheres of investments have not varied since its incorporation.

Argus Corp. is a holding company that has, from its inception in 1945, always diversified its portfolio. Argus holds stock in a small number of companies, exerts minority control over them and is represented by a varying number of directors that never exceed half of any subsidiary's board. Argus' original investment portfolio was as follows:[77]

TABLE 8

Canadian Breweries	39%	Dominion Malt	3%
Massey-Ferguson	13%	Orange Crush	3%
Canadian Food Products	9%	Others	6%
Standard Chemical	9%	Cash	11%
Dominion Stores	7%	Total	100%

Its investments have remained much the same throughout its short history. Canadian Breweries, the company of Argus' founder E.P.

Taylor, left the group in 1968 when Rothman's of Pall Mall bought a controlling interest in it. Argus has maintained its control of Dominion Stores and Massey-Ferguson. When Standard Chemical was absorbed by Domtar in 1951, Argus gained enough shares in it to acquire controlling interest. Also in 1951, Argus liquidated its interest in Orange Crush, Control of several other companies was acquired over the years. B.C. Forest Products and Standard Radio (since renamed Standard Broadcasting Corp.) came under Argus' control in 1946 and 1960 respectively. Both Hollinger and the St. Lawrence Corp. entered the group in 1955 and left in 1961.

A final example of a Canadian holding company is C.P. Investments, set up by the CPR in 1962 to handle CPR subsidiaries unrelated to transportation. Among these we find Algoma Steel, one of the Big Three in Canadian steel, Cominco, Fording Coal and Can Pac Minerals in mining, C.P. Hotels, Great Lakes Paper and Marathon Realty.

The above-mentioned holding companies are merely a few outstanding examples of a form of financial organization that has been widespread in Canada since the 1920's. Many others could also be cited, like the Weston Group's Loblaw Companies Ltd. in food products, Canadian International Power (itself a subsidiary of United Corporation of Delaware) in public utilities both in Canada and, through subsidiaries in Latin America, and Trizec in real estate. We are now in a position to begin looking at how holding companies fit into the finance-capital schema.

It is significant to find that a certain confusion surrounds the notion of holding companies, even in the analyses of such a serious student of various Canadian financial groups as Wallace Clement.[78] Clement reviews the banks, insurance and investment companies, but without distinguishing the three types of the latter that we have discussed above. He implicitly justifies his focus on the holding companies in the following terms:

"Investment companies represent a collage of corporations operating in several different sectors. The one thing they do share in common is that their main activity is that of holding companies with assets in more than one sector."[79]

In fact, the holding companies are only *one* kind of investment company, and their assets are almost exclusively made up of common stock. Holding companies do not have assets outside the financial sector (unless they are *mixed* holdings or simply non-financial corporations with subsidiaries). This confusion leads Clement to draw up a table (page 402) in which investment companies such as Argus Corp., Power Corp. and C.P. Investments, that are holding companies, are thrown in pell-mell with industrial corporations that happen to own subsidiaries, like the Moore Corp. In the same table, Clement compares the assets of companies like Argus and Power, that do not consolidate their subsidiaries' balance sheets with their own, with those corporations like Brascan and Alcan Aluminium that do, at least in part. Irony of ironies, this makes Argus and Power the dwarfs of the holding-company league in Canada! Investors Group, the largest Canadian holding of open-end investment companies, is alternately classified by Clement as a mortgage company (on pages 137 and 406) and a mutual fund (on page 264). Likewise, he begins by defining Brascan as a utility on page 32, and winds up referring to it as an investment company on page 162, in spite of the fact that the very authoritative *Moody's* declares Brascan to be "a holding company owning no physical property" and an "investment-management company which, through operating subsidiaries, supplies public-utility services in southeastern Brazil."[80]

The fact of the matter is that the holding company is an import from the American financial system. The British tradition is one of investment trusts having no control over the companies in which they hold stock. In contrast, holding companies have been, in the U.S. and Canada, a means of gaining control of companies with minimal investment, in order to refinance them and to reduce competition without resorting to out-right merger (whether because of the provincial registration of some companies, as in hydro-electricity, or to get around antitrust legislation or to out-manoeuvre actual or potential share-holder resistance to the idea of a merger). From the point of view of control and cohesion, holdings lie about halfway between a gentlemen's agreement and an outright merger. As can be seen by the examples of U.S. Steel (1901) in manufacturing, Electric Bond and Share (1905) in public utilities, and I.N.C.O. (1902) in mining, holdings were to be found in all sectors of the American economy by the end of the 19th century.[81]

Our preceding examples indicate that this is almost the case in Canada now. Here, the promoters of holding companies have in some instances been investment bankers (Nesbitt Thomson and Co. initiated Power Corp.), while in others, holding companies have been used to reorganize existing conglomerates, as was the case with C.P. Investments, Loblaw Companies and Alcan Aluminium. Not infrequently, financier-industrialists like Brascan's Sir William MacKenzie or Argus Corp.'s E.P. Taylor were the prime movers. In other words, one can hardly claim that holding companies have been either the exclusive prerogative of American and Canadian bankers, or even financiers, or their preferred means of gaining control of the Canadian economy. Holding companies have simply been *one* technical tool for centralizing, controlling and financing companies; other such tools are gentlemen's agreements, combines, pools, mergers, and the like.

The Investment Banks

The classic Marxist finance control theory bases its explanation of banking's domination of industry on various mechanisms, the founding of corporations and their reorganization and long-term financing through security issues being among the more important. Both of these financial activities correspond in Canada and the United States to the operations of investment houses.

In the U.S., the investment banks that developed during the last half of the 19th century played a key role in the centralization of the railroad companies and the 1896 to 1905 wave of industrial mergers.[82] American investment bankers frequently secured positions of control in companies they reorganized or for which they were long-term creditors. We have already seen that several of the American financial groupings described by Rochester in 1936, Sweezy in 1939 and Perlo in 1961, were set up by investment bankers like J.P. Morgan, Goldman Sachs, Lehman Bros., and Kuhn Loeb. Not only Sweezy, Baran, Magdoff and O'Connor, but also non-Marxists like V. Carosso, agree that the investment bankers have lost much of their influence over industry since the 1929 Crash.

In Canada, there have been at least three major waves of mergers in this century, from 1909 to 1913, from 1924 to 1929, and from the end of the Second World War to 1951.[83]. Canadian investment bankers played a central role in the first two waves by actively promoting the fusions; they have also been prominent in corporate stock and bond issues since the First World War. Do they then occupy a position similar to that of their American counterparts in the reorganization and financing of Canadian industry, and thereby wield control in the big corporations in this country? To answer these questions, we must first examine the development of the investment sector in Canada and then appraise the evolution of five of the largest Canadian investment firms.

Compared to those in the U.S., the Canadian investment houses were definite late-comers. Whereas J.P. Morgan and Co. or Drexel and Co. had already cut out for themselves a substantial slice of the American financial market and established international links with European firms by 1880, the major Canadian firms arose only in the late 19th and early 20th centuries: A.E. Ames and Co. in 1889; Dominion Securities Corp. in 1901, Royal Securities Corp. in 1903; Wood, Gundy and Co. in 1905; and Nesbitt Thomson and Co. in 1912. Following the American and European example, the latter were either private corporations or partnerships, completely owned by a few associated owner-directors and exempted from the obligation to publish their balance sheets or financial statements.

The activities of these firms were for the most part undifferentiated. They acted as underwriters for private and public security issues and corporate reorganization (mergers, refinancing), as brokers in the Montréal and/or Toronto stock exchanges, and as security retailers. In federal and provincial bond issues, the investment bankers competed with the chartered banks, which carried out such functions in the 19th century, even though most of the sizable Canadian public and private loans were negotiated directly in New York or London with foreign investment houses. The Canadian firms only took on significant proportions during the First World War, for until then the London and New York houses with their well-entrenched distribution networks had relegated Montréal and Toronto to something less than second fiddle. From 1904 to 1914, for instance, only 18% of Canadian bonds were sold in Canada, as compared to 73% in the United Kingdom and 9% in the U.S. Between 1915 and 1920, however, the proportions changed to 67%, 3% and 30% respectively.[84] The War, closing off the British capital market and repatriating long-term financing to Canada, had set the Canadian investment industry on its feet.

The Canadian firms modelled themselves after their American counterparts. Following the move of the American investment bankers, who formed the Investment Bankers Association of America in response to increasing public criticism and calls for restrictive legislation, the Canadians established the Bond Dealers Association of Canada with thirty-two members in June 1916. By the time this Association changed its name to the Investment Bankers Association of Canada in 1925, its membership had grown to 108. Although an amendment made to the Bank Act of Canada in 1934, prohibiting investment companies from calling themselves "banks" but leaving untouched the operations universally associated with "investment banks, " led the Association to incorporate itself as the Investment Dealers Association of Canada, this in no way affected their real activities. (That is why we call them "banks" in this book, instead of "brokers.")

Throughout the first third of the 20th century, the investment banks were highly active in promoting mergers in Canadian industry. Many of the mergers were carried out by the senior partners of the investment firms searching for new securities to market. (The usual procedure was to buy out competitors or companies producing related products and then carry out a merger.) On other occasions, a holding company was set up to buy most or all of the voting stock of the companies in question, while allowing them to function as legally but not economically independent entities. Occasionally, one of the associates to be merged was used as an operating holding company to administer the other companies that had been absorbed.

Those who have studied the question and pointed out the role of the financial promoters in the consolidation processes that occurred in Canada between 1900 and 1930 do not agree on the amount of control sought by these promoters of mergers. The Royal Commission on Price Spreads, of 1935, concluded that cheap control was as important to bankers as the pursuit of an ongoing supply of securities to sell:

> "To the owners of the vendor company, 'refinancing' is merely an operation which enables them to 'sell out' on terms which appear to them to be advantageous. To the promoter or investment dealer, it is a device used for one or more of the following purposes: to create a supply of securities which may be sold to the public at a profit, to secure control of the vendor business, and to acquire a claim to profits without sharing any losses. . ."

"The promoter gains control and a claim to profits without risk of loss by selling to the public non-voting securities with fixed interest or dividend and reserving for himself the whole or a majority of the voting shares in the new company." [85]

The Commissioners of 1935 thus appear to have been firm supporters of Hilferding's finance capital theory. Yet for all their interesting statistics on 374 mergers that took place between 1900 and 1930, there was not the slightest clue as to the actual extent of control by bankers over the newly-formed companies. The three examples put forward by the Commission—the reorganizations of Simpsons Co. by Wood, Gundy and Co; of Burns and Co. by Dominion Securities Corp.; and of Canadian Canners by Avern, Pardoe and Co.—naturally support the conclusion that the investment banks controlled the reorganized firms.

In a thorough study bearing on the period 1909-1913, A.E. Epp takes the opposite point of view, stating that the financiers were interested only in the quick profits to be had from the sale of fresh securities.

"The financiers who helped to organize these companies only rarely, however, retained any control over them once they were organized. . . Among the principals of firms involved in reorganization of these industries, Alfred Ernest Ames and Cawthra Mulock remained involved with the new companies. The principals of other merger-financing firms did not achieve any new industrial dominance by means of this organization of mergers." [86]

H.G. Stapells took a more qualified position. [87] Accordig to him, the financiers' objective was the promoter's profit and not control, but the latter was easily acquired at small cost. Sometimes the bankers would keep it, more often, however, they would give it up, for it was in the resale of the securities that they would realize their own profits. Moreover, the Stapells study, of the period 1900-1922, presents the mergers as the work not of the investment houses as such, but rather of the principal partners of the firms. It was the latter who were sometimes able to retain positions of control. It was not Wood, Gundy and Co., but James H. Gundy; not Royal Securities but Lord Beaverbrook and then Izaac W. Killam; not the Nesbitt Thomson investment house but Alfred J. Nesbitt and Peter A. Thomson.

"Promotion has not been the chief function of the security or investment concerns in Canada. From the very nature of the task, promotion must be a personal rather than an institutional undertaking. What the promoter needed and what these financial houses supplied was the connection and facilities for marketing the securities of the new concern. It is in this role, rather than in that of the promoter, that the securities and investment houses have a claim to a place in the consolidation movement." [89]

Our examination of the history of the five largest Canadian investment firms confirms Stapells' hypothesis. It will be seen that in some cases the investment bankers carved out real empires for themselves whereas in others their activity amounts to no more than the search for quick profits. These examples will also enable us to show in detail that it was indeed the promoters themselves and not the investment houses that obtained the profits and/or control resulting from the mergers and reorganizations. It is not, of course, easy to separate the promoters from the investment banks given that the latter are private companies owned by the financiers. Nevertheless, careful scrutiny of the examples eventually leads us to the real villain of the piece. Last but not least, we shall support our contention that, as in the United States, the Canadian investment banker no sooner reached the zenith of his power than it began to decline, the zenith in this case being the 1929-1933 crisis. All of this will be illustrated by the case histories of the Big Five in Canadian investment banking at the end of the 1920's: Wood, Gundy and Co., A.E. Ames and Co., Nesbitt Thomson and Co., the Dominion Securities Corporation and the Royal Securities Corporation.

Founded in 1889 by Alfred Ernest Ames, the son-in-law of Senator George Cox from Toronto, Ames and Co. intervened in the organization of Imperial Life and of National Trust in 1898. The following year, the firm announced its first issue of industrial stock:

"$300 000 of Dunlop Tire and Rubber Goods Company 7% Preferred Stock. The issue was an immediate success and established the firm as an issuing house. It paved the way for a succession of other issues, the earliest of which included preferred stocks of Carter-Crume Company, now part of Moore Corporation. . . WM A Rogers Ltd. and City Dairy Company, now part of the Borden Company.''[89]

Later came F.N. Burt and Co., American Sales Book and other companies during the 1909 to 1913 stock market boom. At the end of his career in 1931, Alfred Ames was on the boards of directors of 24 companies, including those he had reorganized.[90] Yet not one of the other principal partners of A.E. Ames and Co. was a member of the board of one of the reorganized companies. Hilton R. Tudhope, the successor to Ames' position as president when the founder died in 1934, had been a director of only a few companies while vice-president of Ames and Co. in 1931. Another 1931 vice-president and director of Ames and Co. was an outside director of only three companies, all of secondary importance. During the 1924 to 1929 boom, Ames and Co. was the investment house that displayed the least interest in corporate securities, and 70% of the issues it underwrote were in public securities, the highest percentage for all the large investment firms (see Table 9).

During the 1930's, Ames and Co. was the investment house that suffered the smallest losses in the Depression, (see Table 9), somewhat of a paradox given that the reason was the absolute and relative increase of its business with corporations. Several former clients of Ames and Co. were still able to borrow on the capital market (in spite of the banker's aid) and the list of corporate clients continued to grow. Among the companies that regularly enlisted the services of Ames and Co., and continued to do so during the crisis, were International Milling, which issued $4,500,000 worth of stock in 1935, Cosmos Imperial Mills which issued $1,010,000 worth in 1936, and Hamilton Cotton, which sold $1,150,000 worth of debentures in 1938. (H.R. Tudhope, who became president of Ames and Co. in 1934, was also a director of the last two companies.) There were also some new clients, such as British American Oil ($5,000,000 in debentures in 1930 and $4,000,000 in 1935), but Ames and Co. partners did not sit on the boards of these foreign subsidiaries.

Although corporate stock issues were very rare during the Second World War, Ames and Co. succeeded in maintaining some of its old clients and even in attracting a few new ones. The old ones included British American Oil ($6,000,000 in debentures in 1939, $3,000,000 in 1943), Cosmos Imperial Mills ($380,000 in debentures in 1940), Victoria Realty Corp. ($436,000,000 in 1941), Hamilton Cotton ($850,000 in debentures in 1943 and $1,500,000 in 1945), and Building Products ($1,000,000 in debentures in 1945.) The most important new client was Alcan, with $4,250,000 in debentures in 1945.

Ames and Co. attracted new clients after the war, including Bell Telephone, Imperial Tobacco, Dominion Textiles and Dunlop Tire and Rubber, but Ames and Co. directors did not secure directorships in these companies and through the 1950's maintained directorships only in older client companies such as Hamilton Cotton, Monarch Knitting, Toronto Brick and Brantford Cordage. As for the companies with which Ames and Co. has done business since World War II, neither the investment house nor its partners participate in their board. Moreover, Ames and Co's old partners have been disappearing (A.E. Ames died in 1934, H.R. Tudhope left the presidency in 1949 to sit as chairman of the board until 1957, and Roy Warren was president from 1950 to 1957), and the new ones hold few outside directorships. Of the eleven members of the A.E. Ames and Co. Ltd Board in 1975, only two held outside directorship and those two did not include the chairman of the Board, (E.C. Lipsit), the company president (P.D. Harris), or the executive vice-president (P.M. Fisher). All of this leads us to believe that the early partners of Ames and Co. acquired shares in the companies they had reorganized or financed between 1900 and 1930, but that A.E. Ames and Co. *as such* held no stock in client companies.[91]

These hypotheses are confirmed by the study of the history of Royal Securities Corporation, founded in 1903 as a private corporation by a group of Halifax capitalists and initially managed by Max Aitken. The other partners were all Nova Scotian financier-politicians: John Stairs (president of the Union Bank and the Nova Scotia Steel and Coal Co., and provincial chairman of the Conservative Party), Honorable Robert E. Harris (later Chief Justice of the province) and Charles H. Cahan (later provincial State Secretary for the Conservatives). Stairs, the first president and principal shareholder of Royal Securities, was the one who supported Aitken. When he died in 1904, the other partners demanded of Aitken that he pay higher dividends and present

TABLE 9

STRUCTURE OF THE OPERATIONS OF THE FIVE MAJOR INVESTMENT FIRMS (1924-1929 AND 1930-1937)
(IN MILLIONS OF CURRENT $C AND %)

	Government Bonds		Corporate Bonds and Debentures		Shares		Total	
1. Wood, Gundy & Co.								
1924-1929	150	(29%)	218	(43%)	142	(28%)	510	(100%)
1930-1937	293	(64%)	157	(35%)	3	(1%)	453	(100%)
2. Dominion Securities Corporation								
1924-1929	276	(64%)	96	(22%)	60	(14%)	432	(100%)
1930-1937	151	(75%)	49	(24%)	2	(1%)	202	(100%)
3. Royal Securities Corporation								
1924-1929	5	(3%)	128	(77%)	34	(20%)	167	(100%)
1930-1937	2	(3%)	57	(95%)	1	(2%)	60	(100%)
4. Nesbitt Thomson & Co.								
1924-1929	2	(1%)	109	(65%)	58	(34%)	169	(100%)
1930-1937	18	(19%)	69	(73%)	7	(8%)	94	(100%)
5. A.E. Ames & Co.								
1924-1929	72	(69%)	11	(11%)	21	(20%)	104	(100%)
1930-1937	47	(54%)	17	(20%)	23	(26%)	87	(100%)

Source: Monetary Times, Yearly Issues, 1925-1938.

clearer and more complete accounts. Rather than comply, Aitken withdrew from Royal Securities and bought Montréal Trust in 1906, only to sell it again to a group of capitalists connected with the Royal Bank.[92] During his early period of tenure with Royal Securities, Aitken bought and reorganized a number of public utilities in Latin America—Trinidad Electric, Puerto Rico Railways, Demerara Electric and Camaguey Electric—as well as Calgary Power, in Canada. The shares of these companies were divided among the shareholders of Royal Securities, but Aitken saw to it that he held firm control.

In 1903, Aitken bought Royal Securities from his former partners in Halifax and moved the company to Montréal, where at the time he had as employees, but not as partners, three future Canadian millionaires: Richard B. Bennett, future Prime Minister of Canada, Arthur J. Nesbitt, who was to become president of Nesbitt Thomson and Co., and Izaac W. Killam, future president of Royal Securities. In 1910 Aitken and Royal Securities organized the formation of Canada Cement and the Steel Co. of Canada, two of the most resounding mergers of the time. In each case, Aitken received payment for his services in both money and shares, but he preferred to let go of the latter, little by little, without availing himself of the control it conferred. The same year he departed for London, leaving the presidency of the company to Izaac W. Killam in 1915 and finally selling it to him in 1919 for $6,000,000 (Nesbitt had already left to found his own investment bank in 1912). Aitken also sold his hydro-electric stock.[93] In 1920, Bennett was president of Calgary Power, the other directors being Killam, Aitken (now Lord Beaverbrook), V.M. Drury (from the Westmount family of millionaire politicians, in-laws of Aitken), and two company employees. In 1925, Killam organized a holding company, International Power, of which he assumed the presidency, to manage his utilities in Latin America.[94]

In the meantime, Killam brought new partners into Royal Securities. By 1929, these included H.J. Symington (a lawyer for the Grand Trunk Pacific, Price Bros., Canadian Marconi and many other companies, who was to become a director of Canadian National Railways and Trans Canada Air Lines and a senior Liberal civil servant during the Second World War), A.F. Culver, S.B. Hammond, N.S. Brooke and J.C. McKeen. None of them, however, were more than junior partners, for Killam held a majority share of Royal Securities' stock. Killam later hired several engineers, such as G.A. Gaherty and F. Krug, who eventually became minor associates and directors of Royal Securities.

As far as the structure of its activities is concerned, Royal Securities has always specialized in corporate financing, and it is for this reason that it was the investment house hardest hit by the Depression (see Table 9). Between 1924 and 1937, 97% of its public activities consisted of the purchase of corporate stock and debenture issues. From 1919 to 1929, it participated in the issues of at least sixty different companies, some of which were controlled by Killam or his associates

(Calgary Power, International Power and its subsidiaries, etc.), and others, including Price Bros., Riordon Co., Fraser Co. and Moirs Ltd. (in which Royal Securities had directorships) that had already done business with the firm. From 1930 on, Royal Securities was reduced to issues of companies under its control and those of its most loyal clients. During the Second World War it handled only a few public utility issues (Nova Scotia Light and Power, Newfoundland Light and Power), plus those of companies under its control, plus the odd new client (New Brunswick Telephone, Northern Telephone, Saskatoon Pipelines and a few others). By this time Royal Securities had become the smallest of the big brokerage houses. In 1954, the year before his death, Killam sold the company to his junior partners, Alan S. Gordon and J.R. Hughes among others, along with his interests in hydro-electricity. The empire built by Aitken and held together by Killam was slowly dissolving. In 1964 the Delaware-based United Corp. bought a majority block of shares in International Power. Merrill Lynch, New York's and the world's largest investment firm, bought Royal Securities in 1969, and this first case of absorption of a major brokerage house by an American company was met with cries of indignation.

Under its presidents Aitken and Killam, Royal Securities had operated as "finance capital" in the purest tradition of the American investment banks. There are, however, a number of important differences that should be pointed out, the first being that its focus on the control of public utilities, especially hydro-electricity through Calgary Power and International Power, seems to indicate that it had little access to the industrial sector. The second is that many of these public utility companies were located outside Canada, in Latin America. Third, even in comparison with the American public utility empires, that of Royal Securities is second rank, in terms both of the number of companies under its control and of their size. It is clearly a case of finance capitalism, but just a clearly of peripheral finance capitalism.

Turning to Dominion Securities Corporation, we find an investment house founded in 1910 by a group of Toronto financiers consisting of Senator George A. Cox (the principal shareholder of Central Canada Loan and Savings, president of Canada Life, director and shareholder of Imperial Life, the Canadian Bank of Commerce, the National Trust, etc.), Henry Pellatt (a long-time associate of William MacKenzie), Edward R. Wood (vice-president of Central Canada Loan and a director of the Bank of Commerce), and others. Three hundred thousand dollars of the authorized capital of $1,000,000 were issued, with Central Canada Loan taking $115,000, Pellatt $80,000 and E.R. Wood $ 50,000. Wood was president from 1901 to 1903, and, following the death of Cox, from 1912 to 1932. George H. Wood and James H. Gundy, who were respectively secretary and accountant, left the company in 1905 to form their own investment bank, Wood, Gundy and Co.

Dominion Securities specialized from the outset in the guaranteed purchase and distribution of Government of Canada, provincial and municipal bonds, as can be seen in Table 9, but did not turn its back on the occasional corporate transaction. A case in point is that of Burns and Co. Ltd., a corporation founded in Calgary in 1890 by Pat Burns that dealt with Dominion Securities as its banking house and organizer of stock issues. When Burns decided to retire in 1928, he called upon Dominion Securities to organize a new company whose assets were to be over-evaluated so as to water-down the share-capital. The spoils from this operation were divided up between Burns and Dominion Securities, the latter also receiving "all of the common stock, as consideration for its 'services' in the refinancing."[95]. The financial performance of Burns and Co. was disastrous, and another reorganization was necessary in 1934 to "deflate" its assets and share-capital. At that time Dominion Securities still owned 60% of Burns and Co. common stock. Other corporate clients in which Dominion Securities had a director, generally the president himself, were St. Lawrence Paper, Beauharnois Power (starting with its founding in 1929), General Steel Wares and Toronto Elevators.

Under the presidency of E.R. Woods and his successor after 1933, Arthur F. White, the company remained in the orbit of the big Toronto financial concerns until the Second World War. During the War it passed progressively into the hands of career employees. Harry Bawden, who inherited the presidency from A.F. White, was in turn replaced by a professional investment dealer, Geoffrey Phipps, in 1953. After the War, Dominion Securities attracted a number of large-scale clients such as Shawinigan Water and Power Corp., Consumers' Gas, Steinberg's, Canadian Canners and Great Lakes Paper, but none of its directors sat on the boards of these companies. In fact, Dofasco is, with H. Bawden on its board, the only big company that is linked by directorship to Dominion Securities (though Bawden is no longer the latter's president but still a board member). In 1973, Dominion Securities merged with Harris and Partners, a Canadian Investment firm founded in 1932 in which two London merchant banks (Baring Bros. and Morgan, Grenfell and Co.) had interests. As a result of this merger, Dominion Securities now has British shareholders, but it is impossible to determine the extent of their participation.

In contrast to Royal Securities, Dominion Securities is much closer to the London than to the American investment banks. By far the majority of its business is in public securities, despite a few issues that gave it a certain amount of control over industrial and utility companies in the 1920's and '30's. Yet it did not seek to maintain these privileged relations nor to establish a holding company to hold onto the stock it received from them. So it would appear that up until the Second World War, Dominion Securities was more or less an appendage of the Toronto group made up of the Bank of Commerce, the National Trust and Central Canada Loan.

The history of Wood, Gundy and Co. is both shorter and more complex. Founded in 1905 by two former employees of Dominion Securities, within twenty years it had become and has remained the largest investment bank in Canada. Table 9 indicates that it was primarily involved in corporate financing during the 1924-1929 period. It had arrived on the scene too late for the 1909-1913 wave of mergers, but it participated fully in the 1924-1929 corporate reorganizations. Its "creations" include Canada Power and Paper (founded in 1928 and evolving into Consolidated Paper in 1931 and Consolidated Bathurst in 1967), the holding company Simpson's Ltd., the giant British Empire Steel Corp. that it reorganized in 1928 and gave the new name of Dominion Steel Corporation, and formed Canada Cement, in 1927. Wood, Gundy and Co. set up four closed-end investment companies between 1925 and 1929. Other important clients at that time were Dominion Tar and Chemical (for which Wood, Gundy issued securities in association with Greenshilds and Co.), Howard Smith Paper Mills, Great Lakes Paper, and Montreal Light, Heat and Power. Wood, Gundy and Co. worked briefly in association with Holt, Gundy and Co., a short-lived investment house that existed only between 1928 and 1931. There seems to have been a certain division of labor between the two, with Holt, Gundy and Co. handling the mergers and Wood, Gundy and Co. distributing the securities of the newly-consolidated companies. The former company was the child of Sir Herbert Holt, the all-powerful president of the Royal Bank and Montreal Heat, Light and Power, associated with James H. Gundy and several corporate lawyers such as George Montgomery. Thanks to their watering down technique of reorganization, the tandem Holt, Gundy and Co.—Wood, Gundy and Co. succeeded in bringing about some of the most spectacular bankruptcies in the history of Canadian industry, of which it is sufficient to recall the collapse of Dosco, of Canada Power and Paper in 1931, and of Great Lakes Paper. The consequences of these bankruptcies, however, were much less disastrous for the investment dealers. The creation of Simpson's Ltd. gave Wood, Gundy 40% of the voting shares of the new holding company. [96] As a result of all these operations, J.H. Gundy was on the boards of about 50 of the biggest Canadian corporations by 1931—Canada Power and Paper, Dominion Steel Corp., Simpson's Ltd., Dominion Tar and Chemical, Canada Cement Co., Massey-Harris Co. and their major subsidiaries. [97] On the other hand, neither G.H. Wood, the president of Wood, Gundy until his retirement in 1933, nor his vice-presidents, G.T. Finch and A.W. Scripture, participated in the management of the client companies, [98] although there are a few cases where Wood, Gundy directors A.H. Williamson and A.D. Cobban did so.

The Depression cut into Wood, Gundy and Co's business, but did not reduce the volume of securities handled by more than about 15%. The primary consequence of the Crash was to reorient the Toronto firm in the direction of government securities. Of course, those old clients lucky enough to escape bankruptcy remained loyal (Canada Cement, Simpson's Ltd., Dominion Tar and Chemical, Massey-Harris, and Howard Smith Paper Mills), and Wood, Gundy directors continued to sit on their boards. The firm even succeeded in winning a few new clients like Great Lakes Power and Canadian Food Products, and the investment dealers' principal partners gave to these companies' boards the benefit of their experienced presence as well.

James H. Gundy handed the presidency of the company over to his son Charles in 1948, and remained chairman of the board until his death in 1951. He was replaced as chairman of the board by his nephew, William P. Scott. In 1967 William Price Wilder took over the presidency of the company from Charles L. Gundy, who continued the family tradition by becoming chairman of the board that same year. Throughout the whole post-war period, members of the Gundy family, as principal partners in the firm, continued to sit on the boards of the "old" client companies that Wood, Gundy had refinanced or reorganized during the 1920's—except, of course, those that had collapsed during the Depression. Thus, in 1955 and 1964 respectively, we find first Charles L. Gundy and then William Scott on the boards of Simpson's Ltd. and Simpson's Sears, the former also following in his father's footsteps as a member of the boards of Domtar, Canada Cement, Abitibi Power and Paper, Massey-Ferguson and Dominion Life. Scott tended to be on the boards of "new" clients like Great Lakes Power Corp., Trans Canada Pipelines and Canadian Food Products. In 1975, Charles L. Gundy, by then honorary chairman of the board, was still on the boards of the "old" clients, and C.E. Medland, president and managing director, along with vice-chairman of the Board, John N. Cole, was on the boards of the "new" ones. Medland is also a director of Distillers Corp.-Seagram and the Interprovincial Pipeline Co. (among others) and Cole is on the boards of Bombardier Ltd., Sherwin-Williams of Canada and Belding-Corticelli (among others)[99]. Here was have confirmation of Stapells' contention that it was the senior partners of the investment firms who acquired dominant positions through reorganizations, refinancing operations and security issues, rather than the investment firms themselves. For all the years mentioned above, several Wood, Gundy vice-presidents occupied no directorships whatsoever outside of the firm. This is all the more striking because Wood, Gundy remains the number one investment bank in Canada and acts, as the examples have shown, as an intermediary for many of the largest Canadian corporations.

Nesbitt Thomson and Co. was founded in 1912 by the former Royal Security employee Arthur J. Nesbitt and Peter A. Thomson. The two partners were respectively president and vice-president of the firm until 1952. As with Wood, Gundy and Co., the principal partners were members of the founders' families. James M. Aird, the father-in-law of A.J. Nesbitt, was also a vice-president from 1931 to 1956; in 1952, the presidency was assumed by Alfred's son Arthur D. Nesbitt, and in 1966 by P.A. Thomson's son, Peter Nesbitt Thomson, making it without any doubt a family concern. Nesbitt Thomson has specialized in corporate financing, in spite of a certain reconversion to public securities after

1930. In the private sector it had long dealt with hydro-electric companies and, through succeeding issues of shares or debentures Nesbitt Thomson acquired or received in partial payment voting shares in the companies concerned. This is how the investment house went about organizing Power Corporation as a holding company in hydro-electricity in 1925 (see above). Power Corp. remained under the control of the Nesbitt and Thomson families until the arrival of the Desmarais-Parisien group in 1968. For 43 years, Nesbitt Thomson continued to feed Power's portfolio with shares received from its financing of issues. In 1925, Power controlled nine hydro-electric companies, including Canada Northern Power, Ottawa and Hull Power, Ottawa River Power, East Kootenay Power, Southern Canada Power, Winnipeg Electric Co., Dominion Power and Transmission and Manitoba Power. Several of these owned, or later formed, subsidiaries in the mining industry. Nesbitt Thomson added to Power's portfolio substantial interests in the British Columbia Power Corp., Canada Steamships Lines (beginning in 1926), Canadian Celanese (also in 1926), Bathurst Power and Paper Co. (beginning in 1928), Canadian Oils Co. (beginning in 1940), and Trans-Canada Pipelines (beginning in 1957). Nesbitt Thomson also formed its own closed-end investment companies: the Foreign Power Securities Corp. in 1927, the Great Britain and Canada Investment Corp. in 1929, and Canada Power and Paper Investments in 1920. Not only did Nesbitt Thomson issue the securities of these companies, but its principal partners and officers also held key positions on the board of Power Corp. and on those of all the companies it controlled or influenced. As a result, Nesbitt Thomson's president Arthur J. Nesbitt held 20 directorships, P.A. Thomson 21, but vice-president and junior partner James S. Aird only three.[100] Twenty-five years later, in 1955, Arthur D. Nesbitt, president of the firm, held 11 directorships, Peter N. Thomson, vice-president and managing director 28, and two minor associates and vice-presidents, D.K. Baldwin and R.H. Dean, 4 and 5 respectively.[101] In all cases the directorships related to client companies whose share and debenture issues had been financed by Nesbitt Thomson. Lastly, the firm attracted a number of important clients other than Power Corporation and its subsidiaries after the War, the main one being Trans-Canada Pipelines for which Nesbitt Thomson organized through syndicates two issues of debentures in 1957, the first for $54 million and the second for $105 million. From then on there has been a continuous stream of issues, and senior partners of Nesbitt Thomson have taken their places on the pipeline company's board. During the 1960's, the Nesbitt and Thomson families sold part of their shares in Power Corp., thereby handing over control to the French-Canadian group led by Paul Desmarais. Only A.D. Nesbitt remains on Power's board, and in the capacity of an ordinary director.

Just as Royal Securities had done, during the 1920s and 30s the principal partners of Nesbitt Thomson and Co. created a public-utilities empire, managed by Power Corp. By operating as finance capitalists in the "marginal" sectors of the economy, A.J. Nesbitt and P.A. Thomson gave birth to a Canadian conglomerate second in size only to that of Canadian Pacific.

Having thus reviewed the history of the five largest Canadian investment houses of the 1924 to 1929 period, it is now time to draw a few general conclusions and look at the overall situation. Our first observation is that not all investment houses operate on the same principles or in the same markets. Two of the five firms we have studied— Nesbitt Thomson and Royal Securities—built financial groupings; two others—Dominion Securities and A.E. Ames and Co.—were only fractions of broader financial groups, in which the investment firms were far from being the most important institutions. The fifth, Wood, Gundy and Co., falling somewhere between the two preceding types, did exert some influence over several companies but never formed a holding company to manage the shares it held in them. Our second conclusion is that the investment banks have undergone a decline. Those that had created financial groups abandoned them during the 1960's, and it is now rare to find investment-firm directors on the boards of major companies—though Wood, Gundy and Nesbitt Thomson are somewhat of an exception in this respect. Canadian investment bankers have, along with their American colleagues, been losing momentum since 1930. There are four main reasons for this decline.

First, there was a steep drop in the volume of corporate securities issued by Canadian companies after 1930. Whereas $788 million-worth of shares were offered publicly between 1924 and 1929, for a yearly average of $131,300,000, the total from 1930 to 1937 was a mere $145,000,000, for a yearly average of only $18,100,000. (see Table 11). The *Monetary Times* stopped publishing figures on Canadian share issues in 1937, but all available data indicate that the market showed no improvement from 1938 to 1946 over the 1930 to 1937 period. Canadian sales of corporate bonds and debentures (including the railways) between 1920 and 1929 amounted to $2,334.7 million, for a yearly average of $233.5 million. From 1930 to 1939, they slumped to $1,548.2 million, of $155 million per year. [102]

Second, the investment bankers suffered from the creation of the Bank of Canada, which began to play an increasing role in the marketing of federal loans, and from the massive incursion of the Canadian chartered banks into federal securities investment (the federal government became during the Depression and the Second World War the principal issuer of bonds in Canada—See Table 11).

Third, the period of reorganization of the industrial base of Canada ended in 1930. According to Weldon, there were 315 consolidations between 1924 and 1930, with a volume of $968 million (volume is calculated or based on the gross assets less depreciation of the absorbed firms), while only 232 consolidations took place between 1931 and 1945, for a volume of $306 million. [103] From that point on, the financiers were faced with big corporations in practically every important sector

TABLE 10

MAJOR CANADIAN STOCK ISSUES BY BROKERAGE HOUSE (1924-1937) [1] (IN MILLIONS OF CURRENT $C AND %)

	1924	1925	1926	1927	1928	1929	1924-29	1930-37
Wood, Gundy & Co.	—	4.3	9.2	84.4[2]	12.5	31.9	142.3	3.4
Dominion Securities	—	—	0.8	10.1	47.5	1.5	59.9	1.5
Nesbitt Thomson & Co.	4.5	5.5	8.1	13.5	20.5	5.9	58.0	7.1
Royal Securities Corp.	7.0	—	7.0	2.3	8.1	9.9	34.3	0.6
A.E. Ames & Co.	0.6	3.8	6.1	0.9	3.9	5.9	21.2	22.5
Subtotal for the five ($)	12.1	13.6	31.2	111.2	92.5	55.1	315.7	35.1
Subtotal for the five (%)	24%	23%	32%	61%	37%	38%	40%	24%
Total ($)	50.7	59.6	97.0	183.5	253.5	143.8	787.8	145.2

Source: Monetary Times, Yearly issues 1924-38.
(1) Figures include issues organized by each brokerage firm operating on its own or at the head of a financial syndicate.
(2) Including $81 millions from the issue of preferred stock in Canada Cement organized by Wood, Gundy & Co. without the help of a syndicate.

TABLE 11

RESPECTIVE SHARE OF THE VARIOUS CHARTERED BANKS AND THE BANK OF CANADA IN GOVERNMENT OF CANADA BOND ISSUES (1924-1940) (IN MILLIONS OF CURRENT $ C$)

	1924	1925	1926	1927	1928	1929	1930	1931	1932	1933	1934	1935	1936	1937	1938	1939	1940
Chartered Banks	—	—	45	45	—	—	40	—	85	80	15	444.3	510	585	674.9	820	1075
American Banks	90	70	40	—	—	—	100	—	60	60	50	136	48	85	88.7	20	—
Bank of Canada	—	—	—	—	—	—	—	—	—	—	—	75	100	213.5	139.8	184.5	430
Mixed Syndicates[1]	85	—	20	—	—	—	—	858	81.3	225	265	60	—	—	—	—	—
Investment Bankers	—	75	—	—	—	—	—	—	—	—	—	—	—	—	—	—	—
Others[2]	—	24.3	—	—	—	—	—	—	—	75	70	—	135	—	—	—	575.6
TOTAL	175	169.3	105	45	—	—	140	858	226.3	440	400	739.3	793	883.5	903.4	1024.5	2080.6

Source: Monetary Times, Yearly issues 1925-1941.
(1) Chartered banks and investment bankers.
(2) Sold in London, sold privately, etc.

of manufacturing and mining, and directors on corporate boards were much more difficult to displace than those of the small pre-merger companies.

Fourth, the political and social climate was less and less hospitable to the investment bankers. It is true that the Canadian Royal Commission on Price Spreads was mere child's play in comparison with American government commissions (e.g. the 1932-34 Gray-Pecora Committee in the United States) that financiers elsewhere had sometimes to deal with. All the same, the evolution of the laws in the U.S. and Britain did come to have an effect on Canadian legislation. Prior to 1930, Canadian federal legislation on transferable securities had taken the form of amendments to the Companies Act. These amendments were intended to make companies tendering securities to the public disclose their prospectus, or report on the names of promoters, officers, and underwriters and publish the contract signed with the company that was the object of the promotion. Following British legislative tradition, the provinces included similar provisions in *their* company laws, but they also added an American invention, called "blue sky laws," which as early as 1912 had been requiring the registration of securities and investment companies. With the arrival of the Depression and fundamental changes in British and American legislation on transferable securities, federal and provincial laws on corporations were modified so as to increase the amount of information to be supplied by directors and promoters to the shareholders. The amendments adopted in 1935 permitted any shareholder to obtain information on the transactions in company shares carried out by the directors though, indeed, this right was little exercised. [104] Under the combined impact of a wave of promotion frauds and American government pressure, Ontario adopted another Canadian transferable securities law in 1945.

> "Canadian mining stock offered an almost perfect vehicle for fraudulent promotion, and American operators flocking to Toronto and Montreal were joined by a Canadian 'fringe' element eager to learn the art of milking suckers. Just how much was taken from the gullible (and greedy) is hard to tell, but the S.E.C. annual reports describe the growing seriousness of the 'Canadian problem'." [105]

The law increased both the quantity and the kind of information that the issuer was obliged to disclose before securities could be issued, and the provinces followed suit. All of these concerted developments undoubtedly resulted in a narrowed margin of manoeuvre for the financial promoters with respect to the control of companies.

One final point that should be brought out is the relationship between the investment houses and the chartered banks. With the exception of the first three presidents of Dominion Securities (G. Cox, E.R. Wood and A.F. White), this author has not come across any directorships common to both institution. It must be recognized, however, that investment firms are privately—owned companies or partnerships limited by shares, and the public is denied access to lists of their shareholders. Investment dealers also make use of short-term credit that the chartered banks put at their disposal, and it seems rather obvious that certain associations have been formed right from the beginning of the century between each investment house and the chartered bank that has given it credit preference (e.g. Dominion Securities and A.E. Ames and Co. with the Canadian Bank of Commerce; Wood, Gundy and Co. with the Royal Bank; Nesbitt Thomson and Co. with the Bank of Montréal), even if this is by no means proof that the chartered banks wield any influence over the investment firms.

Conclusion

In this part of our study, we have seen that the major financial institutions in Canada (the chartered banks, trust companies, life insurance companies, and the great majority of investment companies and brokerage firms) are not in a position of control over non-financial corporations. We have observed a few minor developments in this direction with the chartered banks, inasmuch as the trust companies and life insurance companies have tended in the last fifteen years to give over to them the control of some financial and real-estate firms. But the traditional picture of Canadian finance, one of abstention from the founding, reorganization and control of non-financial corporations, has remained unchanged. The main reason for this "abstention" is to be found in the formative and otherwise pervasive influence of the British financial system on financial practices in Canada. Canadian financial legislation, in which (to say the least) bankers themselves have had a hand, has in no way prevented the financial institutions from financing and participating in industry on a long-term basis. It is the institutions themselves that have put this field out of bounds by refusing to imitate the continental and American models of financial control and involvement in industry.

Why is it that the British financial system has had so great an influence on that of Canada? In the first place, because the latter took shape in the 19th and early 20th centuries and transposed the modes of organization current in the metropolis that was dominant at the time. Second, because the Canadian ruling class that built the financial system here in Canada was in its majority of British origin. And third, because a model in which the banks and other financial institutions steer clear of industrial corporate control corresponds perfectly to the dependent structure of the Canadian economy, in which industry is either lagging behind, economically dispersed, or under foreign control. The continued adherence to a financial system modeled after British finance is therefore not the result of any formal or legal imposition on the part of Great Britain, but a reflection of the dependent economic and social structure of Canada.

The only major exception to the picture we have painted seems to be the holding companies modelled on the American system. This kind of financial corporation, however, is far from being the standard way in which industrial companies are controlled in Canada. Of the one hundred largest manufacturing, mining and utility corporations listed by the Financial Post in 1975,[106] only 40 were known not to be under foreign control, and of these 40 companies only six (Massey-Ferguson, Domtar and Noranda Mines for Argus, Canada Steamship Lines and Consolidated Bathurst for Power Corp., and J. Labatt's for Brascan) were controlled by a holding company.

Several cases, such as those of Abitibi over Price and Algoma Steel over Dominion Bridge, showed control by a non-financial firm. Others were family-controlled (the Molson family controls the conglomerate of the same name; the Bronfman family, Distillers-Seagram). As for companies like Bell Canada or Canadian Pacific, no one institution or large block of shareholders appeared to have control. As further evidence, the same page of the *Financial Post* presents a list of the 25 largest financial institutions in Canada by assets, as of December 31, 1974. This list included the seven largest Canadian chartered banks, of which only one is under financial control (the Provincial Bank, controlled by the *Mouvement des Caisses Desjardins*), the four largest trust companies (of which only the National Trust has a large corporate shareholder, Canada Life), the nine largest insurance companies (of which only the Great West is under financial control, that of Power Corp.), the two major mortgage and loan companies (of which only the Canada Permanent Mortgage Corp. is bank-controlled, by the Toronto Dominion and the Bank of Nova Scotia), and the three biggest sales-finance companies, with again only one being under financial control (the Traders Group, controlled by Canadian General Securities). All told, only 5 cases of financial control out of 25, and not one case of non-financial institutional control.

The foregoing shows clearly that the finance capital theory remains useful only as a working' hypothesis. In its original version, that of Hilferding's bank control, it has proven to be inapplicable to the Canadian context. Even in Lenin's more qualified version, which refers to bank-industry interpenetration rather than control, it raises more questions than it answers. If interpenetration simply means "personal connections" at the level of boards of directors, the concept is a trivial one. If interpenetration is meant to refer to actual involvement through shareholding by one corporation in another, it is not hard to show that this is not the case in Canada. Banks and the other financial institutions, with the exception of holding companies, do not control non-financial companies, and non-financial companies do not control financial ones. Finally, if interpenetration at the board level is conceived of as various types of commercial (a bank supplying commercial credit to its industrial clientèle), financial (common directors being individual principal shareholders in the financial and non-financial enterprises they administer) or other relations, such connections must first be detected and then studied. The Marxist theory of financial control can, at best, explain only part of the control of joint stock companies in Canada. It must be supplemented with the Berle and Means[107] theory of internal control, consideration of cases of family or even individual control of corporations, control by non-financial institutions, etc.

Finally, let us stress that control of a company by a holding company does not always mean that the control is financial. Numerous examples, in particular that of C.P. Investments, show that the holding company is often nothing more than a technical-administrative means of centralization and reorganization, used by an already-established interest group. Only a few holding companies—Power Corp. among them—were formed by financiers or brokers. In many cases they are a mere pawn on the checkerboard of a family empire, like that of G. Weston, or of an internally-controlled conglomerate, like Canadian Pacific.

The investment banks, for their part, were heavily involved in the process of consolidation and reorganization that took place in Canadian industry between 1900 and 1930, and it was not uncommon for the principal partners of the investment firms to accumulate positions of control in the refinanced concerns. Nevertheless, it was not the investment houses *as such* that inherited the mantle of industrial power. In addition to this, a whole series of factors sent the investment firms into a long decline after 1930. This led some to merge in order to stave off extinction, while others fell prey to American or British investment banks.[108]

NOTES

(1) R. Hilferding, *Le Capital financier* (1910), Ed. de Minuit, Paris, 1970, p. 180.
(2) Ibid., p. 181.
(3) Ibid., p. 319.
(4) Lenin, *Notebooks on Imperialism*, Complete Works, Vol. 39, Progress Publishers, Moscow, 1976, pp.202 and 333-338; Lenin, *Imperialism, The Highest Stage of Capitalism*, in *Lenin: Selected Works in Three Volumes*, International Publishers, New York, 1967.
(5) Lenin, *Imperialism. . .* (op. cit.), Vol. I, p. 705.
(6) Ibid., p. 716.
(7) A. Rochester, *Rulers of America: A Study of Finance Capital*, F. White Publishers Ltd., Toronto, 1936, p. 13.
(8) V. Perlo, *The Empire of High Finance*, International Publishers, New York, 1961.
(9) P. Sweezy, *The Theory of Capitalist Development*, (1942), Dobson, New York, 1967, and, "The Decline of the Investment Banker" in *The Present as History*, Monthly Review Press, New York, 1955.
     P. Baran & P. Sweezy, *Monopoly Capital*, Monthly Review Press, New York, 1966.
     H. Magdoff, *The Age of Imperialism*, Monthly Review Press, New York, 1967.
     See also, in a similar vein:
     J. O'Connor, "Finance Capital or Corporate Capital" in *Monthly Review*, New York, December 1968. and,
     E. Herman, "Do Bankers Control Corporations?," in *Monthly Review*, New York, 1973.
(10 A. Rochester, *The Rulers of America*, op. cit., Chapters 2 to 5.
(11) V. Perlo, *The Empire of High Finance*, op. cit., Chapter 7.
(12) J.-M. Chevalier, *La structure financière de l'industrie américaine*, Paris, Cujas, 1970, Part II.
(13) P. Baran & P. Sweezy, *Monopoly Capital*, op. cit., p. 18.
14) J.-M. Chevalier, *La structure financière de l'industrie américaine*, op. cit.

(15) Ibid., p. 106.
(16) S. Menshikov, *Millionaires and Managers*, Progress Publishers, Moscow, 1969.
(17) Ibd., pp. 214-215.
(18) R. Fitch & M. Oppenheimer, "Who Rules the Corporations?," in *Socialist Revolution*, (Vol. I, No. 4, 5 & 6), San Francisco, July-December 1970.
(19) P. Sweezy, "The Resurgence of Financial Control: Fact or Fancy?," in *Socialist Revolution* (Vol. II, No. 8), March-April 1972, and in *Monthly Review*, November 1971; as well as J. O'Connor, "Who Rules the Corporations?," in *Socialist Revolution* (Vol. II, No.7, Jan.-Feb. 1971).
(20) R. Fitch, "Repy", in *Socialist Revolution*, (Vol. II, No. 7), January-February, 1971. R. Fitch, "Sweezy and Corporate Fetishism," in *Socialist Revolution*, (Vol. II, No. 12), December 1972.
(21) E.S. Herman, "Do Bankers Control the Corporations?," op. cit.
(22) J. Bouvier, *Un siècle de banque française*, Paris, Hachette, 1973.
(23) Ibid., p. 116.
(24) P. Barret Whale, *Joint Stock Banking in Germany*, McMillan & Co., London, 1930.
(25) R. Cameron (ed.) *Banking in the Early Stages of Industrialization*, Oxford University Press, New York, 1967.
(26) A. Gerschenkron, *Economic Backwardness in Historical Perspective*, F.A. Prager, New York, 1965.
(27) B.D. Nash, *Investment Banking in England*, A. Shaw & Co., Chicago & New York, 1924. pp. 42-43.
(28) Ibid. p. 45.
(29) A.T.K. Grant, *A Study of the Capital Market in Britain From 1919 to 1936*, (2nd Edition), A.M. Kelley, New York, 1967, p. 173.
(30) V.P. Carosso, *Investment Banking in America*, Harvard U.P., Cambridge 1970.
(31) J.C. Bonbright & G. Means, *The Holding Company*, (1932), A.M. Kelley & Co., New York, 1969.
(32) V.P. Carosso, *Investment Banking in America*, op. cit., Chapters 17 to 19.
(33) D.J. Baum & N.B. Stiles, *The Silent Partners: Institutional Investors and Corporate Control*, Syracuse U.P., New York, 1965.
(34) F. Morin, *La structure financière du capitalisme français*, Paris, Calman-Lévy, 1975.
(35) J. O'Connor, "Finance Capital or Corporate Control," op. cit.
(36) J. Bouvier, *Un siècle de banque française*, op. cit., loc. cit.
(37) F. & L. Park, *The Anatomy of Big Business*, (1962), Toronto, J. Lewis & Co., 1973.
(38) Ibid., p. 71.
(39) Ibid., p. 73.
(40) Ibid., p. 79.
(41) Ibid., p. 80.
(42) Ibid., pp. 84-85.
(43) Ibid., p. 74.
(44) T. Naylor, *The History of Canadian Business 1867-1914*, Toronto, J. Lorimer & Co., 1976, 2 Volumes.
45) Ibid., Volume I, Chapter VI.
(46) E.P. Neufeld, *The Financial System of Canada*, Toronto, MacMillan 1972, pp. 612-621.
(47) Ibid., loc. cit.
(48) Among other titles on this subject, see:
  H. Marshall et al, *Canadian-American Industry*, (1936), McClelland & Stewart, Toronto, 1976.
  H. Aitken, *American Capital and Canadian Resources*, Toronto, 1961.
  K. Levitt, *Silent Surrender*, Montreal, 1971.
(49) E.P. Neufeld, *The Financial System of Canada*, op. cit., pp. 114-116.
(50) House of Commons Select Standing Committee on Banking and Commerce, Session of 1928, p. 101.
(51) House of Commons Select Standing Committee on Banking and Commerce, Session of 1934; of particular interest is the testimony of Sir Charles B. Gordon.
(52) *Royal Commission on Banking and Finance*, 1964, Ottawa, The Queen's Printer, Chapter 7.
(53) Among others, see: E.P. Neufeld, *The Financial System of Canada*, op. cit., pp. 105-138.
(54) Other later shareholders include financiers W.H. McDonald, Michael Boyd and C. Howard Eaton, corporations such as Alcan, Time, Edper Investments (owned by Edward and Peter Bronfman), the Air Canada and Canadian Pacific pension funds. Duke Sealbridge (owned by the Guinness family of England), and the Houston, Willoghby & Co. investment house. (See *La Presse*, June 3, 1976 Edition, p. A-13).
(55) E.P. Neufeld, *The Financial System of Canada*, op. cit., p. 310.
(56) Ibid., p. 312.
(57) Royal Commission on Banking and Finance, op. cit., p. 194.
(58) D.J. Baum, *The Investment Function of Canadian Financial Institutions*, Praeger, New York, 1973, p. 71.
(59) E.P. Neufeld, *The Financial System of Canada*, op. cit., pp. 306-307.
(60) F. & L. Park, *The Anatomy of Big Business*, op. cit., p. 244.
(61) *Monetary Times*, several articles published in February and March, 1882.
(62) Among others, see the statements of bankers appearing before the House of Commons Select Standing Committee on Banking and Commerce, Sessions of 1928 and 1934.
(63) *Royal Commission on Banking and Finance*, op. cit., p. 195.
(64) Ibid., loc. cit.
(65) Part of the agency funds are administered as mutual funds. The data on the shares held in these funds, of which the largest is in the Royal Trust "m" Fund, indicate that the share portfolios are remarkably dispersed and that there are practically no personal connections between the trust companies and the companies of which they are shareholders. In particular see the *Financial Post Survey of Investment Funds* directory, 1962-1976.
(66) *Moody's Bank and Finance*, 1958 & 1959. For a description of the attempt to take over Sun Life between 1950 and 1956 and the subsequent conversion of the company into a mutual company, see J. Schull, *The Century of the Sun*, MacMillan of Canada, Toronto, 1971.
(67) S. Schwarzchild & A.E. Zubay, *Principles of Life Insurance*, R.C. Irwin & Co., Illinois, 1964, Vol. II, pp. 4-16.
(68) E.P. Neufeld, *The Financial System of Canada*, op. cit., pp. 260-261.

(69) On this question see: the *Report of the Royal Commission on Life Insurance* (1907); T. Naylor, *The History of Canadian Business*, op. cit., Vol. I, pp. 192-197; J. Schull, *The Century of the Sun*, op. cit., pp. 15-22.
(70) J. Schull, *The Century of the Sun*, op. cit., pp. 58-59. In 1927, 55% of the assets of Sun Life were in shares.
(71) E.P. Neufeld, *The Financial System of Canada*, op. cit., p. 241.
(72) For a description of the major companies, see: H. Bullock, *The Story of Investment Trusts*, New York, Columbia University Press, 1959.
(73) *Report of the Royal Commission on Price Spreads* (1935), Ottawa, Printer to His Majesty the King.
(74) H. Bullock, *The Story of Investment Trusts*, op. cit., p. 25. On the parallel development of mutual funds, or unit trusts, in Britain, see K.T. Grant, *A Study of the Capital Market in Britain from 1919 to 1936*; for the United States, see: J.S. Warner & C. Russel Doane, *Investment Trusts and Funds*, Mass., 1955.
(75) *Moody's Bank and Finance*, New York, 1964.
(76) F. Marshall et al, Canadian-American Industry (1936), McClelland & Stewart, Carleton Library, 1976.
(77) *Moody's Bank and Finance*, New York, 1946, p. 1066.
(78) W. Clement, *The Canadian Corporate Elite*, McClelland & Stewart, Carleton Library, Toronto, 1975.
(79) Ibid., p. 135.
(80) *Moody's Public Utility*, 1973, p. 2243.
(81) J.C. Bonbright & G. Means, *The Holding Company* (1932), A.M. Kelley Publ., New York, 1969.
(82) V.P. Carosso, *Investment Banking in America*, op. cit.
(83) Royal Commission on Price Spreads (H. H. Stevens, Chairman), 1935, Ottawa, Printer to His Majesty the King. J. C. Weldon, "Consolidations in Canadian Industry, 1900-1948", in L.A. Skeoch, *Restrictive Trade Practices in Canada*, Toronto, 1966, pp. 228-279.
(84) E.P. Neufeld, *The Financial System of Canada*, op. cit., p. 492.
(85) *Royal Commission on Price Spreads* (1935), op. cit., p. 33.
(86) A. Ernest Epp, *Cooperation Among Capitalists: The Canadian Merger Movement, 1909-1913*, Ph.D. Thesis, Johns Hopkins University, Baltimore, Maryland, 1973.
(87) H.G. Stapells, *The Recent Consolidation Movement in Canadian Industry*, M.A. Thesis, University of Toronto, 1922, p. 313.
(88) Ibid., pp. 70-71.
(89) *A.E. Ames & Co., 1899-1949*, Toronto, 1950 (Private publication).
(90) *Financial Post Directory of Directors*, 1931, Toronto, pp. 11-12.
(91) The data on A.E. Ames & Co. were taken from the yearly issues of the *Monetary Times* (1915-1962), the *Financial Post Directory of Directors* (1931-1975), several annual reports of A.E. Ames & Co. and the *Canadian Who's Who* (1928-1969).
(92) A.J.P. Taylor, *Beaverbrook*, Penguin Books, London, 1974, Chapters 1 and 2; *Commercial Register of Canada*, The Globe Publishing Co., London, 1930, pp. 123-125.
(93) A.J.P. Taylor, op. cit., p. 37.
(94) *Annual Financial Review*, Houston Publ. Co., Toronto, 1920 and 1926.
(95) *Royal Commission on Price Spreads* (1935), *Report*, p. 384.
(96) Ibid., p. 337 and thereafter.
(97) *Financial Post Directory of Directors*, 1931, p. 150.
(98) *Commercial Register of Canada*, op. cit., pp. 127-28.
(99) *Annual Reports,* Wood, Gundy ! Co., 1955, 1964, 1973.
(100) *Financial Post Directory of Directors*, 1931, pp. 8, 276, and 369.
(101) *Financial Post Directory of Directors*, 1955, pp. 20, 94, 299 and 399.
(102) *Monetary Times*, Yearly issues, 1931 to 1940.
(103) J.C. Weldon, "Consolidations in Canadian Industry, 1900-1948," op. cit., p. 233.
(104) C.A. Ashley & J.C. Smyth, *Corporation Finance in Canada*, Macmillan, Toronto, 1956, p. 203.
(105) J.P. Williamson, *Securities Regulation in Canada*, University of Toronto Press, 1960, p. 380.
(106) *Financial Post*, July 26, 1975, p. 13.
(107) A. Berle Jr. & G. Means, *The Modern Corporation and Private Property* (1932), Harcourt, Brace and World, New York, 1968.
(108) See the article intitled Brokers, the Battle for Survival" published in the *Montreal Star* on October 26, 1974, p. G-1.

CHAPTER II

INTERNAL CONTROL, CONGLOMERATES AND OTHER FORMS OF CONTROL

THE THEORY OF INTERNAL CONTROL, or of control by professional managers, is in direct opposition to the theory of finance capital. All versions of this latter theory hold that power in large industrial and commercial corporations tends to concentrate outside the corporations and inside financial institutions—in banks, in particular. According to the theory of internal control, however, a process of share-dispersal has caused power in large corporations to pass from shareholders to the company's senior management and non-ownership directors. Control of large enterprises by families, individual capitalists or small groups of associates is in the process of disappearing, or already a thing of the past. Once detached from the grasp of their owners, companies characterized by internal control would no longer be oriented to the maximization of profits; their managers would become a neutral technocracy, administering the companies according to the pressures exerted by consumers, governments, workers and shareholders.

The managerialist doctrine goes on to attack classical and neoclassical economic thinking. Almost nowhere in economic thinking is control even an issue: the capitalist or entrepreneur would make the key decisions in the firm, but he would do so according to the impersonal laws of the market, laws set by the free play of supply and demand. If he chose not to obey those laws, he would disappear. Whatever their form of control, companies were condemned to seek maximum profit.

The managerialist trend was established in 1932 with the publication of *The Modern Corporation and Private Property*, by Adolf A. Berle Jr. and Gardiner C. Means.[1] Berle and Means attracted many followers in the economic and sociological academic communities, including—to name only the best-known—James Burnham, Ralph Dahrendorf and John K. Galbraith. There were critics as well, however, from the ranks of both orthodox economists and Marxist economists and sociologists. In the first section of this chapter we shall review the arguments *pro* and *con* and then draw our own conclusions. In the second section we shall test this theory in the Canadian context, using 1975 data on the ownership of shares in the 136 largest Canadian companies in the sectors of finance, industry, commerce, utilities and transportation and real-estate development.

The Theory of Internal Control and Its Critics

In their book, which laid the basis for the managerialist theory, Berle and Means proceeded as follows: they claimed and demonstrated that (a) the most basic economic unit in the contemporary capitalist system is the corporation; (b) corporations centralize a growing proportion of the assets of all sectors of economic activity; (c) ownership of shares in these companies has a tendency to become dispersed among thousands of shareholders and, as a consequence, the great majority of shareholders has lost any possibility of effective control over the companies; and (d) the proxy vote requested by the sitting board of directors, tends to reinforce the power of these directors and make the oligarchies practically unassailable. Berle and Means define control as follows:

> "Control lies in the hands of the individual or group who have the actual power to select the board of directors (or its majority), either by mobilizing the legal right to choose them—controlling a majority of the votes directly or through some legal device—or by exerting pressure which influences their choice."[2]

Berle and Means reviewed the methods of controlling the 200 largest non-financial companies in the United States and concluded that internal control, that is (in their terms), control by corporation directors and senior officers, was increasingly the dominant method of control.

> "Separation of ownership and control becomes almost complete when not even a substantial minority interest exists, as in the American Telephone and Telegraph Company, whose largest holder is reported to own less than one percent of the company's stock. Under such conditions, control may be held by the directors or titular managers who can employ the proxy machinery to become a self-perpetuating body, even though as a group they own but a small fraction of the stock outstanding."[3]

The authors draw a good many conclusions from their observations. Among the most important is the rejection of the theory of profit maximization as the determining influence on large companies. Shareholders are interested in profit but they no longer hold power in the large companies. Since directors are no longer obliged to seek profit maximization, the behaviour of companies in the market is no longer under this form of determination, especially since monopoly and oligopoly are the usual methods of competition. Thus, classical and neo-classical theories of the setting of prices and allocation of resources no longer apply. However, Berle and Means do not believe that directors hold unlimited power. New constraints are being formed: pressures by salaried workers, consumers and government are such that this unassailable body of directors distributes the fruits of production in an equable manner.

> "It is conceivable—indeed it seems almost essential if the corporate system is to survive—that the 'control' of the great corporations should develop into a pure neutral technocracy, balancing a variety of claims by various groups in the community and assigning to each a portion of the income stream on the basis of public policy rather than private cupidity."[4]

In a later work, *Power Without Property*,[5] Berle reaffirms his theories of internal control, but introduces some important changes. According to this new version, control in large corporations goes through four stages: the first is that of majority control by the founding shareholders and lasts only one generation; the second is that of *de facto* working control in which an individual or group holds a minority of the shares but retains influence over the other directors and company; the third is that of internal control which, he says, characterizes American industry today. He predicts that this stage will also be a transitory one and will give way to control by financial institutions.

> "Now appears the fourth stage. In this situation emerge the newer mechanisms, the fiduciary institutions, by which these dispersed stockholdings are once more concentrated. . . But as distribution of income increases voting power becomes increasingly concentrated."[6]

The concentration of stockholding in financial institutions does not change Berle's conclusions, as set out in the earlier book. First, because the process has only just begun. Second, because bank, insurance company and mutual-fund directors are just as removed from their stockholders as are the directors of industrial companies. Finally, because in finance as in industry, the forces for equilibrium (the consumers, workers and the State) are developing as quickly as the powers of the corporate directors.

The reader will have recognized in our outline all the elements of the theories of John K. Galbraith on countervailers and technostructures.[7] The differences between Berle and Galbraith are too slight to mention. To some extent, it was Galbraith who popularized the results of the research done by Berle and Means, for his books are more easily read by the public than theirs.

James Burnham came up with a somewhat different theory of internal control.[8] Like Berle and Means, Burnham holds that control of joint-stock companies has been removed from the hands of the stockholders and concentrated in those of the managers, but Burnham is referring to a different sort of "manager" and he explains the process differently. For Burnham, the power of the managers is strengthened, not by the progressive dispersal of shares, but by the growing complexity of technology and of company-administration. Furthermore, when he talks about the "managers" he is not talking about the members of the board of directors who have inherited the control of large companies, but rather, about the technocrats of senior management. This variant on the theory of managerial control was worked out in 1940 under the combined influences of the rise of fascism and the doctrines of Berle and Means, and has not won many followers. It is the Berle and Means versions which has been at the base of an entire school of thought.

R.J. Larner is one of the most important defenders of this theory.[9] Larner replicated the 1929 research using the same definitions, classifications and procedures as had Berle and Means, but with 1963 data. His results confirmed the tendency towards internal control in the 200 largest non-financial companies in the United States. While in 1929 44% of these companies were under internal control, Larner stated that by 1963 the figure had risen to 84.5%. The tendency seemed even more marked in terms of total assets: in 1929, internally-controlled companies centralized 58% of the assets of the 200 largest firms. In 1963, the proportion was 85%. Larner's figures therefore supported the theory of Berle and Means and helped it continue to flourish in academic circles.

Ralph Dahrendorf adopted the Berle and Means theory as well. He claimed that the divorce between ownership and control of corporations is one of the main characteristics of contemporary industrial society.[10] According to this German sociologist, this phenomenon has spread throughout the most advanced Western countries, i.e. the United States, France, Germany and the U.K. Dahrendorf draws imaginative conclusions about the social structure which results from the separation of ownership and industrial control, notably the appearance of a new upper class, distinct from that of the capitalists and formed by the managers who are no longer recruited by class, but for competence.

Berle and Means' work has been repeated in Great Britain,[11] where the theory of internal control has been adopted, among others, by the Labour Party. In the United States, the main elements of their theories are to be found in the doctrine of "people's capitalism," which is widely propagated by business circles. This, therefore, is an ideology and a theory with widespread currency in the contemporary capitalist world.

The Critique of Internal Control

We may now turn to those who—whether it be from an academic perspective or a Marxist one—have sought to invalidate the theories of Berle and Means. One of the most important critics is Edward S. Mason. In a now-famous article, Mason attacked the conclusions of the managerialist approach to economic theory.[12] Yet, for him, the extension of internal control is an irreversible fact.

> "The attenuation of ownership and the expansion of the area of managerial control in large corporations are other significant developments rightly emphasized in the managerial literature."[13]

Mason points out, however, that the Berle and Means theory does not explain the mechanisms by which, in a system of internally controlled oligopolistic enterprises, resources are allocated, factors of production rewarded or prices determined. The managerialists also fail to explain what will prevent abuses of power by large corporations. For Mason, "countervailance" is an inadequate argument.

> "The 'countervailers' have never been able to explain why countervailance does not lead merely to a sharing of monopoly profits at the expense of the rest of the economy. If fear of adverse government action is the limitation, what government action is feared and what evidence is there that it can and will be taken? Nor does the conscience of corporation management, duly instructed by public opinion, appear to be a particularly reliable reed."[14]

Marxists and radicals direct their criticism more at the issue of control itself than at its eventual consequences for the workings of the capitalist economy.[15] They show that share-dispersal is far from being as pronounced as the managerialists have claimed it to be. For example, the amount held by the top one percent of American shareholders has risen from 61.5% in 1922 to 76% in 1953.[16]. Furthermore, the major shareholders are well represented on the boards of directors of the large corporations, either in person or through their lawyers or trustees: thus, the separation of ownership and control only means that the great bulk of *small* shareholders has lost control. Example after examples proves that managers cannot withstand the opposition mounted by large shareholders in those rare cases where one of their decisions goes against the interests of that group. Also, many managers, hired for their technical, legal or financial competence, buy shares in the companies which employ them and thus themselves become large shareholders. None of these critics, however, question the assertion that the proportion of directorships held by professional managers has risen over the years.

> "As industrial corporations grew and developed in complexity, more skilled persons were required to keep affairs running smoothly. Moreover the rapid technological developments of this century have placed greater demands on the management of large concerns. Decisions based on technical understanding became more frequent and the demands on management increased in direct proportion. Thus a very large fraction of these executives rose through the ranks as specialists of one sort or another."[17]

The Marxist critique emphasizes that, whatever may be the method of control, large corporations have no choice about seeking maximization of profits: they must do so because high profits are the key to their growth (through the reinvestment of undistributed dividends) and to self-financing through the sale of company stock (low profits mean low dividends which mean low prices for their shares on the stock exchange). In other words, the market behaviour of the big companies is structurally determined by the conditions of oligopolistic rivalry. No company can escape these constraints.[18]

Conclusions

The criticisms directed at the theory of internal control seem conclusive as far as the question of the behaviour of internally-controlled companies is concerned. The Berle and Means theory does not explain the mechanisms of price formation, allocation of resources or the remuneration of work and capital under such a system. The managerialists' view of the social responsibility and beneficient neutrality of the managers has very openly the appearance of an ideology which seeks to justify certain traits of the monopolist stage of advanced capitalism.

Moreover, according to the final works by the very father of this theory, Adolf Berle, share dispersal is being nullified by the growing concentration of shares in the finance departments of commercial banks, life-insurance companies and mutual funds. Berle assumes throughout the elaboration of his thesis that these financial institutions are themselves in the process of falling under the control of their managers, but he furnishes no empirical proof for this assumption. His 1929 study, like that of Larner in 1963, concerns itself only with non-financial institutions; nothing justifies their assumption that the same process is underway in financial ones.

At the methodological level, one can raise many questions about the "data" of those who defend this theory. How many of the companies which Berle and Means or Larner classify as being under internal control are so in fact? In how many cases are we really dealing with a lack of information (complete lists of shareholders not being available) or incorrect classification of the information? Those who wield power in large enterprises rarely seek to publicize their dominant position, and their modesty is facilitated by a variety of mechanisms of minority control and by the use of dummy corporations, private investment companies, foundations and the like. The type and quantity of sources used by the researcher, therefore, can enormously influence his results. As an example, let us compare Larner's figures for 1963 with those of Chevalier for 1965-66. The former found that 169 of the 200 largest non-financial institutions in the United States were internally controlled[19]; the latter found only 80 such cases among the 200 largest industrial companies,[20] whereas Larner had claimed that 91 of the 117 industrials on his list fell into this category. It is hard to determine how much of this discrepancy is due to the sources and how much to the nuances in the operational definitions employed. On this latter point, one should note that Larner's definition of "internal control" is broader, with a threshold of under 10%, whereas in the Chevalier study the threshold for internal control was 5%.

In the following section, we shall study the extent of internal control to be found in a list of the major financial and non-financial institutions in Canada. We have eliminated the subsidiaries of foreign companies, since the study of the ultimate control of these corporations would cause us to extend our analysis to the parent companies abroad. We shall make no prior assumptions about the market behaviour of the firms or about the responsibility of their directors either to the companies they administer or to society as a whole. In fact, we shall not deal with these issues at all. Like Berle and Means, Larner, Villarejo or Chevalier, we shall study the type of corporate control, whether it be internal or not, and we shall distinguish among the types of control that we find. In other words, the degree (whether greater or lesser) of internal control that we find will neither confirm nor invalidate the managerialists' conclusions about the "managerial revolution," "corporate conscience" or the social responsibility of the directors. Like Baran and Sweezy, we believe that the market behaviour of companies (and of their directors) is structurally determined, unaffected by the nature of company control. In this work we wish to test only the essence of the theory of internal control, namely, that a large majority of large corporations are controlled by professional directors (managers). If the theory of Berle and Means proves false, we may briefly consider the composition of the Canadian big bourgeoisie, the class which owns and administers the major companies in this country.

Internal Control, Conglomerates and Other Forms of Control in Canada

We shall test the validity of the theory of internal control by referring to statistics on ownership of company shares. We shall first set forth the sources and methods used to arrive at those statistics and our conclusion. We shall study in some detail the major examples of companies which we find to be internally-controlled, in order better to understand that category as a whole. We shall then discuss the companies excluded from that category, namely, family companies and those under individual or group control. Finally, we shall examine the rise of conglomerates, for we believe this phenomenon to be the major present trend countering that of share dispersal. Even if all our statistics come from one moment in time (December 1975), we shall put forth several hypotheses about apparent trends, over time, in the different forms of control.

Sources and Methodology

Our goal is to understand control of *Canadian* companies. We therefore eliminated from our lists all subsidiaries of foreign companies whose immediate control is generally either absolute or at least majority in form and whose ultimate control lies beyond our borders. In order to carry out this process of elimination, we drew on the 1976 editions of the Financial Post Survey of Industrials, the F.P. Survey of Mines, the F.P. Survey of Oils, Moody's Industrial Manual, Moody's Bank and Finance Manual, Moody's Transportation Manual and Moody's Utility Manual, and, finally, the lists of major Canadian corporations as published in the Financial Post of 31 July 1976. These statistics were confirmed by those of the monthly Bulletins issued by the Ontario and Quebec Securities Commissions.[21]

We had next to limit our list of Canadian-controlled companies by size. We settled on a minimum of $100 million in total assets and so came up with a manageable list which could be compared to studies done elsewhere, notably, in the United States. If we had instead chosen a lower limit—say, minimum assets of $50 million—we would have had a much longer list that included medium-sized companies but could not possibly be compared to those studied by Larner or Chevalier.

Our list included the 50 largest industrial corporations (mining and manufacturing)—i.e., all Canadian-controlled companies with total assets of $100 million or more. It also included 50 financial institutions—the seven chartered banks, the Savings Bank of the City and District of Montréal,[22], the ten largest insurance companies under domestic control, the eleven largest trust companies owned by Canadians, the nine biggest holding companies and ten other financial institutions (the biggest finance companies, mortgage-loan companies, fixed-term investment companies, mutual funds and the largest brokerage firm). We have also included the fifteen largest utility and transportation companies and the fifteen largest real-estate development companies. In these last three sectors, as with industrials, our list included every company under Canadian control with total assets of $100 million or more in December 1975.

The statistics on assets were taken from the final financial statement of 1975 which, in most cases, carried the date of 31 December. For a few companies, primarily banks and trusts, the date was 31 October instead. In a few other cases we had to use the latest available statement, whatever its date of presentation to shareholders. Table I, annexed to this chapter, gives the complete list of companies studied, their assets and the date of the financial statement used.

We also had to decide whether or not to include the subsidiaries of companies already on the list which themselves had assets of $100 million or more. Berle and Means included such companies only if they also had a pyramidal structure worthy of analysis. Larner, in 1966, followed the same criterion, but he also included subsidiaries under the majority control of parent companies which were smaller than their subsidiaries and not themselves on the list. In other words, he treated such subsidiaries like independent companies under majority control. We have included all those subsidiaries with at least $100 million in assets, whether or not the parent corporation was on our list (i.e. whether or not the parent company itself had $100 million of assets) and whatever might be the form of control employed (absolute, majority or minority). We eliminated only those subsidiaries whose financial statements were consolidated with those of their parent companies and thus impossible to disaggregate. We therefore eliminated companies like Canada Permanent Trust, a wholly-owned subsidiary of Canada Permanent Mortgage Corporation, and Shawinigan Industries Ltd., a wholly-owned subsidiary of Power Corporation of Canada. In these two cases, the financial statement of the subsidiary was consolidated with that of the parent company and no separate report on its own assets was available. Our list therefore included 81 independent companies, 55 subsidiaries of these independent companies, seven chartered banks (which publish no figures on ownership of their shares) and two subsidiaries of these chartered banks. Finally, we did not include Crown Corporations (like Canadian National Railways) or corporations either wholly-owned or partially-owned by provinces (Sidbec and Churchill Falls Labrador Corporation, respectively). This is because, even were a process of share-dispersal underway (leading to internal control), it wouldn't affect companies wholly or partially owned by the state.

We assumed that corporate control rests with the board of directors and, like Berle and Means, Larner, Chevalier and others, we defined control as the power to choose the board of directors or a majority of its members. Since the board is chosen by the holders of voting shares, we shall define the types of control according to the percentage of the vote held. Berle and Means, and subsequently Larner, classified companies under five types of control: 1) private or semi-absolute, in which an individual, family or group of associates holds 80% or more of the voting shares; 2) majority, in which the major shareholder owns between 50% and 80%; 3) minority, in which the major shareholder owns between 20% and 50%; 4) control via legal procedures such as pyramidal structures, the issuing of non-voting stock and of stock with too high a requirement for the vote, and voting trusts; and 5) managerial, in which no individual, group or family holds more than 5% of the voting stock and the company in question may therefore be considered under the control of its directors.

Larner introduced only minor changes in this classification system. He raised the threshold between minority control and managerial control to 10%, in order to avoid the difficulties of classifying companies whose controlling interests held between 5% and 20% of the stock. Chevalier (1970) went further. First, he insisted that no large American company today is under absolute control. The distinction between absolute and majority control, therefore, served no purpose and he fused the two categories. Second, pyramidal structures could lead either to majority control, minority control or to managerial control. Chevalier demonstrated this by reminding his readers of the distinction between initial and ultimate control—a distinction which applies to subsidiaries and which designates respectively the type of control exercised by the parent company over its subsidiary and the type of control of the parent company itself. To take an example, Bell Canada holds 69.2% of the voting stock of Northern Electric Company and so the initial control of this subsidiary is majority control. Bell Canada itself, however, is under managerial control and so, ultimately, Northern Electric is as well. Chevalier also proposed to change the dividing-line between minority control and managerial control to 5 percent.

We shall classify the types of control in Canadian companies according to the criteria of Berle and Means and Chevalier. We shall maintain the distinction between semi-absolute control and majority control since, while Larner and Chevalier didn't find any large American company under 80%- plus control on their lists, we found 10 independent Canadian companies that fell into this category. We shall, however, adopt Chevalier's proposed threshold of 5% to distinguish between minority control and managerial control. We shall also eliminate the category of "control via legal procedures," reducing it to situations of majority, minority or managerial control. In dealing with subsidiaries, when both the subsidiary and its parent company have total assets of $100 million or more we shall classify the subsidiary twice: once by initial or immediate control (the percentage of control held by the parent company) and once by ultimate control (the type of control of the parent company itself). Subsidiaries of companies not on our list (cases in which the parent company has less than $100 million of assets but the subsidiary more) shall be included in the list as independent companies. Finally, subsidiaries under initial minority control by a company itself under majority control will be classified as being under ultimate minority control. For example, Domtar, a company 16.9% controlled by Argus Corporation (itself 60% controlled) will be classified as being under ultimate minority control.

We have taken the interlocking of directors as an additional criterion in several borderline cases. Canada Life Assurance Company holds 4.9% of the shares of National Trust and *a priori* we would have had to classify the latter as a company under managerial control, since no group, individual or family holds more than that 4.9%. However, two members of the Canada Life Assurance board of directors—the chairman of the board and the chairman of the executive committee—also sit on National Trust's board of directors, holding the positions of vice-chairman and honorary chairman respectively. We therefore concluded that Canada Life Assurance Company controls National Trust. In reaching this conclusion, we have followed the criteria of Berle and Means, Larner and Chevalier.

Our main source of statistics was the monthly Bulletins published by the Ontario and Quebec Securities Commissions. These Bulletins list the transactions (public and private) carried out that month by directors and executive officers of companies listed on the Toronto, Winnipeg and Montréal stock exchanges. The date for our analysis being December 1975, we took the total shares held at that date by each director, plus those held by any other declaring individual or institutional shareholder (the threshold for this group being 10%). We corroborated and complemented this information with data published by the Financial Post surveys and the manuals of the Moody Company of New York. In a few cases, we drew on the financial and daily papers. Each such case and its source of information will be identified. Information about boards of directors came from the Financial Post Directory of Directors of 1976, which gives 1975 information, though the exact date is not specified.[23]

Presentation of the Overall Results

Tables II and III, annexed to this chapter, present the data on the control of each of the 136 Canadian companies for which we could assemble information. One must always bear in mind that we do not have complete lists of shareholders but rather, information about shares held by company managers, directors and all those holding blocks of 10% or more of the voting shares (whether or not they are represented on the board of directors or the executive committee). Our statistics should be taken with as much caution as those of Berle and Means, Larner, Villarejo or Chevalier. Our results justify to some extent, we believe, the methods and definitions we have employed.

The summary tables on the following pages give the essential details of the information presented in Tables II and III of the appendices. First, one notes the existence of companies under private or semi-absolute control in virtually all sectors of the economy, though primarily in commerce and real-estate development, sectors which have more recently undergone concentration and in which the average size of assets is smaller. The fact that companies under either private or semi-absolute control exist in almost every sector of the economy justifies our maintaining this category distinct from that of majority control.

Second, one notes that the lower the percentage of control, the greater the number of cases to be found in that category. Only in one sector (utilities and transportation) is the majority of companies under managerial control. In every other sector, most companies are under minority control. Internally-controlled companies are to be found in three sectors, primarily those which centralize the most substantial assets: they account for 57% of the total assets of the 136 companies on our list. If one examines the situation sector by sector, one notes that in finance fewer than one-quarter of the companies are internally-controlled but that these companies hold almost half the total assets of this sector. In industry, only 38% of the companies are under managerial control but they control 56% of that sector's assets. No real-estate development company is under managerial control. In this sector, as in commerce, most companies are minority controlled. However, one may conclude from our statistics that companies under managerial control are the largest ones in every sector where they exist at all.

Our statistics seem to suggest that, as far as the growth of managerial control is concerned, the Canadian situation more closely resembles that described by Chevalier than by Larner. Managerial control does not seem as widespread as the managerialists found it to be in the United States of 1963, or even of 1929. Of course, there is one factor which makes any comparison between Canada and the United States very difficult, and that is, the sheer size of the companies in question. The American companies studied by Larner in 1963 were much larger than the Canadian ones of 1975. If we had included only companies of comparable size, our list would have been much shorter and the percentage of cases of managerial control much higher. Nonetheless, the companies we included, even if smaller than the average American ones, were still the largest corporations under Canadian control in this country.

Now let us look at these companies and the characteristics of their control.

TYPE OF ULTIMATE CONTROL OF THE 136 largest companies owned by Canadians, BY SECTOR OF ECONOMIC ACTIVITY, 1975[1]

Type of control \ Sector	Finance	Industry	Transportation & utilities	Commerce	Real-Estate development	All sectors
Semi-absolute	3	3	—	3	3	12
Majority	16	3	1	5	3	28
Minority	12	25	—	6	9	52
Internal	9	19	14	2	—	44
TOTAL	40	50	15	16	15	136

Type of control \ Sector	Finance	Industry	Transportation & utilities	Commerce	Real-Estate development	All sectors
Semi-absolute	8%	6%	—	19%	20%	9%
Majority	40%	6%	7%	31%	20%	21%
Minority	30%	50%	—	38%	60%	38%
Internal	22%	38%	93%	12%	—	32%
TOTAL	100%	100%	100%	100%	100%	100%

Sources: Tables II and III.
(1) This table excludes the chartered banks, for which we do not have the statistics, as well as their subsidiaries whose ultimate control, therefore, remains unknown.

TYPE OF ULTIMATE CONTROL OF THE 136 LARGEST COMPANIES OWNED BY CANADIANS, ACCORDING TO TOTAL ASSETS, BY SECTOR OF ACTIVITY (1975) (MILLIONS OF $ AND %)

Type of control \ Sector	Finance	Industry	Transportation & utilities	Commerce	Real-Estate development	All sectors
Semi-absolute	3,463	441	—	673*	742	5,319
Majority	10,893	445	394	2,108	812	14,652
Minority	11,529	11,800	—	1,818	2,629	27,776
Internal	24,105	16,411	19,417	1,613	—	61,546
TOTAL	49,990	29,097	19,811	6,212	4,183	109,293

Type of control \ Sector	Finance	Industry	Transportation & utilities	Commerce	Real-Estate development	All sectors
Semi-absolute	7%	1%	—	11%	18%	5%
Majority	22%	2%	2%	34%	19%	13%
Minority	23%	41%	—	29%	63%	25%
Internal	48%	56%	98%	26%	—	57%
TOTAL	100%	100%	100%	100%	100%	100%

Sources: Tables I, II and III.
(*) T. Eaton Co. does not make public its financial statements. We therefore have an under-estimation of semi-absolute control both in the commerce sector and in the economy as a whole.

Companies Under Managerial Control

We have just indicated that the largest companies in each sector, with the exception of real-estate development, are under managerial control. This holds true for each type of institution in the financial sector. For example, the ten insurance companies under Canadian control on our list have each total assets average $2,062 million, but the total average assets of each insurance company under managerial control reach $2,587 million. The eleven trust companies on the list have average assets of $915 million, but the two trusts under managerial control (Royal Trust and National Trust) have average assets of $2,300 million.

The same phenomenon is found among holding companies: the nine firms on our list have average assets of $850 million but the one holding company under managerial control (C.P. Investments) is the largest in Canada, with total assets of $3,511 million. While internally-controlled companies in the finance sector are distinguished by their size, they are not necessarily the oldest: Royal Trust (founded in 1892) and National Trust (1898) are about as old as Montréal Trust (1889) and Crown Trust (1897). C.P. Investments, incorporated in 1962, is one of the *newest* holding companies in Canada. Life-insurance companies present an even more striking contrast with the theory of the progressive dispersal of shares: the six companies which we have classified as being under managerial control are the six mutuals—North American Life, Sun Life, Manufacturers Life, Canada Life, Confederation Life and Mutual Life. Four of these companies became mutual societies in the 1950s and 1960s—in other words, recently—while Mutual Life from its incorporation was a company without share capital. The transformation of life-insurance companies from joint-stock companies to mutual funds was a transformation which, as we saw in the previous chapter, is often thought by the experts to have been due to the *concentration* of shares in the hands of a few shareholders, who wished to realize capital gains. Whatever may be the reason (and one would have to study the question in more depth to be sure), the transformation of insurance companies into mutual funds was *not* due to the mechanism invoked by Berle and Means, i.e., share dispersal.

The directors of institutions under managerial control are not major shareholders. (This whole question clearly does not arise in the case of those life-insurance companies which have no share capital.) One finds, instead, that the major shareholders are the *inside* directors, those who also hold senior executive positions with the company itself (chairman of the board, president, vice-president, chairman of the executive committee, etc.). These inside directors hold important blocks of shares and have, without any doubt, a decisive influence on the company and its choice of outside directors.

Company	Average number of shares per director	Average value of shares per director	Average number of shares per inside director
Royal Trust	3,970	$ 88,576	8,758
National Trust	2,226	$ 36,173	3,764
C.P. Investments	4,619	$ 68,107	10,217

We find the same characteristics with companies under managerial control in the industrial sector. The firms run by non-ownership managers are the biggest in the sector. While the average total assets of the fifty industrial firms under Canadian control are $582 million, the assets of management-controlled firms reach $864 million. Once again, the management controlled companies are not particularly old. Take, for example, the paper industry. Abitibi Paper, management controlled, was founded in 1914 while Consolidated Bathurst Corporation (of the Power Corporation group) and Maclaren Power and Paper (of the Maclaren family) both date from the 19th century. In the steel industry, Stelco, which is management controlled, was founded in 1910 and is virtually the same age as Dofasco, a minority-controlled company incorporated in 1912.

The case of Abitibi Paper illustrates two points very well. One is the ambiguity of the category of management control as a basis for a theory of managerial power. The second is the problem of data sources. We classified Abitibi Paper as a management controlled company on the basis of declarations furnished to the Ontario Securities Commission. The twenty members of its board of directors declared a total of 149,447 voting shares in December 1975, which amounts to 0.8% of the vote. No company declared that it held stock in Abitibi Paper but then, no declaration is necessary unless the owner holds 10% or more of the total voting stock. The newspaper *Le Devoir* gave the same picture as the Bulletin of the Ontario Securities Commission in its economic and financial section of 14 December 1974:

> "Many people own Abitibi stock but nobody holds an important block of shares; the average number of shares per person is 700. Technically speaking, control would be very easy to acquire."

One week later, however, the newspaper *La Presse* published a list of the major shareholders in Abitibi Paper, plus the number of shares held by each. We reprint the list in its entirety.

Principal Shareholders	Number of Shares
Royal Trust (in trust)	1,362,000 (approximately)
Montréal Trust (trustees)	575,000 (approximately)
Bank of Montréal (dummy)	1,000,000 (approximately)
Bank of Commerce (dummy)	460,000 (approximately)
Royal Bank (dummy)	1,094,000 (approximately)
Gilbert Securities Ltd.	400,000
Beckow Investments	175,000
Investors Growth Fund	180,000
Dayton Newspapers Inc. (Ohio)	400,000
Canada Permanent Trust	250,000 (approximately)
Grator & Co.	250,000 (approximately)[24]

Eleven institutional shareholders in this paper company hold 6,146,640 shares, that is, 34% of the vote—despite the judgment of *Le Devoir's* financial analysts to the contrary. It is worth noting that not one of the institutional shareholders holds 10% or more of the Abitibi voting stock and thus, none are required to declare its holdings to the Securities Commission. However, the three chartered banks figure on the list simply as dummies. We do not know the identity of the beneficiaries of those stocks, the real shareholders hidden behind the banks. We have been able to confirm part of the information published by *La Presse*. The Financial Post Survey of Funds of 1975 corroborates the number of shares held by Investors Growth Fund. Furthermore, one of the directors (L. Norstad) of Abitibi Paper comes from Dayton Newspapers Inc. in Ohio, a long-standing relationship:

"Abitibi until recently had as its chairman G.H. Mead of Dayton, Ohio, and as its president Alexander Smith of Chicago. It is believed that the Mead interests have had a large investment in Abitibi, which would account for the presence of the Americans on the board."[25]

Norstad is the only Ohio director on the Abitibi board. However, we found three directors from the Thompson Newspaper Ltd. group: Lord Thompson of Fleet, the Honorable K.R. Thompson (son of Lord Thompson) and John A. Tory. Thus, the possibility exists that the banks and/or the trusts mask control by the Thompson chain, or by the Ohio group, or by the two newspaper interests together. Available sources do not permit us to settle this question. The category of "managerial control" thus seems to us at least partly a residual category where, through lack of information, one classifies the companies which could not be placed elsewhere.

As in the financial sector, the directors of management controlled companies own few shares, with the exception of those who also hold senior management positions with the company concerned.

Company	Average number of shares per director	Average value of shares per director	Average number of shares per inside director
Abitibi Paper	7,474	$ 74,254	10,690
Alcan Aluminium	5,956	$ 135,111	11,540
Canada Packers	10,166	$ 191,883	10,166
Canron	2,626	$ 47,268	8,898
Dominion Textile	3,876	$ 30,524	5,598
Inco Ltd.	4,576	$ 117,260	7,629
Moore Corp.	10,275	$ 472,650	24,842
Steel Co. of Canada	4,977	$ 142,467	5,181
Hiram Walker	12,984	$ 478,785	34,578

In a number of these companies, however, one may well question the degree of management control. We have already shown the ambiguities of control in the case of Abitibi Paper. With Alcan Aluminium, the situation is almost as confused. Until 1928, it was a wholly-owned subsidiary of Alcoa, the American aluminum giant. That year, American anti-trust legislation forced Alcoa to hive off its subsidiary. It did so by distributing to its own shareholders one Alcan Aluminium Ltd. share for each three shares held in the parent company. In 1934, Fortune magazine wrote the following about the shareholders of Alcoa and Aluminium Ltd:

"So the two companies, technically separate, were owned by the same people. The identity of stockholders no longer continues to a 100 percent degree, but Aluminium's president, Edward K. Davis, is the brother of Aluminium's (Alcoa) chairman, Arthur Vining Davis, and the two companies are brotherly in other respects as well."[26]

"We have seen that the Mellon family owns about a one-third interest in Aluminium Co./Alcoa. The Aluminium Co. is not a Mellon company in the popular sense of the word. . . A one-third interest does usually amount to an operating control. But it might not in the case of the Aluminium Co. because most of the remaining two-thirds is also closely held by the Davises, the Hunts and other early managers and sponsors."[27]

In December 1931, four Alcoa shareholders, plus their families, held more than 50% of the shares in Aluminium Ltd.[28] In the early 1950s, anti-trust lawsuit judgments in the United States ordered the four families (the Mellons, the Dukes, the Hunts and the Davises) to sell their stock in one or other of the companies. In 1951, a public offering was made on the New York and Canadian markets of 333,000 common shares in Aluminium Ltd., for a total value of $30,000,000. The offering included 223,000 shares from the Mellon family, 100,000 shares from Arthur V. Davis and 10,000 shares from Roy A. Hunt. Messrs A.V. Davis and R.A. Hunt held onto both their shares and their executive positions with Alcoa Ltd.[29] It appears, however, that members of the Davis family have continued to own major blocks of shares in Alcan Aluminium Ltd. as well. Along with Nathaniel V. Davis, son of Edward K. (Alcan president since 1947 and chairman of its board since 1971), other members of the family are represented in the company's senior management. H.R. Davis is in Alcan management and B.L. Davis is a director of Aluminium Co. of Canada, Alcan's operating subsidiary. The Davises who sit on the board of directors and the executive committee of Alcan do not appear to hold many shares. In 1957, N.V. Davis and H.R. Davis held only 0.1% of the shares issued by the company and they were the two largest shareholders on the board and the executive committee. It is not known if other members of the family (those without executive position) hold Alcan shares. The other founding families do not hold positions on the board and the executive committee. Whether Alcan is a Canadian or American company is a minor issue. 43.1% of the shares are held in the United States, 42% in Canada and 14.9% elsewhere. The board of directors consists of eight Canadians, four Americans and four Europeans. The headquarters are in Montréal. One can probably say that Alcan is a Canadian-American company.

The other giant in this sector is Inco Ltd., the world's largest nickel producer. Founded in 1902, the company was originally incorporated in New Jersey and, as part of the Morgan group, controlled by the world's biggest steel manufacturer, United States Steel. In 1916, it was incorporated in Canada but the control remained unchanged. The Ontario Commission of Inquiry into Nickel established in 1917 that 96% of the common stock was held in the United States and that the entire board of directors was American.[30] The Canadian-held percentage of stocks rose in the years 1917-1928. In 1928, Inco Ltd. absorbed Mond Nickel Company, its major rival on the North-American continent, through an exchange of shares. The English family, Mond, which controlled both Mond Nickel and Imperial Chemical Industries, received a huge block of these shares. The Mond stockholders, with one-seventh the total Inco shares, won the right to choose five of 25 directors of the new company which, moreover, was to transfer its headquarters to Canada in order to avoid anti-trust legislation in the United States. In the new International Nickel Company of 1928, Canadians had the right to elect three directors and that year chose J.P. Bickell, James A. Richardson and J.W. McConnell (of the Holt group).[31] The proportion of Canadian-owned shares has been rising ever since that 1928 reorganization of the company. In 1975, Canadians held 48% of the shares, vs. 37% held by Americans and 15% by Europeans. The board of directors has 14 Canadian members, among them G.T. Richardson (son of James A. and brother of the former federal Liberal cabinet minister), who is the major stockholder on the board. There are also eight Americans holding key positions (including those of chairman and vice-chairman of the board and president of the company), and one English director. Two Inco Ltd. directors sit on the board of United States Steel.

In other management controlled industrial companies as well, one find an important family aspect to the evolution of the boards of directors. Canada Packers Ltd. was founded in 1927 as a holding company in order to acquire four abattoirs; it became an industrial company in 1932 through a consolidation of its assets. At the time of its foundation, two members of the McLean family were on the board of directors, which consisted in total of seven people. James S. McLean was president of the company from 1927 to 1954, when he was succeeded by his son and current president, William F. McLean. William F. holds in his own name 128,667 shares or 2% of the voting stock issued by the company; he is by far the biggest shareholder on this board which is composed entirely of inside directors. Moreover, in 1954, three members of the family sat on the board. It is difficult to escape the conclusion that the McLean family controls the company, an assumption which Porter himself made in 1960[32]. Peter C. Newman makes the same claim.[33]

Dominion Textile Ltd. was incorporated in 1905 as the merger of various cotton-fabric producing companies, and went on to become the largest textile company in Canada. Sir Charles B. Gordon was president for several decades and then succeeded by his son, G. Blair Gordon, who held the position from 1939 to 1965. Early in the 1960s, Frank H. Sobey bought a block of shares in the company and became a company director. He was succeeded by his son, David F. Sobey, who is now the largest shareholder on the board. It is not known if Frank H. still holds the 300,000 shares which he owned in 1972 but if that is the case, Dominion Textile is under the control of the Sobey family.

Hiram Walker-Gooderham Worts was incorporated in 1927 as a holding company for two distilleries. H.C. Hatch was named president and remained president for 20 years. In 1964, H. Clifford Hatch, his son, became in turn president. With 0.7% of the shares, he is the largest shareholder on the board.

Steel Co. of Canada was incorporated in 1910 by Max Aitken, in order to merge several Ontario and Québec foundries and producers of related products. Ross McMaster was named to its board of directors in 1914 and later became both president and chairman of the board. He was succeeded by his son, D. Ross McMaster, the largest shareholder on the board.

In Moore Corporation and Canron Ltd., we found no sign of directorships passing from one generation of a family to the next; in other companies, it was very difficult to judge the true weight of the founders' descendants. In many cases, however, management control could turn out to be, in fact, minority family control for which the data are not published.

In the commerce sector, an "independent" company seems to be management controlled. The company in question is Simpson's Ltd., originally founded in 1925 as a holding company to take over Robert Simpson Co., the commercial firm which had been established in 1872. Simpson's Ltd. was reorganized in 1929 by Wood, Gundy & Co., with the investment broker receiving 41.7% of the voting stock in exchange for his services. [34] The Gundy family still furnishes the major shareholders on the board of directors: Charles L. Gundy, for example, son of James H., holds 571,536 shares in his own name, plus 283,668 in trust, plus 249,666 in trust for his children, which make a total of 1,104,870 shares for a value of $7-10 million in 1975. Then there's his brother-in-law, William P. Scott and Scott's son. William P. declared in December 1973, while he was a director, that he held 300,000 shares; his son today acknowledges holding 110,000 shares and is on the board of directors. In sum, the Gundy-Scott families hold not less than 2% of the voting stock of Simpson's Ltd. The Burton family, descendants of the company manager of the first part of this century, have two family members on the board, and declare almost 400,000 shares, which is less than 1%. In all, board members hold more than 4% of the shares in Simpson's Ltd. If other members of the Gundy—Scott and Burton families hold other blocks of shares in the company, the company could then be said to be under the minority control of these two families.

As in the financial and industrial sectors, the management controlled commercial companies are not necessarily the oldest. Simpson's Ltd. is about the same age as the family companies of Steinberg's Ltd. or Canadian Tire Corporation, founded respectively in 1930 and 1927. It would appear that, once again, Berle's theory of the three stages of company control (individual, family, management) has been disproven by the facts.

In Simpson's Ltd., as in the management controlled financial and industrial companies, the inside directors are the largest shareholders. While the average number of shares per director is 142,472 (worth in 1975 more than a million dollars), the management people on the board hold an average of 268,672 shares each. Finally, if one looks at the size of the company, Simpson's Ltd. and its half-owned subsidiary, Simpsons-Sears Ltd., are significantly larger than the average of the major commercial companies' the assets of these two are worth respectively $562 million and $1,051 million, vs. an average of $481 million for all the companies on the list.

Two companies stand out by reason of size in our list of utilities and transportation: Bell Canada and Canadian Pacific. The former was incorporated in Canada in 1880 as a subsidiary of the American Bell Telephone Company, which was later absorbed in the American Telephone and Telegraph Co. system. The parent company has for a long time held on to minority control (a declining percentage since 1890) in its Canadian subsidiary.[35] In 1905, a Select Committee investigated the relationship between the American parent and its Canadian subsidiary and the advantages and disadvantages of this relationship. While the Committee studied the possibility of recommending the nationalization of Bell Telephone Co. of Canada, in the end it did not do so. Throughout the 20th century, AT&T has slowly been relinquishing its control of the Canadian company. In 1910, it held 38.6% of the shares; in 1928, 23.7%; in 1948, 14.8%;[36] and, according to Porter, in 1960, only 3.5 percent. The American company has made no declarations in the 1960s and 1970s to the Canadian Securities Commissions; no sign of AT&T ownership of Bell Canada stock could be found; no Bell director in 1975 was linked to the former parent company. No other sizeable shareholder, whether institutional or individual, seems to be represented on the board of the Canadian telephone company. The only two inside directors in the firm, the chairman of the board and the president, are former senior executives who have made their careers in Bell since 1937 and 1940 respectively. The others are directors recruited from outside the company among the president and vice-president of other large corporations. They hold a negligible amount of stock.

Canadian Pacific was founded in 1881 with very concentrated capital: nine shareholders held 79% of the initial offering of shares.[37] Among them were George Stephen, Richard B. Angus and Donald Smith (Lord Strathcona) of the Bank of Montréal, all of whom remained for many years on the railway company's board of directors. Later, they were to bring other directors to the company from the bank, but also from Stelco, Royal Trust and Sun Life. The founding directors bought a major portion of subsequent stock offerings. Until World War II, most CPR directors came from top layer of Montréal and Toronto financial circles. The most durable connection—now more than a century old—has been with the Bank of Montréal: each year five or six bank financiers sit on the boards of the two companies. However, the inside directors of Canadian Pacific today, like those of Bell Canada, are employees who have had long careers with the company. The "control group" (as Chodos so aptly termed it) seems always to have been Canadian, even if, until very recently, most shares were held in England.[38]

Two other management controlled utilities, Calgary Power and Newfoundland Light and Power, were part of the group of hydroelectric companies controlled by Izaac W. Killam, owner of Royal Securities Corporation, who had bought them from Max Aitken. A number of former Killam employees now sit on the boards of the two companies and have bought shares in them.

The following table shows the shares held by directors of internally-controlled utility companies.

Company	Average number of shares per director	Average value of shares per director	Average number of shares per inside director
Bell Canada	678	$ 30,212	2,488
Calgary Power	2,449	$ 61,531	5,552
C.P. Ltd.	4,983	$ 74,097	5,175
Consumers' Gas	7,660	$ 106,742	2,606
Newfoundland Light & Power	6,346	$ 69,806	13,189
Norcen Energy Resources	8,934	*	20,816
Union Gas	26,583	$ 214,259	1,177

* Having been incorporated at the end of 1975, there was no market value established for its shares.

The above table shows that, with the exception of Consumers' Gas and Union Gas,[39] shares are concentrated in the hands of the inside directors.

The major utilities and transportation companies are almost all under management control. Canada Steamship Lines is the one exception: it belongs to the Power Corporation group. But these companies did not all arrive at their present situation via some hallowed process of share dispersal, as the Berle and Means theory would have us believe. For example, the voting stock of Alberta Gas Trunk Line (created in 1954), which amounted to only 1,699 shares by 31 December 1975, is held by other utilities and by companies that produce, export, and transport natural gas. Each shareholder possesses only a few shares. This dispersal was planned by the company from the moment of its foundation and has absolutely nothing to do with the process described by Berle. Furthermore, AGTL voting stock is not quoted on the exchange and three of its directors are named by the Lieutenant-Governor of Alberta in Council. As far as Norcen Energy Resources is concerned, it was incorporated in 1975 to seize control of Northern and Central Gas Corporation which had been founded in Ontario in 1954. Its shares were relatively dispersed by 1966-67, when Power Corporation bought more than 2,000,000 (18% of the voting stock), only to sell them once again in 1970 to Canadian and British institutional investors.[40] The dispersal of the shares of Calgary Power and of Newfoundland Light and

Power Co. didn't begin until 1955, after the death of Killam who had controlled both companies for more than 30 years. Only Bell Canada, Canadian Pacific, Consumers' Gas (founded in 1848) and Union Gas (founded in 1911) could be said to correspond to the model laid out by Berle and Means.

Having reviewed the major management controlled companies in the different sectors of activity, we may now offer some generalizations about the situation as a whole and point out some common characteristics. First, let us recall that companies under managerial control are distinguished by their size. Both their size and the fact of managerial control may be explained by the many mergers which these companies have undergone over the years. Family control, whether individual or by a small group of shareholders, is difficult to maintain if the company must absorb other companies by an exchange of stock: a good many mergers are carried out by dividing control among the power groupings in the companies involved. This sharing of control necessarily implies a dispersal of the shares of the company that results from the merger. This is one the major means of breaking down large blocks of shares, and also one of the principal methods of growth used by large companies.

Second, one can see that within each sector management controlled companies are just about the same age as those under other forms of control. We can now add that management controlled companies are relatively more numerous in the oldest sectors of activity (utilities, transportation, finance) or those which were first to undergo the process of concentration (utilities, finance, industry). These companies are relatively less numerous in the newer sectors (real-estate development) and those which have centralized more recently (retail commerce).

Third, the major shareholders, with two exceptions, are to be found among the inside directors. In many cases, these inside directors are the descendants of the company's founders or of people who formerly held power in the company. In such cases, only a complete list of shareholders would allow us to decide if these companies are, in fact, under family control.

Fourth, it is not just that the companies do not become management controlled as the result of a linear and sanctified process of share dispersal. As we shall show later on, the post-war formation of conglomerates could very easily reverse any present trend towards the scattering of major blocks of shares. Furthermore, a number of companies ended up in a situation of managerial control as the result of legislative or judicial action: e.g. the 1967 Bank Act, which prohibited chartered banks from holding more than 10% of the shares of a trust company and also prohibited the exchange of directors between them; e.g. the 1950 United States injunction against the Alcan and Alcoa shareholders, which forced them to sell their shares in one or other of the companies; e.g. restrictions imposed on the charter of Alberta Gas Trunk Line. In other cases, it has been a matter of changing juridical status: e.g. the life-insurance companies which became mutuals during the 1950s and 60s. All these different cases show ways in which companies have arrived at a situation of managerial control without passing through the three stages ordained by Berle and Means.

We can better understand the characteristics of management controlled companies if we compare them to companies controlled by a family, by individuals and by groups, and then examine the growth of conglomerates.

Companies Under Family Control

A company is under family control if the principal group of shareholders—the group with 5% or more of the voting shares—comes from one family, whether or not members of this family sit on the company's board of directors. This definition excludes not only companies under managerial control (in which no individual or group holds 5% of the shares) but also companies under personal control and those which are controlled by a non-familial group of associates. We shall look at this last category later on. For the moment, it is enough to say that individual and group control are transitory forms of control, forms which end with the lives of the capitalists involved and which may evolve into family control or, through share dispersal, into internal control.

Companies under family control have certain distinctive characteristics. First, they are not very old. Only six of the 37 family companies on our list were in existence at the turn of the century. The patriarch of the group is undoubtedly Molson Companies Ltd: its antecedents go back to 1786 and it became a public company only in 1945. Until then, the entire share capital was held by members of the Molson family, who thereby occupied all the seats on the board of directors. Today, various family members hold, directly and indirectly, 36.3% of the shares and only two Molsons sit on the parent-company's board (see Table II annexed to this chapter). The commercial firm T. Eaton Company, founded in 1869, is the third-oldest family company. It is still a private company, with all the shares held by members of the Eaton family via a private holding company, Eaton's of Canada Ltd. The most important subsidiary, in terms of its assets, is the T. Eaton Acceptance Co., established in 1954 and wholly-owned by T. Eaton Co. It, too, is on our list, being the fourth-largest finance company in Canada. Somewhat less well-known than the first two examples, but also of great importance, is London Life Insurance Company. It was established in London, Ontario in 1874 by Joseph Jeffery and Edward Harris, with Jeffery as the first president. His sons, Albert Oscar and James Edgar, followed him into the senior management of the company. The three sons of James Edgar today hold the positions of chairman of the Board, president and director. London Life's share capital is not quoted on the stock exchange, even though it is the third-largest insurance company in Canada, with December 1975 assets of $2,392 million. F.P. Publications is a private company founded in 1898 by the Liberal minister and fund-raiser, Clifford Sifton. It belongs to the Sifton and Bell families which, however, have left the administration to R.H. Webster, a shareholder since 1965. F.P. Publications has outstripped both Southam Press and Power Corporation to become the largest newspaper chain in Canada. Finally, Maclean-Hunter, founded in 1891 and controlled by the Hunter family, and Hugh Russel Ltd., founded in 1826 and controlled by the Russel family, are two other old, family establishments. All the rest were begun in the 20th century.

A second important characteristic: family companies are relatively more numerous in the field of commerce, where they comprise 44% of our list and hold 48% of the assets. There is no family company to be found among the major utilities and transportation companies. Family companies form 26% of our industrial-sector list, 20% of real-estate development and 32% of finance.

Third, their size. In both commerce and real-estate development, family companies are larger than the average; in finance, they are of equal size; in manufacturing and mining, they are among the smaller companies (see Table I). The group of family companies includes the largest commercial company in Canada (G. Weston Ltd.), the largest real-estate development company (Cadillac Fairview Corporation), the largest brokerage firm (Wood, Gundy & Co.), the major fixed capital-investment company (Canadian General Investments), the third-largest insurance company (London Life Insurance Co.), the largest finance company (IAC Ltd.), the largest distillery company (Seagram Co.) and the major newspaper chain (F.P. Publications). One might say that family capitalism is doing very nicely here in Canada.

Fourth, let us note that family companies include very few outsiders. A few families are the exception to this rule, notably the Searle-Leaches and the Bronfmans. The former holds 36.7% of the shares of Federal Insurance Ltd. This company, founded in 1929 under the name of Federal Grain, was under the minority control of the Sellers family when, in September 1966, it absorbed Searle Grain Co. through an exchanges of shares. The Searle-Leach family received thereby more than one-third of the shares of Federal Grain and so became its principal shareholder. Today, four members of the family sit on the board of directors of Federal Industries and hold senior management positions in the company. The Bronfmans established Distillers Corporation in 1924, which soon became the largest distillery in Canada. In 1928, they created a holding company, Distillers Corp-Seagrams Ltd, to absorb (through an exchange of shares) the former Joseph E. Seagram & Sons distillery of Waterloo, Ontario. From this holding company, in which the Bronfman family today holds about one-third of the shares, the Bronfmans have gone on to other fields of activity. In the real-estate development sector, they founded Cemp Holdings in 1958, which went public in 1972 under the name of The Fairview Corporation. They also acquired control over Cadillac Development Corporation and merged it, in 1974, with The Fairview Corp. and with Canadian Equity and

91

Development, a subsidiary of Cadillac Development Corp. Bronfmans hold more than one-third the shares of the resulting company, Cadillac Fairview Co., and are its principal owners.[41] In the financial sector, the family bought control of IAC Ltd. in 1974. This finance company is about to organize a chartered bank, to be called the Continental Bank of Canada.

Fifth, members of the family which controls a company normally hold the top positions in the direction and management of the company. In other words, the families delegate family members to positions on the board of directors, primarily as inside directors. The following table supports this conclusion.

Sixth, one notes that twelve of the family companies are under absolute control or are private companies, seven are under majority control and the other 22, under minority control. Family empires show no signs of disappearing after the first generation, as the Berle-Means theory would have it: on the contrary, a number of family companies have now reached the second or third generation. Moreover, several of the most dynamic groups—in terms of growth, diversification and acquisition of other existing companies—are under family control. The most remarkable examples in this regard are the Bronfman and Eaton families. In very few of the companies is family control showing any signs of declining to the point of disappearing. Some of the companies which we have listed under managerial control were formerly under family control: Alcan Aluminium Ltd., Canada Packers and Hiram Walker-Gooderham & Worts. In other cases, family companies have been absorbed into conglomerates, as was the case with John Labatt and Massey-Ferguson. Some family companies have passed into the control of individuals or groups of associates, such as Burns Food, which was long the property of the Burns family and is now under the control of R.H. Webster. In most cases, however, transformation from a private to a public company has not resulted in loss of control by the families involved. Thus, Steinberg's (which went public in 1955) and Oshawa Group (1960) remain under the absolute control of, respectively, the Steinberg family and the Wolfe family. In other companies, absolute family control became majority control with the change to public-company status: this was the case with G. Weston Ltd. (which became a public company in 1928), Canadian Tire Corp. (1944), and Bombardier Ltd. (1969). Finally, in some circumstances, private family companies have been transformed into companies under minority control: this is what happened to Distillers Corp.-Seagram and Maclaren Power & Paper, which went public with their reorganization in 1928, and with Molson Companies, which sold its first stocks and bonds on the market in 1945.

Transitory Forms; Individual and Group Control

Control by either individuals or by groups of associates is not an outdated form of control of joint-stock companies. It has existed in all stages of Canadian capitalism and has not necessarily been associated with the founding era of the company. Among other examples, one can point to Sir James Dunn, who from 1935 to 1956 was absolute master of Algoma Steel but who did not take control of the company until it was already twenty years old. Or again, the case of Izaac Killam, who controlled a hydro-electric empire from the 1920s to 1954, an empire which he bought from Max Aitken. However, this form of control, as the Dunn and Killam examples show, is not a long-lasting one. In all the companies on our list which are under this form of control, the acquisition of individual or group control has been of recent date.

There are many new companies, whose founders are the major shareholders and directors. This is the case with a number of large real-estate development companies and their owners, such as Campeau Corp. (R. Campeau), S.B. McLaughlin Assoc. (S.B. McLaughlin) and Unicorp Financial Corp. (G.S. Mann). In the financial sector there is Argus Corporation, set up in 1945 and still in the hands of a small group of associates (E.P. Taylor, J.A. McDougald, E. Phillips and M.W. McCutcheon in 1945; Taylor, McDougald, G. Black, A.B. Matthews and M.C.G. Meighen at the end of 1975).

Outsiders have managed to seize control of a number of already-functioning companies. The most remarkable outsider is undoubtedly Paul G. Desmarais, the major shareholder in Power Corporation. Peter Newman has already written a detailed and lively account of the steps which Desmarais took to acquire control of Power.[42] We shall here restrict outselves to the major steps only, and add a few important figures. On more than one occasion, Desmarais used the technique of the reverse take-over: as described above in the case of Federal Grain, he would each time exchange a smaller company for a larger one. He began in 1950 with a small family bus company and, by 1961, had control of Provincial Transport. That same year Gatineau Power founded Gelco Enterprises Ltd., a holding company, with the $12.5 million received from the government of New Brunswick for the nationalization of its assets in that province. The shareholders of Gatineau Power received one common share in Gelco for each share they held with Gatineau. Still in that same year, Desmarais bought 20% of the Gelco stock for $450,000 and later gained control of the company by exchanging Provincial Transport for 6,531,776 newly-issued shares in Gelco. In 1963, he held 80% of the Gelco shares. In 1964, the holding company acquired control (51.2%) of Imperial Life, one of the largest life-insurance companies in Canada. The following year, Desmarais exchanged 100% of the Provincial Transport shares and all his Imperial Life shares for 56% of the stock of an even larger holding company, Trans Canada Corporation Fund. Gelco took control of this other holding company which, in turn, held the shares of Provincial Transport and Imperial Life. In 1954, Trans Canada, which had been founded by Jean-Louis Lévesque, controlled a dozen medium-sized businesses throughout the country. In 1968, Desmarais exchanged control of Trans Canada for 4,136,810 preferred shares at 5% of Power Corporation, each share being a voting share (1 vote each). These shares, specially offered by Power Corporation in order to acquire Trans Canada, did not give Desmarais control of

FAMILY-CONTROLLED COMPANIES
MEMBERS OF THE OWNERSHIP FAMILY ON THE BOARD OF DIRECTORS AND BOARD OF OFFICERS

A — FINANCE

Canadian Corporate Management	W.L. Gordon (chairman of the board)
Canadian General Investments	M.C.G. Meighen (chairman of the board)
	T.R. Meighen
City Savings and Trust	S. Belzberg (pres.); W. Belzberg (V.P.)
	H. Belzberg
T. Eaton Acceptance Co.	A.Y. Eaton; J.W. Eaton
E-L Financial Corp.	H.N.R. Jackman (pres.); H.R. Jackman
First City Financial Corp.	S. Belzberg (pres.); W. Belzberg (v.p.)
	H. Belzberg
Huron & Erie Mortgage Corp.	M.C. G. Meighen (v.p.)
IAC Ltd.	P.F. Bronfman
London Life Insurance Co.	J. Jeffery (chairman of the board)
	A.H. Jeffery (pres.); G.D. Jeffery
Prenor Group	L.C. Webster (pres.)
Victoria and Grey Trust	H.N.R. Jackman
Wood Gundy & Co. Ltd.	C.L. Gundy (chairman of the board)
	J.M.G. Scott

B — INDUSTRY

Bombardier Ltd.	A. Bombardier (v.p.); L. Beaudoin (pres.)
	J.L. Fontaine (v.p.)
Bow Valley Industries	D.K. Seaman (pres.); B.J. Seaman (exec. v.p.)
	D.R. Seaman (sr. v.p.)
F.P. Publications	none
Federal Industries	A. Searle Leach (chairman of the board)
	S.A. Searle Jr. (pres.); A. Searle Leach Jr. (v.p.)
	C.L. Searle
Irving Oil Co.	A.L. Irving (pres.); J.E. Irving; J.M. Irving
Ivaco Industries	I. Ivanier (pres.); P. Ivanier (exec. v.p.)
	S. Ivanier (v.p.)
Kruger Pulp & Paper	G.H. Kruger (chairman of the board)
	B.J. Kruger (vice-chairman of the board)
	D. Kruger; J. Kruger II

Maclaren Power & Paper	D. Maclaren (v.p.); J.F. Maclaren A.B. Maclaren; A.R. Maclaren; G. F. Maclaren
Maclean-Hunter Ltd.	D.F. Hunter (chairman of the board)
Molson Companies	Hon. H. de M. Molson (hon. chairman of the board); E.H. Molson
Hugh Russel Ltd.	A.D. Russel (chairman of the board and chief executive officer)
The Seagram Co.	E.M. Bronfman (chairman of the board); Ch. R. Bronfman (pres.); A. Bronfman
The Southam Press	St. Clair Balfour (chairman of the board) G.N. Fisher (pres.); R.W. Southam (v.p.) G.H. Southam; G.T. Southam

C — COMMERCE

Canadian Tire Corp.	A.D. Billes; A.J. Billes; A.W. Billes; D.G. Billes
T. Eaton Co.	J.W. Eaton (v.p.); A.Y. Eaton
Kelly, Douglas & Co.	W.G. Weston
Oshawa Group	M. Wolfe (hon. chairman of the board) R.D. Wolfe (chairman of the board) H.S. Wolfe (pres.); L. Wolfe (exec. v.p.) J.B. Wolfe (v.p.); H.J. Wolfe (secretary)
Steinberg's Ltd.	M. Dobrin (pres.); M.M. Dobrin (v.p.) S. Steinberg (chairman of the board) N. Steinberg (vice-chairman of the board) A. Steinberg (exec. v.p.)
C. Weston	W. Galen Weston (chairman of the board) W. Garfield Weston (vice-chairman of the board); G.H. Weston
Woodward Stores	C.N.W. Woodward (chairman of the board)

D — REAL-ESTATE DEVELOPMENT

Block Bros. Industries	A.J. Block (chairman of the board) H.J. Block (pres.)
The Cadillac Fairview Corp.	Ch. R. Bronfman
Daon Development Corp.	G.R. Dawson (chairman of the board) J.W. Poole (pres.)
T. Eaton Realty	J.W. Eaton
Orlando Corp.	Orey Fidani (pres.); E. Fidani (v.p.)

Power, since the Power capitalization also included 6,198,550 common voting shares and 1,194,570 preferred shares at 6% (each worth ten votes). As soon as he held the preferred stock at 5%, Desmarais made a public offer of 1 and 1/3 shares at 5% for each share at 6 percent. In November 1968, when the offer expired, he had amassed 500,000 shares at 6%, which gave him 5 million votes and he still had 2,600,000 shares at 5 percent. He had become the major shareholder in Power, followed closely by Peter N. Thomson, who had not accepted his offer of purchase and who still held 600,000 shares at 6%. Desmarais bought these shares in 1969 for $7.2 million, thus acquiring majority control of the second-largest conglomerate in Canada.[43]

Lesser known but equally active outsiders are such men as H. Ruben Cohen and Leonard Ellen who in 1975 discreetly acquired a minority block of Crown Trust, one of the oldest trust companies in Canada (founded in 1897), although they were not at the time on the board of directors. Through a recent series of mergers, they have acquired almost half the stock of Central & Eastern Trust, which in 1975 became the fifth-largest trust company in Canada.

Burns Food, incorporated in 1890 and under the control of the Burns family for sixty years, was taken in hand in 1965 by R.H. Webster, who today owns less than one-third its shares. In 1953, Stephen B. Roman bought minority control in Denison Mines, set up in 1936 by a group of associates, a control which Roman holds to this day. Dominion Foundries & Steel Corp. was founded in 1917 by the American Sherman family. Today, the chairman of the board is a Sherman, but the major shareholder on the Board is J. Daniel Leitch. His father was a director and minority shareholder of Dofasco from the days of World War II. It is not know whether or not the Sherman family still holds a significant block of shares in the company.

The "independent" companies under individual or group control are among the smallest on our list. Apart from Dofasco in the industrial sector and Central & Eastern Trust in finance, only Argus and Power merit any special attention, and then only because they are at the head of two of the most important conglomerates in Canada. On the other hand, there are a number of subsidiary companies which dominate various branches of the economy. We shall return to them in the next chapter.

As far as their distribution among the various sectors of the economy is concerned, the "independent" companies under this form of control are relatively more numerous in the real-estate development business: nine of the 15 companies on our list were either under individual or group control. This is less frequently the case in finance, industry or commerce. In all, there were in 1975, 26 independent companies under this form of control with assets of more than $100 million; if their subsidiaries are counted as well, there were 44. As with family companies, the principal owners of independent companies under individual or group control usually hold key positions on the board of directors and the executive committee.

96

INDEPENDENT COMPANIES UNDER INDIVIDUAL OR GROUP CONTROL POSITIONS OCCUPIED BY THEIR OWNERS ON THE BOARDS AND EXECUTIVE COMMITTEES

A — FINANCE

Argus Corp.	J.A. McDougald (chairman of the board and press[1]); M.C.G. Meighen (v.p. and chairman of the executive committee); G.M. Black Jr. (v.p.) A.B. Matthews (exec. v.p.)
Brascan Ltd.	J.H. Moore (pres.)
Central & Eastern Trust	H.R. Cohen; L. Ellen
Crown Trust	none
Crown Life	C.F.W. Burns (chairman of the board) H.M. Burns (v.p.); J.J. Jodrey
Jannock Corp.	G.E. Mara (chairman of the board) D.G. Willmot; M. Tannenbaum; W.M. Hatch
Power Corp.	P.G. Desmarais (chairman of the board)
Trust Général du Canada	Jean-Louis Lévesque (v.p.)
United Trust	G.S. Mann (chairman of the board)

B — INDUSTRY

Burns Food	R.H. Webster
Denison Mines	S.B. Roman (chairman of the board and chief executive officer)
Dofasco	J.D. Leitch
Neonex International	J. Pattison (chairman of the board, pres.)

C — COMMERCE

Acklands Ltd.	L. Wolinsky (chairman of the board), W. Starr (exec. v.p.) H. Bessin (pres.)
Finning Tractor & Equipment	none
Westburne International Industries Ltd.	J.A. Scrymgeour (chairman of the board)

D — REAL-ESTATE DEVELOPMENT

Allarco Developments	Charles Allard (chairman of the board, pres.)
Bramalea Consolidated Development	J.A. Schiff (pres. and chief exec. officer)
Campeau Corp.	R. Campeau (chairman of the board and chief exec. officer)
Deltan Corporation	R.J. Prusac
S.B. McLaughlin Assoc.	S.B. McLaughlin (pres.)
Nu-West Development Corp.	R.T. Scurfield (pres.); C.J. McConnell
Oxford Development Corp.	G.D. Love (pres.); G.E. Poole; J.E. Poole
Unicorp Financial Corp.	G.S. Mann (pres.)

Again, as with family companies, most independent companies are under minority control (twelve cases out of twenty), while two are under semi-absolute control and six under majority control.

The Growth of Conglomerates

There is no consensus on the concepts to be used in defining the firms and groups of firms which are simultanously active in different, and non-related, markets. Certain authors use the term "conglomerate" to identify the huge, diversified, multi-divisional company[44]. Others prefer such expressions as "interest groups" or "financial groups", and apply these terms primarily to the collections of companies which are legally independent, yet under one single control.[45] In the Marxist tradition, the concept of a "financial group" refers to a group of companies under the control of a financial institution—more precisely, under the control of a bank. In the following analysis, we assume that the two types of enterprises (huge diversified companies and groupings of independent companies under one control) are not fundamentally different, and that the dissimilarities of superficial organization are often the result of a combination of circumstances —such as legislation governing companies (which varies from country to country and even from province to province), or fiscal or accounting practices. We shall use the term "conglomerate" to refer both to the larger company producing many different products, and to groupings of large firms under a single control, whatever may be the type of company which exercises that control.

There have been conglomerates in the Canadian economy throughout the 20th century: Canadian Pacific is the example that comes immediately to mind. But the process of forming these conglomerates has accelerated very rapidly since World War II, especially during the 1960s. In this sense, the Canadian economy follows the organizational contours of American capitalism, which underwent a parallel and similar restructuring of the monopolist system.

The point which we wish to stress, however, is that the formation of conglomerates reverses the trend towards the dispersal of shares. Conglomerates try to obtain control of those already-operational companies which may most easily be absorbed and that means those whose stock is most widely dispersed. Canadian conglomerates are formed either by setting up new companies or by taking over existing ones. The two forms of growth are not mutually exclusive, but the second has recently become much more important than the first.

Of the three big Canadian conglomerates, it is Argus Corporation which has most systematically grown by absorbing internally-controlled companies. The conglomerate's founder, E.P. Taylor, explains his group's strategy:

> "I look for companies where no very large shareholder exists. With my partners, I buy enough stock to give us effective control. Then the Company holds our view."[46]

A striking example of this strategy was the way in which Argus took over the largest producer of agricultural machinery in Canada, Massey-Harris (now Massey-Ferguson). Massey-Harris was born in 1891 of the merger of two family companies; the Massey family, which had held control from the time of that merger, withdrew in 1927. Wood, Gundy & Co. bought their block of shares on behalf of a syndicate and quickly dispersed them. In the absence of major shareholders, John H. Gundy retained operational minority control of Massey-Harris until 1942. In that year, E.P. Taylor and his associates began to buy shares. With the foundation of Argus in 1945, they—with less than 10% of the voting stock—were the major shareholders in Massey-Harris. In 1948, when the majority of the Massey-Harris executive committee members came from Argus, it was obvious that the holding company had gained control of the agricultural-machinery company.[47] A similar example is the case of Dominion Stores, in which E.P. Taylor and his associates bought 35,000 Treasury shares in early 1945, which gave them a total of 11.8% of the vote. Four Argus group members were immediately named to the board of directors of Dominion Stores, with one of them as chairman. Argus counts on the dispersal of the rest of the shares to allow it to retain control of its subsidiaries from a minority position.

There is another take-over technique widely used by Canadian conglomerates—notably by Canadian Pacific and by Power Corp.—and that is to purchase a minority block of shares where such a block exists and then make a public offer to purchase the rest of the target company's shares (or enough of them to gain majority control of the absorbed company). Canadian Pacific used this technique to acquire Algoma Steel Corp. in 1973 and 1974. In August 1973, C.P. Investments, the holding company of the C.P. group, bought 25% of the shares offered by Algoma Steel, Canada's third-largest steel producer, from Mannesman A.G. of Dusseldorf, Federal Republic of Germany. In June 1974, the holding company made a public offer to purchase 2,500,000 shares of Algoma Steel at $32 each. This offer, widely accepted by the steel company's shareholders, gave to C.P.I. more than 50% of the vote in Algoma Steel, which then became its subsidiary along with Algoma's *own* subsidiary, Dominion Bridge.[48] Power Corp. used the same method to bring off the majority of its take-overs: in each case, it first acquired a minority block of shares and then made a public offer to purchase, in order to gain majority or even absolute control. In May 1963, Power bought from Algoma Steel a minority group of shares in Canada Steamship Lines; in three successive steps it acquired more than 50%; in January 1972 it assured itself absolute control of the company by means of a public offer to purchase.[49] The same technique was used in the case of Consolidated Paper. In March 1965, Power bought 13% of the shares in the Québec paper company from St. Regis Paper of New York, which had been the major shareholder since 1960; in April 1970 Power launched a public offer to purchase 2,300,000 shares of Consolidated-Bathurst, a purchase which would have given Power majority control of the paper company. The offer did not meet with the desired response and Power came out of the affair with only a somewhat enlarged minority control of 34%.[50] In May 1967, Power and Consolidated Paper set out to absorb Dominion Glass by making a successful joint offer to purchase majority control of the company, a company in which the purchasers already had "substantial interests."[51] In the take-over of Great West Life through Investors Group in March-April 1969, Power Corp. bought 19.4% of the Winnipeg insurance company's shares from a holding company of the Bronfman family; subsequently, Investors Group bought 307,000 shares in a public offer and thus acquired 50.1% of the shares of Great West Life.[52]

It seems to be much more difficult, however, to acquire a company which is already under tight control. The aborted efforts to acquire McIntyre Mines and Argus Corp. should have convinced Power of the obstacles to be faced when challenging a well-entrenched control group. At this point we may introduce a damning piece of evidence against the Berle-Means theory: *financial concentration primarily takes place at the expense of companies under internal or minority control. One sees in this the development of a counter-tendency to the share-dispersal on which the Berle and Means theory is based.*

As well as reaching this theoretical conclusion one can, in looking at charts I to VII, make a few methodological observations. The different groups or conglomerates use a variety of means of control: Bell Canada and Power Corp. prefer majority control of their subsidiaries; Argus Corp. and Canadian General Investments operate through minority participation. In other conglomerates, the level of control of subsidiaries varies according to no set pattern. Moreover, there is no correlation between the number of directors in common between a parent company and its subsidiaries, and the degree of control exercised by the parent company.

Bell Canada has majority control of all its subsidiaries, but only has directors in common with Northern Electric. C.P. Investment has one director in common with Algoma Steel, which it controls 51%, and two with McMillan Bloedell, in which it has only 13.4% of the voting shares. Here we see examples of the imprecision of using interlocking directorships as a criterion for deducing anything at all about company relationships. In other words, the exchange of directors cannot be taken into account without immediate reference to financial control, to the ownership of the stock. We shall be returning to this point.

Conclusion

The theory of managerial control with its four stages of evolution in corporate control (individual, family and internal control and finally control by financial institutions) seems not to fit the Canadian context. Of course, it does not apply at all to the subsidiaries of foreign com-

CHART NO. I: THE BELL CANADA GROUP

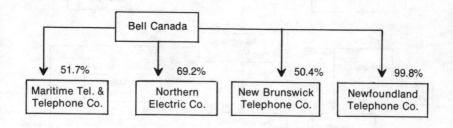

THE BRASCAN GROUP LTD. (in Canada)

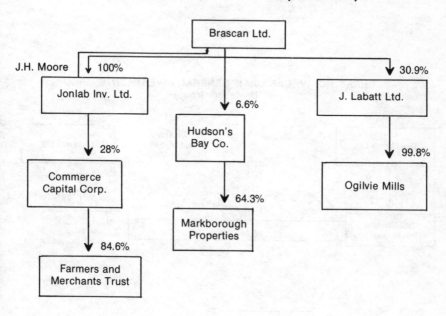

Sources: Financial Post Directory of Directors, 1976
Additional tables no. 2 and 3

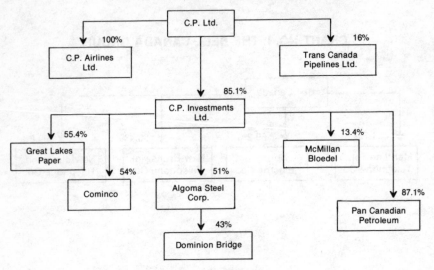

CHART NO. II: THE CANADIAN PACIFIC GROUP

Sources: Financial Post Director of Directors, 1976 Tables 2 and 3

CHART NO. IV: CANADIAN GENERAL INVESTMENTS GROUP
(Meighen Group)

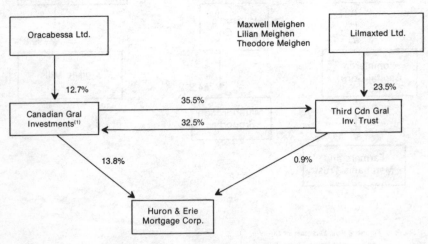

Sources: Financial Post Directory of Directors, 1976 Tables 2 and 3

CHART NO. III: THE ARGUS CORPORATION GROUP

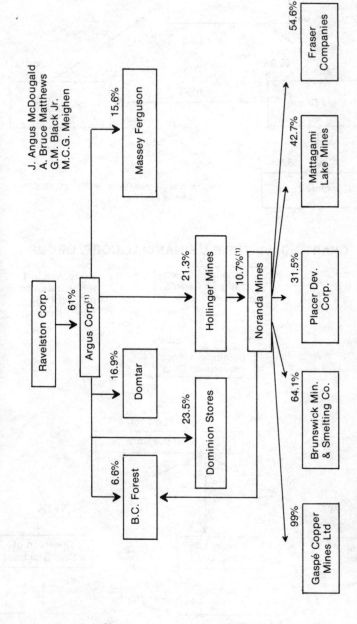

J. Angus McDougald
A. Bruce Matthews
G.M. Black Jr.
M.C.G. Meighen

Ravelston Corp. → 61% → Argus Corp.(1)

Argus Corp.(1) → 15.6% → Massey Ferguson
Argus Corp.(1) → 21.3% → Hollinger Mines
Argus Corp.(1) → 16.9% → Domtar
Argus Corp.(1) → 23.5% → Dominion Stores
Argus Corp.(1) → 6.6% → B.C. Forest

Hollinger Mines → 10.7%(1) → Noranda Mines

Noranda Mines → 31.5% → Placer Dev. Corp.
Noranda Mines → 42.7% → Mattagami Lake Mines
Noranda Mines → 54.6% → Fraser Companies
Noranda Mines → 64.1% → Brunswick Min. & Smelting Co.
Noranda Mines → 99% → Gaspé Copper Mines Ltd

Sources: Financial Post Director of Directors, 1975 Tables 2 and 3

(1) Including the 815,310 shares of Noranda Mines held by Labrador Mining & Exploration Co., a subsidiary of Hollinger Mines

103

CHART NO. V: CANADIAN GENERAL SECURITIES GROUP

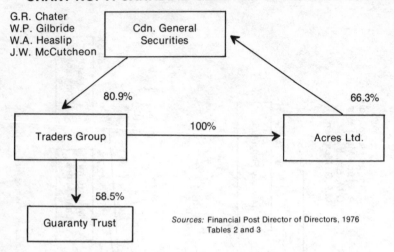

G.R. Chater
W.P. Gilbride
W.A. Heaslip
J.W. McCutcheon

Cdn. General Securities

80.9%

66.3%

Traders Group

100%

Acres Ltd.

58.5%

Guaranty Trust

Sources: Financial Post Director of Directors, 1976
Tables 2 and 3

CHART NO. VI: THE E-L FINANCIAL CORP. GROUP

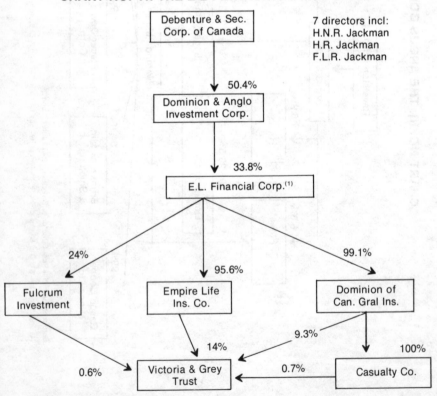

Debenture & Sec. Corp. of Canada

7 directors incl:
H.N.R. Jackman
H.R. Jackman
F.L.R. Jackman

50.4%

Dominion & Anglo Investment Corp.

33.8%

E.L. Financial Corp.[1]

24%

95.6%

99.1%

Fulcrum Investment

Empire Life Ins. Co.

Dominion of Can. Gral Ins.

0.6%

14%

9.3%

100%

Victoria & Grey Trust

0.7%

Casualty Co.

Sources: Financial Post Directory of Directors, 1976 Tables 2 and 3

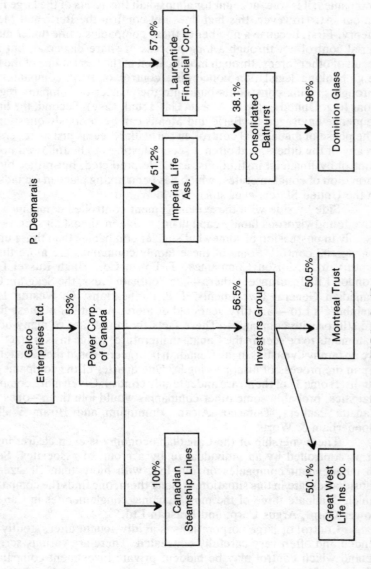

CHART NO. VII: POWER CORPORATION GROUP

Gelco Enterprises Ltd. —53%→ Power Corp. of Canada

P. Desmarais

Power Corp. of Canada:
- 57.9%→ Laurentide Financial Corp.
- 51.2%→ Imperial Life Ass.
- 38.1%→ Consolidated Bathurst
- 56.5%→ Investors Group
- 100%→ Canadian Steamship Lines

Consolidated Bathurst —96%→ Dominion Glass

Investors Group:
- 50.5%→ Montreal Trust
- 50.1%→ Great West Life Ins. Co.

Sources: Financial Post Directory of Directors, 1976 Talbes 2 and 3

105

panies, which are generally under the very firm control, whether absolute or majority, of their parent companies abroad.

Nor does it apply very well to large Canadian-owned companies, of which only one-third seem to be under managerial control. These companies, it is true, account for almost half the assets of the large firms on our list. However, this fact does not confirm the Berle and Means theory. First, because a number of these companies came under managerial control not through a long process of share dispersal, but as a result of other forces: through modification in the legal status of the firm (e.g. banking legislation concerning control of trust companies) or through specific constraints built into the charter or company regulations (e.g. United Grain or Alberta Gas Trunk Line). Second, the linear sequence envisaged by Berle and Means can be seriously questioned. The phase of managerial control, in particular, seems just as reversible as any of the others, and often it seems destined to be followed not by control by financial institutions, as Berle predicted, but rather by the formation of conglomerates, which has been taking place in Canada, as in the United States, ever since World War II.

Side-by-side with these management controlled companies, we have found vigorous family capitalism, active in almost all sectors and usually in possession of somewhat smaller companies than those under managerial control. Some of these family companies are more than a century old: Molson Companies, T. Eaton Co., Hugh Russel Ltd., London Life Insurance. Others—like Southam Press, the Seagram Co., Canadian General Investments, F.P. Publications, G. Weston Ltd., Steinberg's Ltd.—are fifty years old or more. A number of these firms are still private companies. These facts fly in the face of many of the statements to be seen in the Canadian literature, which insists that there are no family dynasties in the Canadian bourgeoisie or, if they exist, they are in the process of disappearing.[53] One quarter of the companies on our list, some 37 of them, are under family control. Given more complete statistics, probably some other companies would join them—ones like Canada Packers, Dofasco, Alcan Aluminium and Hiram Walker-Gooderham & Worts.

The ownership of the Canadian economy is even clearer in the firms controlled by an individual or by a group of associates. Some 26 independent companies on our list, with more than 20 sizeable subsidiaries, are in this situation. Among them, one finds the companies which dominate three of the most dynamic conglomerates in Canada: Power Corp., Argus Corp. and Brascan Ltd.

Control of large corporations is avidly sought after, stoutly defended and often very carefully concealed. There are various screens behind which control may be hidden: private investment companies, charitable foundations, trust companies or even chartered banks acting as dummies. Sometimes a complete list of the trustees declaring their shares still does not permit a full knowledge of the true owners, who may be cloaked by a variety of pseudonyms. The sources at our disposal allow us to recognize who really holds power in a good number of companies, but others remain a mystery. We do not know, moreover, anything at all about the control of the biggest companies in all Canada—the chartered banks.

In the previous chapter we stated that among financial institutions, only holding companies play a permanent role in the control of joint-stock companies. We can now add that these holding companies are merely legal mechanisms through which individual capitalists or groups of capitalists exercise control over a collection of companies, using a pyramidal structure.

NOTES

(1) MacMillan Co., New York, 1932. The quotations are taken from an edition revised by the authors and published in 1968 by Harcourt Brace & World, New York.
(2) A.A. Berle Jr and G.C. Means: *The Modern Corporation and Private Property*, op. cit., p. 66.
(3) *Ibidem.*, p. 6.
(4) *Ibidem.*, p. 312.
(5) A.A. Berle Jr.; *Power Without Property*, Harcourt Brace & Co., New York 1959.
(6) *Ibidem.*, p. 74.
(7) J.K. Galbraith: *American Capitalism*, Houghton Mifflin Co., Boston 1952; *The New Industrial State*, Houghton Mifflin Co., Boston 1967.
(8) J. Burnham: *The Managerial Revolution* (1942), Penguin, London, 1962.
(9) R.J. Larner: "Ownership and Control in the 200 Largest Non-Financial Corporations, 1929 and 1963" in *American Economic Review*, Sept. 1966, pp. 777-787.
(10) R. Dahrendorf: *Classes et conflits de classes dans les sociétés industrielles* (1957), Paris, Mouton, 1972.
(11) P. Sargant Florence: *Ownership, Control and Success of Large Companies*, London, 1961.
(12) E.S. Mason: "The Apologetics of 'Managerialism'" in *The Journal of Business of the University of Chicago*, vol. XXXI, January 1958.
(13) *Ibidem.*, p. 10.
(14) *Ibidem.*, p. 8.
(15) V. Perlo: "People's Capitalism and Stock Ownership" in *American Economic Review*, June 1958, pp. 333-347.
    D. Villarejo: "Stock Ownership and the Control of Corporations" in *New University Thought*, Autumn 1961, Winter 1962.
    G. Kolko: *Wealth and Power in America*, Praeger Publ., New York, 1962.
    P. Sweezy: *The Theory of Capitalist Development*, Monthly Review Press, New York, 1942.
(16) D. Villarejo: "Stock Ownership and the Control of Corporations", *op. cit.*, Autumn 1961, p. 44.
(17) *Ibidem.*, Winter 1962, p. 52.
(18) P. Sweezy: *Monopoly Capital*, Monthly Review Press, New York, 1966, Chapter II.
(19) R.H. Larner: "Ownership and Control in the 200 Largest Non-Financial Corporations, 1929 and 1963," *op. cit.*, p. 781.
(20) J.-M. Chevalier: *La structure financière de l'industrie américaine*, Cujas, Paris, 1970, p. 65.
(21) We have taken as a foreign subsidiary any company whose control group or headquarters is located outside Canada. It did not matter to us whether the control was absolute, majority or minority, or whether it it was exercised directly or through other companies.
(22) We eliminated from our list the Bank of British Columbia, since 10% of its shares are held by Metropolitan Trust, which is controlled 10.8% by Cardigan Holdings, N.V. of Curacao. The Mercantile Bank of Canada is controlled by the First National City Bank of New York.
(23) An exception to this general rule has been the board of directors of Central & Eastern Trust, a finance company born of the merger of Central & Nova Scotia Trust with Eastern Canada Savings and Loan Co. in May 1976. The board of directors of the more important of the two merged companies, Central & Nova Scotia (itself the product of an amalgamation in May 1974), has never presented a report to the Securities Commissions. So as not to have to strike this large company from our list, we took the composition of its board of directors and the distribution of its shares from the July and August 1976 issues of the Bulletin of the Ontario Securities Commission. The information about its assets is equally *pro-forma*.
(24) *La Presse*, 21 December 1974, p. A 9.
(25) H. Marshall et al: *Canadian American Industry* (1936), McClelland and Stewart, Toronto, 1976, p. 47.
(26) *Fortune*, September 1934, p. 105.
(27) *Ibidem.*, p. 106.
(28) D.H. Wallace: *Market Control in the Aluminium Industry*, Cambridge, Harvard Univ. Press, 1937, pp. 75-76.
(29) *Moody's Industrial Manual*, 1959, pp. 2-48.
(30) Ontario Legislature: *Report of the Nickel Commission*, 1917 Sessional Papers, Part XI, pp. 73-75.
(31) O.W. Main: *The Canadian Nickel Industry*, Univ. of Toronto Press, 1955, pp. 100-106 and 156-157.

(32) J. Porter: *The Vertical Mosaic*, Univ. of Toronto Press, 1965, p. 592.

(33) P.C. Newman: *The Canadian Establishment*, vol. 1, McClelland and Stewart, Toronto, 1975, p. 187.

(34) Royal Commission on Price Spreads: *Report*, King's Printer, Ottawa 1936 pp. 377-382.

(35) R.C. Fetherstonhaugh: *Charles F. Sise*, Gazette Printing Co., Montreal 1944, p. 208.

(36) Sources for 1928, 1938 and 1948: *Financial Post Survey of Corporate Securities* and *Financial Post Survey of Industrials*.

(37) J. Lorne McDougall: *Canadian Pacific*, McGill University Press, p. 60.

(38) R. Chodos: The CPR: *A Century of Corporate Welfare*, 1973 J. Lorimer & Co., Toronto, p. 136.

(39) In Consumers' Gas, lawyer and director A.H. Zimmerman administers 112,903 shares passed down from former company directors. In Union Gas, R.M. Barford owns 330,000 common shares and sits on the board of directors. Neither one nor the other, however, is an inside director.

(40) *Wall Street Journal*, 19/11/1970, p. 16 and 9/12/1970, p. 7.

(41) In May 1976 the Bronfman family acquired control of Trizec Corp., the largest real-estate development company in Canada, which until then had been owned by English interests.

(42) P.C. Newman, *The Canadian Establishment*, op. cit., chap. II.

(43) *F.P. Survey of Industrials*, 1955 to 1969.

(44) J.M. Blair: *Economic Concentration*, World Brace & Jovanovitch, New York 1972 chap. III.

(45) J. Houssiaux: *Le pouvoir de monopole*, Sirey, Paris, 1958, pp. 106-111.

(46) P.C. Newman: *Flame of Power*, McClelland and Stewart, Toronto 1959, p. 224.

(47) E.P. Neufeld: *A Global Corporation: A History of the International Development of Massey-Ferguson Ltd.*, Univ. of Toronto Press 1969, p. 42.

(48) *Wall Street Journal*, 22/8/1973 p. 2; 10/6/1974 p. 14, 10/7/1974 p. 7.

(49) *Wall Street Journal*, 10/5/1963 p. 11; 28/1/1972 p. 16.

(50) *Wall Street Journal*, 12/3/1965 p. 22; 4/3/1970 p. 6; 3/6/1970 p. 5.

(51) *Wall Street Journal*, 1/5/1967 p. 12; 12/5/1967 p. 27; 25/5/1967 p. 3.

(52) *Wall Street Journal*, 30/1/1969 p. 19; 5/3/1969 p. 7; 10/3/1969 p. 14.

(53) For example, in *The C.P.R.*, op. cit., by R. Chodos, p. 134, one reads:
"Canada has no equivalents of the Rockefellers, the Du Ponts, the Mellons, the Morgans and the other American Corporate dynasties. . . Control of the Canadian economy is in large measure anonymous."

TABLE I

MAJOR COMPANIES UNDER CANADIAN CONTROL
AND THEIR ASSETS (1975)

A) Financial Institutions	Total Assets (millions of $)	Date of Financial statement
BANKS		
Royal	25,211	(1)
Canadian Imperial Bank of Commerce	22,259	(1)
of Montréal	18,243	(1)
of Nova Scotia	16,006	(1)
Toronto-Dominion	13,577	(1)
Canadienne Nationale	4,872	(1)
Provincial of Canada	3,059	(1)
Savings Bank of the City and District of Montréal	968	(1)
Unity of Canada	172	(1)
LIFE-INSURANCE COMPANIES		
Sun Life Assurance Co. of Canada	4,699	(2)
Manufacturers Life Ins. Co.	3,083	(2)
London Life Ins. Co.	2,392	(2)
Great West Life Ass. Co.	2,349	(2)
Canada Life Ass. Co.	1,887	(2)
Mutual Life Ass. Co. of Canada	1,782	(2)
Confederation Life Ass. Co.	1,485	(2)
Crown Life Ins. Co.	1,205	(2)
North American Life Ass. Co.	1,024	(2)
Imperial Life Ass. Co. of Canada	714	(2)
TRUST COMPANIES		
Royal Trust Co.	3,436	(2)
Victoria & Grey Trust Co.	1,296	(1)
National Trust Co.	1,163	(1)
Guaranty Trust Co. of Canada	1,086	(2)
Central & Eastern Trust Co.	885	(2)
Montréal Trust Co.	768	(2)
Trust Général du Canada	411	(2)
City Savings and Trust Co.	276	(2)
Farmers & Merchants Trust	263	(2)
Crown Trust Co.	240	(2)
United Trust Co.	237	(2)
BROKERAGE COMPANIES		
Wood, Gundy & Co.	693	(2)
FINANCE COMPANIES		
I.A.C. Ltd.	2,391	(2)
Traders Group Ltd.	1,024	(2)
Laurentide Financial Corp.	429	(2)
T. Eaton Acceptance Co.	378	31-1-76
First City Financial Corp.	302	(2)

109

MORTGAGE COMPANIES

Canada Permanent Mortgage Corp.	2,726	(2)
Huron & Erie Mortgage Corp.	2,626	(2)

MUTUAL FUNDS

Investors Group	636	(2)

INVESTMENT COMPANIES

Canadian General Investments	118	(2)

HOLDING COMPANIES (DIVERSIFIED)

Canadian Pacific Investments	3,511	(2)
Brascan Ltd.	2,247	(2)
Power Corp.	579	(2)
Commerce Capital Corp.	316	(2)
E-L. Financial Corp.	282	(2)
Prenor Group	261	(2)
Argus Corp.	205	30-11-75
Canadian Corporate Management	130	(2)
Jannock Corp.	122	(2)

B) Industrial Companies (and specialized holding companies)	Total Assets (millions of $)	Date of financial statement
Abitibi Paper Co.	871	(2)
Alcan Aluminium Ltd.	3,012	(2)
Algoma Steel Corp.	851	(2)
Bombardier Ltd.	145	31-1-75
Bow Valley Industries Ltd.	101	31-5-75
British Columbia Forest Products Ltd.	369	(2)
Brunswick Mining & Smelting Corp. Ltd.	151	31-12-74
Burns Food Ltd.	135	1-3-76
Canada Packers Ltd.	273	29-3-75
Canron Ltd.	183	(2)
Cominco Ltd.	870	(2)
Consolidated-Bathurst Ltd.	662	(2)
Denison Mines Ltd.	219	(2)
Dominion Bridge Co.	327	(2)
Dominion Foundries & Steel Corp. Ltd.	944	(2)
Dominion Glass Ltd.	107	(2)
Dominion Textiles Ltd.	348	30-6-75
Domtar Ltd.	721	(2)
F.P. Publications Ltd.	142	(2)
Federal Industries Ltd.	107	31-3-75
Fraser Companies	130	(2)
Gaspé Copper Mines Ltd.	166	31-12-74
Great Lakes Paper Co.	205	(2)
Hollinger Mines	148	(2)
Home Oil Co.	398	(2)
Inco Ltd.	3,026	(2)
Irving Oil	150	31-12-71
Ivaco Industries Ltd.	188	(2)
Kruger Pulp & Paper Co.	149	13-12-74
John Labatt Ltd.	426	30-4-75

Maclaren Power & Paper Co.	105	(2)
Macmillan Bloedel Ltd.	1,198	(2)
Massey-Ferguson Ltd.	1,982	(1)
Mattagami Lake Mines Ltd.	164	31-12-74
Maclean Hunter Ltd.	112	(2)
Molson Companies	407	(2)
Moore Corp.	737	(2)
Neonex International	100	(2)
Noranda Mines	1,980	(2)
Northern Electric Co.	590	(2)
Ogilvie Mills	161	30-4-75
Pan Canadian Petroleum Ltd.	382	31-12-74
Placer Development Ltd.	242	31-12-74
Price Corp.	356	(2)
Hugh Russel Ltd.	137	(2)
The Seagram Co.	1,991	31-7-75
Southam Press Ltd.	145	(2)
Steel Co. of Canada	1,678	(2)
United Grain Co.	193	31-7-75
Hiram Walker-Gooderham & Worts Ltd.	913	31-8-75

C) COMMERCIAL COMPANIES

Acklands Ltd.	181	30-11-75
Canadian Tire Corp.	359	(2)
Dominion Stores	263	(2)
T. Eaton Co.	—	(3)
Finning Tractor & Equipment	147	30-8-75
Hudson's Bay Co.	822	31-1-76
Kelly Douglas & Co.	173	3-1-76
M. Loeb Ltd.	151	25-1-76
Oshawa Group	255	25-1-76
Simpson's Ltd.	562	7-1-76
Simpsons-Sears Ltd.	1,051	7-1-76
Steinberg's Ltd.	418	26-7-75
United Westburne Industries	116	31-3-75
Westburne International Industries	214	31-3-75
G. Weston Ltd.	1,248	(2)
Woodward Stores	252	31-1-76

D) Transportation companies and utilities	Total Assets (millions of $)	Date of Financial statement
Alberta Gas Trunk Lines	658	(2)
Bell Canada	6,588	(2)
Calgary Power	760	(2)
Canada Steamships Lines	394	31-12-74
Canadian Pacific Airlines	324	(2)
Canadian Pacific Ltd.	6,236	(2)
Consumers' Gas Co.	741	30-9-75
Gaz Metropolitain Inc.	252	(2)
Maritime Telegraph &Telephone Co.	355	(2)
New Brunswick Telephone Co.	251	(2)
Newfoundland Light & Power Co.	193	(2)
Newfoundland Telephone Co.	141	(2)
Norcen Energy Ressources	916	(2)
Trans Canada Pipelines	1,572	(2)
Union Gas	430	31-3-75

E) Real-Estate Development Companies

Allarco Developments	101	(2)
Block Bros Industries	147	31-1-76
Bramalea Consolidated Dev.	297	31-1-76
Cadillac Fairview Corp.	921	28-2-75
Campeau Corp.	482	(2)
Carma Developers	103	(2)
Daon Development Corp.	210	(1)
Deltan Corp.	390	(2)
T. Eaton Realty Co.	103	31-1-76
Markborough Properties	142	(2)
S. B. McLaughlin Assoc. Ltd.	256	(2)
Nu West Development Corp.	187	(2)
Orlando Corp.	120	(2)
Oxford Development Group	475	(2)
Unicorp Financial Corp.	249	(2)

(1) 31-10-75.
(2) 31-12-75
(3) T. Eaton Co. does not publish any Financial statement.

TABLE II

CONTROL IN "INDEPENDENT" CANADIAN COMPANIES (1975)

Name of the Company	Type of Control	Holder of Control (and % of vote)
A) FINANCIAL INSTITUTIONS		
Argus Corp.	Majority	Ravelston Group Corp. (61%)
Brascan Ltd.	Minority	Jonlab Investments of J.H. Moore & Assoc. (8%)
Canadian Corporate Management	Minority	The board of directors holds 15.9% of the shares; Walter L. and Duncan L. Gordon (13.1%); L.C. Bonnycastle (3.6%); B.H. Rieger (3.3%)[1]
Canadian General Investments	Majority	Third Canadian Gral Inv. Trust (32.5%); Oracabessa Ltd. (12.7%); M.C.G. Meighen and T.R. Meighen (4.9%)
Central & Eastern Trust Corp.	Majority	H.R. Cohen and L. Ellen (49.7%); other directors (5.3%)
Crown Life Ins. Co.	Minority	Scotia Investments, of J.J. Jodrey & Assoc. (11.8%); Kingfield Investments of H.M. Burns and others (12%)
Crown Trust	Minority	H.R. Cohen and L. Ellen (20.4%)[2]
E-L Financial Corp.	Minority	Dominion & Anglo Investment Corp. (33.8%); P.S. Gooderham (5.8%); W.L. Knowlton (2.9%)
First City Financial Corp.	Majority	Belzberg family (68.8%)
Jannock Corp.	Minority	D.G. Willmot (17%); G.E. Mara (10%); M. Tannenbaum (7.6%); W.M. Hatch (4.2%); rest of directors (5%)
London Life Ins. Co.	Semi-absolute	Jeffery Family
Power Corp.	Majority	P. Desmarais (53%) through Gelco Enterprises Ltd. and Nordex Ltd.
Prenor Group	Joint-Majority	L.C. Webster and family (41.3%); Norlac Financial Group (29.9%)

113

	Type of Control	Holder of Control (and % of vote)
Royal Trust	Managerial	The board of directors holds 1% of the vote
Trust Général du Canada	Minority	Jean-Louis Lévesque (10.5%)
United Trust	Majority	G.S. Mann (70.6% of the vote)
Wood, Gundy & Co.	Semi-absolute	Gundy-Scott family

(1) Duncan L. Gordon, brother of Walter L., is not a member of the board of directors.
(2) Messrs Cohen and Ellen are not members of the board of directors of Crown Trust.

B) INDUSTRIAL COMPANIES

	Type of Control	Holder of Control (and % of vote)
Abitibi Paper Co.	Managerial	The board holds 0.8%
Alcan Aluminium	Managerial	The board holds 0.3%
Bombardier	Majority	Les Entreprises J.A. Bombardier Ltée (74.9%) Bombardier family
Bow Valley Industries Ltd.	Minority	Donald R., Daryl K. and Byron J. Seaman (14.7%)
Burns Food	Minority	R.H. Webster (32%)[1]
Canada Packers	Managerial	The board holds 2.4%
Canron	Managerial	The board holds 1.6%
Denison Mines	Minority	Roman Corp. (26.2%); S.B. Roman (4.3%)
Dominion Foundries & Steel	Minority	J.D. Leitch (4.8%); rest of board (0.4%)
Dominion Textile	Managerial	The board holds 0.5%
F.P. Publications	Semi-absolute (private)	Bell Foundation (22.5%); heirs of J.W. Sifton (22.5%); R.H. Webster (22.5%)[2]
Federal Industries	Minority	Searle-Leach family (36.4%)
Inco Ltd.	Managerial	The board holds 0.15%
Irving Oil Co.	Semi-absolute (private)	K. Irving (100%)
Ivaco Industries	Majority	Isin, Paul and Sydney Ivanier hold 33.6%; M. Herling (10.5%); J. Klein (12%)
Kruger Pulp & Paper	Semi-absolute (private)	Kruger family
Maclaren Power & Paper	Minority	Maclaren family (19.6%)
Maclean-Hunter	Majority	D.F. Hunter (49.8%); rest of board (9.1%)
Molson Companies	Minority	Molson family (36.3%); D.G. Willmot (11.2%)
Moore Corp.	Managerial	The board holds 0.3%
Neonex International Ltd.	Minority	J. Pattison (29.4%)
Hugh Russel	Minority	A.D. Russel (18.4%)
The Seagram Co.	Minority	Bronfman family (32.6%)

(1) According to the F.P. Survey of Industrials, this control is 42% (1976 edition, p. 266).
(2) Le Devoir, 11/12/75, p. 15; Financial Post, 4/5/76, p. 5-4.

	Type of Control	Holder of Control (and % of vote)
Southam Press	Minority	G.H. Southam (2.2%); G.T. Southam (1%); W.W. Southam (1%); St. C. Balfour (1.1%); R.W. Swanson (1.3%); G.N. Fisher (1.3%)
Steel Co. of Canada	Managerial	The board holds 0.3% (1)
United Grain	Managerial	
Hiram Walker-Gooderham & Worts Ltd.	Managerial	The board holds 0.9%

C) COMMERCIAL COMPANIES

	Type of Control	Holder of Control (and % of vote)
Ackland Ltd.	Majority	L. Wolinsky, N. Starr, H. Bessin (46.2%); rest of board (6.1%)
Canadian Tire Corp.	Majority	Billes family (60.9%)
T. Eaton Co.	Semi-absolute (private)	Eaton family (100%)
Finning Tractor & Equipment	Majority	J.E. Barker and MM. Young (70.2%)
M. Loeb & Co.	Joint-Minority	Loeb family (15.4%); G. Weston Ltd. (18.7%)
Oshawa Group	Semi-absolute	Wolfe family (100%)
Simpson Ltd.	Managerial	The board holds 4%
Steinbergs Ltd.	Semi-absolute	Steinberg family (100%)
Westburne International Industries Ltd.	Minority	J.A. Scrymgeour (23.5%); rest of board (6%)
G. Weston Ltd.	Majority	Weston family (59% approximately)
Woodward Stores	Minority	C.N.W. Woodward (27.3%); other family members (12.4%)

D) TRANSPORTATION AND UTILITIES

	Type of Control	Holder of Control (and % of vote)
Alberta Gas Trunk Line	Managerial	The board holds 0.07%
Bell Canada	Managerial	The board holds 0.03%
Calgary Power	Managerial	The board holds 0.4%
Canadian Pacific Ltd.	Managerial	The board holds 0.2%
Consumers' Gas	Managerial	The board holds 0.7%
Newfoundland Light & Power	Managerial	The board holds 1.6%
Norcen Energy Resources	Managerial	The board holds 0.6%
Union Gas	Managerial	The board holds 2.3%

(1) Company regulations forbid any shareholder to hold more than 25 shares. Furthermore the rule in shareholders' meetings is: one person, one vote.

115

E) REAL-ESTATE DEVELOPMENT COMPANIES

	Type of Control	Holder of Control (and % of vote)
Allarco Developments	Minority	Ch. Allard (48.2%)
Block Bros. Industries	Minority	A.J. Block and H.J. Block (16%)
Bramalea Consolidated Dev.	Minority	Braminuest Corp. Ltd. (K.S. Field, J. Schiff & Assoc.) holds 20.9%
Cadillac-Fairview Corp.	Minority	Bronfman family (not less than 38% through Cemp Investments)
Campeau Corp.	Majority	Robert Campeau (62.5%)
Daon Development	Majority	J.W. Poole and family (23.8%); G.R. Dawnson and family (21.7%); rest of board (9.8%)
Deltan Corp.	Semi-absolute	R.J. Prusac (94.7%)
S.B. McLaughlin Assoc. Ltd.	Minority	S.B. McLaughlin (46.7%)
Nu-West Dev. Corp.	Minority	R.T. Scurfield (20.8%); C.J. McConnell (20.7%)
Orlando Corp.	Majority	O.R. and E. Fidani (51.2%)
Oxford Development Corp.	Minority	J.E. Poole (6.4%); G.E. Poole (6.4%); G.D. Love (5.8%)
Unicorp Financial Corp.	Semi-absolute	G.S. Mann & Assoc. (82.5%)

TABLE III

CONTROL IN CANADIAN SUBSIDIARIES (1975)

Name of the Company	Initial Control (and ultimate)	Parent Company (and % of vote)
A) FINANCIAL INSTITUTIONS		
Banque d'Epargne de la Cité et du District de Montréal	Minority (no data)	Canada Permanent Mortgage Corp. (10%)
Banque Provinciale du Canada	Minority (Managerial)	Fédération de Québec des Caisses Populaires Desjardins (23%)
Canada Permanent Mortgage Corp.	Joint Minority (no data)	Toronto-Dominion and Bank of Nova Scotia (9.9% each)
Canadian Pacific Investments	Majority (Managerial)	C.P. Ltd. (85.1%)
City Savings and Trust Co.	Semi-absolute (maj.)	First City Financial Corp. (88.4%)
Commerce Capital Corp.	Minority (Minority)	Brascan Ltd. through Jonlab Investments Ltd (28%)
T. Eaton Acceptance Co.	(Semi-absolute)	T. Eaton Co. (100%)
Farmers & Merchants Trust Co.	Majority (Minority)	Commerce Capital Corp. (84.6%)
Great West Life Ass. Co.	Majority (Majority)	Power Corp. through Investors Group (50.1%)
Guaranty Trust Co. of Canada	Majority (Majority)	Cdn. Gral Securities though Traders Group (58.5%)
Huron & Erie Mortgage Corp.	Minority (Minority)	Cdn. Gral Investments (13.8%); Third Cdn Gral Investment Trust (0.9%)
IAC Ltd.	Minority (Minority)	Carena Bancorp Inc. (19.4%)
Imperial Life Ass. Co. of Canada	Majority (Minority)	Power Corp. (51.2%)
Investors Group	Majority (Majority)	Power Corp. (56.2%)
Laurentides Financial Corp.	Majority (Majority)	Power Corp. (57.9%)
Montréal Trust Co.	Majority (Majority)	Power Corp. through Investors Group (50.5%)
National Trust Co.	Minority (Managerial)	Canada Life (4.9% and two directors)
Traders Group	Majority (Majority)	Canadian Gral Securities (80.9%)
Victoria and Grey Trust	Minority (Minority)	E-L Financial Corp. through several companies (24.6%)

B) INDUSTRIAL COMPANIES

Company	Control type	Controlling interest
Algoma Steel Corp.	Majority (Managerial)	C.P. Investments (51%)
British Columbia Forest Products	Joint Majority (Minority)	Noranda Mines (28.5%); Mean Group (15.3%); Brunswick Pulp & Paper (26.6%)
Brunswick Mining & Smelting	Majority (Minority)	Noranda Mines (64.1%)
Cominco	Majority (Managerial)	C.P. Investments (54%)
Consolidated-Bathurst	Minority (Minority)	Power Corp. (38.1%)
Dominion Bridge	Minority (Managerial)	Algoma Steel Corp. (43%)
Dominion Glass	Majority (Minority)	Consolidated-Bathurst (96%)
Fraser Companies	Majority (Minority)	Noranda Mines through Northwood Mills Ltd (54.6%)
Gaspé Copper Mines Ltd.	Majority (Minority)	Noranda Mines (99%)
Great Lakes Paper	Majority (Managerial)	C.P. Investments (55.4%)
Hollinger Mines	Minority (Minority)	Argus Corp. (21.3%)
Home Oil Co.	Minority (Managerial)	Consumers' Gas (49.7%)
John Labatt	Minority (Managerial)	Brascan Ltd. (30.9%)
Macmillan Bloedell	Minority (Minority)	C.P. Investments (13.4%)
Massey-Ferguson Ltd.	Minority (Minority)	Argus Corp. (15.6%)
Mattagami Lake Mines Ltd.	Joint Majority (Min.)	Noranda Mines (34.1% directly plus 8.6% indirectly); Placer Development (27% indirectly)
Noranda Mines	Minority (Minority)	Hollinger Mines (10.7%)
Northern Electric Co.	Majority (Managerial)	Bell Canada (69.2%)
Ogilvie Mills	Majority (Minority)	J. Labatt (99.8%)
Pan Canadian Petroleum	Majority (Managerial)	C.P. Investments (87.1%)
Placer Development	Minority (Minority)	Noranda Mines (31.5%)
Price Co.	Majority (Managerial)	Abitibi Paper Co. (50.7%)

C) COMMERCIAL COMPANIES

Company	Control type	Controlling interest
Dominion Stores	Minority (Minority)	Argus Corp. (23.5%)
Hudson's Bay Co.	Minority (Minority)	Jonlab Investments (6.6%)
Kelly, Douglas & Co.	Majority (Majority)	G. Weston Ltd. (68.1%)
Simpsons-Sears Ltd.	Joint absolute (Managerial)	Simpsons Ltd. (50%); Sears-Roebuck Co. of the U.S.A. (50%)
United Westburne Industries	Majority (Minority)	Westburne International Ind. (95%)

D) TRANSPORTATION COMPANIES AND UTILITIES

Company	Control Type	Parent (%)
Canada Steamship Lines	Semi-absolute (Majority)	Power Corp. (100%)
C.P. Airlines	Absolute (Managerial)	C.P. Ltd. (100%)
Gaz Métropolitain Inc.	Majority (Managerial)	Norcen Energy Resources (81.6%)
Maritime Telegraph & Telephone	Majority (Managerial)	Bell Canada (51%)
New Brunswick Telephone Co.	Majority (Managerial)	Bell Canada (50.4%)
Newfoundland Telephone Co.	Majority (Managerial)	Bell Canada (99.8%)
Trans-Canada Pipelines	Minority (Managerial)	CP Ltd. (16%)

E) REAL-ESTATE DEVELOPMENT COMPANIES

Company	Control Type	Parent (%)
Carma Developers	Minority (Minority)	Nu West Development Corp. (47.8%)
T. Eaton Realty Co.	Semi-absolute (Private)	T. Eaton Co. (100%)
Markborough Properties Ltd.	Majority (Minority)	Hudson's Bay Co. (64.3%)

119

CHAPTER III

Corporate Control
and the Economic Elite

"Elite analysis is popular among sociologists nowadays. Its popularity derives, I believe, quite as much from the things it enables an analyst to avoid, as from the things it enables him to do." Robert Lynd

ELITE THEORY has been used to study the control of big business in Canada. According to this theory, there is an "economic élite" which controls the country's major industrial, financial and commercial companies and utilities. Before taking its place in the Canadian social sciences, élite theory had already been long present in sociology and political science. It is not my intention in this work to trace the evolution of this theory: partly because a number of authors have already done so,[1] partly because it is only recently that people have begun using élite theory to study corporate control. We shall therefore begin with the book which has most profoundly influenced Anglo-Saxon élite sociology, namely, *The Power Elite*, by C. Wright Mills, originally published in 1956.[2] Mills set in motion a radical stream of interpretation which questioned existing analyses of power in large joint-stock companies. This stream is well represented in Canadian industrial sociology and history. Moreover, here as elsewhere, the concept of an élite, particularly that of an economic élite, has become an important element in Marxist theory, even if it was formerly a rival theory.

In the first part of this chapter, we shall trace the main steps in the evolution of the new, radical élite theory as it applies to the question of the control of industry. We shall set forth the critiques and debates to which it has given rise as well as the way in which it has been integrated into Marxist theory—in an effort to explain that integration. In the second part, we shall examine critically the main Canadian works on this subject, always as they relate to the issue of corporate control. This analysis of the élite theory will provide an opportunity to introduce fresh data concerning the administration of major Canadian companies.

The Economic Elite of C. Wright Mills

Numerous authors have demonstrated that the élite theory—as developed in the sociology and political science of this century in the works of Vilfredo Pareto, Gaetano Mosca and others—is in direct opposition to liberal and socialist democratic doctrines.[3] Other, more recent authors, such as Raymond Aron and A. Downs, have used the élite theory to modernize liberal theories about democracy in capitalist society: according to this more current version, pluralist competition for power does not take place between individuals but between élites. Continued competition for positions of power guarantees to the government a choice among worthy candidates.[4]

The originality of C. Wright Mill's work was his effort to develop a radical critique of capitalist society by means of the élite theory. This critique, however, wished to separate itself from Marxism from the very beginning. Mills rejected the concept of the ruling class, which is central to Marxist studies of control of big business and of the state. He believes that class is an economic concept and that the very word suggests the existence of an economic class which governs, directs or imposes its will on the whole of society. Mills does not wish to assume *a priori* the ultimate control by those who govern economic institutions over other spheres of society, such as the state, the armed forces or culture. He therefore chooses a term which he considers to be more neutral, that of the "élite". He assumes the existence of three relatively separate yet inter-related élites, forming a "power élite". There are the economic élite, which dominates big business, the political élite, which manages the state, and the military élite which commands the armed forces.[5]

Though he assumes that the economic, political and military élites are relatively autonomous bodies, Mills believes that the economic élite is *internally* unified. This élite is said to consists of two major groupings: the large shareholders in major corporations (the corporate rich), heirs to the huge fortunes amassed at the turn of the century; and the upper echelons of business management (the chief executives). This latter group in turn consists of those rare entrepreneurs who have managed in mid-20th century to climb to the top of the big companies; managers who have been given positions in companies owned by their own families; lawyers; and career administrators. Mills does not think that these different groups form separate categories: they are united by their interest in the ownership of big business.

"The chief executives and the very rich are *not* two distinct and clearly segregated groups."[6] "The very fact of the spread of ownership among the very rich and the chief executives of the great corporations makes for a unity of the propertied class, since the control of many corporations by means of various legal devices has excluded the smaller, but not the larger, propertied interests."[7]

This economic élite is thus a propertied class and it resembles, in this at least, the bourgeoisie of Marx, even though when Mills uses the concepts of "bourgeoisie" and "ruling class" he is referring to the past, to American history:

"The American élite entered modern history as a virtually unopposed bourgeoisie."[8]

According to Mills, the American economic élite dominated large corporations, the state and the armed forces until World War I. During the Progressive Era and the New Deal, however, political and military spheres gained increasing independence from the business world. The autonomy of each of the three élites prevents Mills from using the concept of "ruling class" in a study which examines the post-war period.

Mills' theory is a radical one. Yet, it has been the object of many critical studies by radical Americans. Robert Lynd and Ferdinand Lundberg are prominent among the socialist opponents to Mills' ideas. Lynd points out the absence of a theory of power and a theory of social structure. What is the basis for unequal division of power? What limits are imposed on power-holders by the structures? Lynd summarizes his critique in this way:

"He does not hold steadily in focus the massive continuities involved in the fact that ours is a capitalist society; the factor of class is belittled; the relative weights of his three institutions in a capitalist society go unassessed; and an unwarranted autonomy is imputed to the several institutions."[9]

F. Lundberg addresses himself more directly to the control of major corporations. Essentially, Lundberg criticizes Mills for having exaggerated the internal unity of the economic élite and for having confused the capitalist with his senior-management employees:

"That the top corporation executive is a person of commanding power in his own right is part of the executive mystique and is uncritically incorporated into his theory of power élite by C. Wright Mills, the American sociologist."[10]

This assimilation of executives, military leaders and politicians into one power élite makes Lundberg think that Mills has adopted the managerialist theories of Berle, Means, Burnham and Galbraith. And Lundberg opposes this assimilation because, according to him, most members of Mills' power élite are merely highly-qualified employees, technicians and consultants in the pay of the big owners.

"Although the situation as projected by Mills creates a complicated and dramatic picture, one must object to it on compelling grounds. Mills has raised what are clearly subordinate advisers and technicians into his élite of power. . . But most of the members in Mills' power élite are readily removable, or may be ignored, by other members. Most of the members of Mills' power élite are indeed no more than advisers and technicians. They were hired and can be fired, hold their position only during satisfactory conduct. This is not to say that while in office they are not powerful. But their power is *derived power, not their own, not autonomous*."[11]

The major Marxist critique of *The Power Elite* is that of Paul Sweezy.[12] He criticizes Mills for failing to explain how these members of the élite gain the positions of power which they occupy and the nature of their relationship to the rest of society. As well, Sweezy claims that Mills' own data show that American political life is controlled by the members of the economic élite which, therefore, constitutes a ruling class. For example, Mills shows that 50 people within the Executive Branch make the key decisions in American government and that, among those 50, one finds 30 who are "linked financially or professionally or both with the corporate world.[13] Like Lundberg, Sweezy claims that the senior officers of the armed forces participate in the direction of major corporations, in a subordinate role to that of the major shareholders. According to Sweezy, the military has never challenged the civilians for economic (or political) control of the United States.

One should add that Mills' approach cannot explain the very existence of these social hierarchies whose summits are occupied by the "élites". Mills claims that the process of economic concentration is at the basis of the formation of an economic élite. Yet this cannot account for the inequality of power within large corporations. It is only through the study of the birth and evolution of the division of labour, first in manufacturing and then in big business, that one can explain the powers concentrated in the hands of the boards of directors of corporations. This division of labour confers all decision-making powers on the capitalists and their salaried managers: power to organize the work, to set its pace and to appropriate its surplus.[14] In other words, the process of technological, economic and financial concentration explains the existence of giant corporations, but it does not explain the monopoly of powers which has been conferred on boards of directors within these corporations. This can only be explained by the intervention of private ownership of the means of production and exchange, the capitalist mode of production and the technical and social division of labour which typifies the monopolist stage. One of the many criticisms addressed to C. Wright Mills will be given a more detailed empirical analysis later in this chapter, because it deals directly with the problem of corporate control. This is Lundberg's critique and, to some extent, that of Sweezy as well: when looking at a board of directors one must not confuse the large shareholders with the legal advisers, financial consultants, technicians and former politicians. Mills held that these chief executives themselves tended to become large shareholders; his critics reply that large companies are commanded by the big owners. Mills gives advisers an equal place within the economic élite to that of the corporate rich. His opponents retort that the legal/financial/technical/political advisers are not in the same league as the major stockholders, neither in share-ownership nor in status on the board of directors. It is not too difficult to test this aspect of Mills' theory. We shall return to it.

Elite Theory and Marxism

Marxists have criticized Mills' élite theory. But many of them have been deeply influenced by this book nonetheless, and have attempted to integrate Mills' perspective into their own concept of Marxism. These efforts at integration have taken place primarily in Anglo-Saxon countries: in the United States, the United Kingdom and in English-speaking Canada.

In a book which he dedicated to the memory of Mills, the English Marxist Ralph Miliband adopted the concept of an economic élite to describe control of major corporations. Even though he rejected the managerialist theories, Miliband claimed that more and more non-owners are to be found on the boards of major joint-stock companies:

"But it is nevertheless true that at the head of the largest, most dynamic and most powerful concerns of the system are now to be found, and will increasingly be found, managers and executives who owe their position not to ownership but to appointment and cooption."[15]

Miliband criticizes the line of reasoning employed by Berle, Means and Galbraith to explain the "social" motivation of professional managers, who were said to be removed from the search for profit. For him, professional managers are among the biggest shareholders; they buy shares regularly through preferential purchasing schemes. Miliband also claims that members of the board of directors are frequently recruited from the members of the propertied classes, but he continues to favour the term "economic élite" to describe the social group which controls big business. Furthermore, he claims that there is not *one* economic élite, but *several*: yet he does not specify exactly what factors (economic, ethnic, regional or other) delineate them.

In sum, Miliband's understanding of the concept of an economic élite is not significantly different from that of Mills. It is the institutional autonomy of the economy from the other spheres of social activity which creates the autonomy of an economic élite, consisting of the major shareholders and salaried chief executives now in the process of being assimilated by the propertied class.

G. William Domhoff[16] adopts the concept of an élite, but in quite another context. Like Mills and Miliband, Domhoff rejects the theory of managerial control of corporations. According to him, the managers identify with the big shareholders because they are buying up shares themselves in the companies they administer. Thus they are gradually assimilated into the upper class. Moreover, the managers, just like the major shareholders, seek the maximization of profits for their companies. So far, Domhoff agrees fully with élite theory. He then proceeds to set himself apart by creating a distinction between the ruling class (or "upper class" or "governing class") and the power élite. He defines his terms as follows:

> "Let me begin by defining two terms, "ruling class" and "power élite". By a ruling class, I mean a clearly demarcated social upper class which:
> a) has a disproportionate amount of wealth and income
> b) generally fares better than other social groups on a variety of well-being statistics. . .
> c) controls the major economic institutions of the country; and
> d) dominates the governmental process of the country.
> By a power élite I mean the 'operating' arm or 'leadership' group or establishment of the ruling class. This power élite is made up of active, working members of the upper class and high-level employees in institutions controlled by members of the upper class."[17]

This distinction between the ruling class and the power élite allows Domhoff to tackle the criticisms levelled at Marxist theory by élite theorists. The major criticism of Marxism is that control of major corporations (and of the state) is not entirely in the hands of the members of the ruling class and that, conversely, not all members of the ruling class are to be found in positions of control in these institutions. To this objection Domhoff replies that one part of the ruling class is completely detached from controlling companies (and the state). Another part, however, is very actively involved, with the help of employees who have been carefully educated in universities administered by members of the ruling class. These employees (managers, lawyers, technicians) control the big companies and the state, side-by-side with the active part of the ruling class. Some of these employees assimilate to the ruling class.

To bolster his thesis, Domhoff studied the social origins of 884 directors of fifteen of the largest banks, fifteen of the largest insurance companies and twenty of the largest industrial companies. He found that 53% of these directors came from the upper class and that the other 47% consisted of salaried executives assimilating to the upper class, of university professionals (engineers, economists, statisticians, etc.) and of non-ownership members of the élite such as lawyers in the big corporations, directors of foundations controlled by ruling-class families, university presidents and former military officers.[18] In sum, for Domhoff, corporate control lies with the ruling class, through its active members in alliance with non-ownership members of the power élite, most of whom are lawyers and technical experts.

It is not difficult to explain these repeated efforts in the Anglo-Saxon world to integrate Marxist theory with the concept of élites. First, there is much more information about ownership and control of big corporations available in North America and Great Britain than in continental Europe or elsewhere in the capitalist world. Thus, many more studies have been done on this subject in these countries. The existing data and studies clearly show the growing number of professional administrators (lawyers, business-school graduates, engineers) to be found on the boards of directors of large corporations. Some of these professional administrators eventually become major shareholders, but not all. Thus, one must find a concept that takes account of this sort of board of directors: a number of Anglo-Saxon Marxists have therefore adopted the term, "élite".

However, the very limited knowledge of historical materialism in North-American and British universities has prevented radical writers like Mills or Marxists like Miliband and Domhoff from using concepts that have already been created in the context of European capitalism to account for the rise of professional administrators. In fact, the Marxist concept of corporate control that Mills rejects and Miliband distorts is an elementary, superficial, practically caricature version of Marxism. Domhoff has in effect reinvented Gramsci's idea of "organic intellectuals" under the conceptual label of Mills' "power élite". Compare, for example, Domhoff's perspective with that of Gramsci:

> "Every social group that originates in the fulfillment of an essential task of economic production creates, along with itself, organically, one or more categories of intellectuals which give their class homogeneity and awareness of its own function, not only in the economic field but also on social and political levels: the capitalist entrepreneur brings forth the industrial manager, the political scientist, the cultural innovator, a new law, and so on. . . If not all entrepreneurs, then at least an *élite* amongst them must be capable of organizing society in general. . . or at least capable of choosing their 'clerks' (specialized employees) to whom they may entrust this organizing activity..." [19]

Gramci's concept of "organic intellectuals of the propertied class" corresponds exactly to Domhoff's theory about the power élite as an "operating arm of the upper class". Both authors conceive of one group of organic intellectuals (or of a power élite) issuing from the ruling class itself, while another group is attracted to and partially assimilated by the ruling class after specialized training. Domhoff studied and set forth the organic ties between the ruling class and its "intellectuals", stressing the control of the ruling class over the major universities which train them, and analyzing the social origins of the directors of the largest corporations.

With Mills, the concept of an élite is set in opposition to the theory of a ruling class; with Domhoff, the concept of a power élite deals with the problem and allows us a deeper study of Marxist theory about control of corporations (and of the state). Mills and Miliband stress the unity and common characteristics of corporation directors. Domhoff, like Lundberg, makes a clear distinction between the owners of these companies and their legal, financial and technical advisers. As far as these last two authors are concerned, control rests solely with the owners.

The Economic Elite in Canadian Sociology: Porter and Clement

John Porter is one of Canada's most prolific sociologists; it is not within the objectives of this present work to evaluate such an abundant and diversified output. What we shall analyse is his concept of the economic élite, the concept which he uses to describe power within large companies in Canada.

In one of his earliest articles, which appeared in 1955, Porter distinguished five types of power: economic, political, bureaucratic, military and ideological.[20] These were the five "functional systems" of complex modern societies, the five role systems. Within each system, there has to be some coordinating and decisional positions. The people who occupy these power positions are designated by Porter as being members of related but distinct élites. The interconnections within each élite gives them a certain homogeneity. While the various élites remain separate and no one of them dominates the others, they can still counter-balance each other. For Porter, this is the situation in western societies. He thus places the Canadian economic élite squarely within a pluralist format. In such a scheme of things, there is rivalry for power in the overall society and no one of the élites wins absolute power at the expense of the others. The economic élite is "the reflection of oligopolistic and monopolistic competition which exists in all industrial systems."[21] It is the members of the boards of directors of large corporations who form the economic élite.

In a second article, which deals directly with the economic élite, Porter puts his definitions into practice.[22] Through a study of the boards of directors of 170 companies dominant in the non-financial sectors, Porter picks out three types of directors: the financiers, the legal experts and the technical experts. He stresses the fact that the three types are of equal importance in the control of large corporations. *Because of the secrecy and the collective responsibility which operates in all these élite collectivities, Porter explicitly adopts Mills' assumption about the equality of power of each director.* This article of Porter's on the economic élite elicited both commentaries and criticisms. Professor Ashley[23] insisted that not all directors have the same power, but he did concede that the confidentiality of data about corporations made Porter's assumptions plausible. Ashley also criticized the distinction between the three types of directors, claiming that within the boards there was very much less specialization than Porter had assumed. Finally, he felt that the Canadian economic élite is composed of many fewer people than Porter thought, namely, the directors of the four biggest chartered banks in the land (the Royal, Montréal, Commerce and Nova Scotia). These 97 people, holding between them more than 900 directorships outside the above-named banks, form the true economic élite of Canada. In sum, Ashley wished to see a different composition of the Canadian economic élite than that given to it by Porter, but he nowhere criticized the basic hypothesis of Porter's work.

In *The Vertical Mosaic*, published in 1965, Porter's economic élite found itself competing with labour, political, bureaucratic and ideological élites. This time, however, the competition was unequal, since company directors could enlarge their own power at the expense of the other élites. Behind the élites, one now saw social classes, but only as statistical categories lacking precise identity, defined according to the varying needs of different chapters of the book and not systematically linked with the élites.[24] The economic élite is defined on the theoretical and operational level in the same way as it had been described in the earlier work devoted entirely to that subject. Its membership consists of the directors of the 170 dominant non-financial companies, the nine chartered banks and the ten biggest assurance companies. Porter rejects the theory of managerial control of large corporations: for him, as for Mills, those who direct the giant firms are often those who hold the major blocs of shares; in the case of subsidiaries, the directors represent the parent company.

> "In Canada, on the other hand, the dispersal of ownership is not characteristic of industry because, as we have noted earlier, many Canadian giants are wholly or 'majority' owned in the United States or the United Kingdom. Moreover, where ownership does appear to lie in Canada, rather than in another country, the ownership of large blocks of stock is linked closely with control. . . . There is little doubt that management control arising from stock dispersal is not nearly as extensive in Canada as it is said to be in the United States.[25] The notion that directors are a kind of window dressing arranged by management follows from the theory of management control. Whether or not this situation applies to American industry as a consequence of the separation of ownership and control is not our concern here. It is doubtful, however, that it satisfactorily describes Canadian corporate power."[26]

In other words, Porter suggests that it is the major shareholders who wield the power in Canadian joint-stock companies. Here one sees the influence of Mills: *The Power Elite* had been published in the interval between Porter's first articles and *The Vertical Mosaic*. Porter's economic élite is, thereafter, an ownership élite. In this, it resembles Marx's ruling class, but there are nonetheless important differences between the two:

(a) Porter's economic élite has no history, no more than have the hierarchies on which this élite has come to roost (the oligopolies and the monopolies).

(b) The economic élite forms a homogenous unity, within which one does not distinguish between the owners and their legal, financial and other advisers. Porter assumes that *all* members of the economic élite own large companies and in this, agrees with Mills.

(c) The economic élite does not rule and it does not control either the production or the diffusion of ideology.

In his chapter on the economic élite and social structure, Porter studies the method of recruitment used for this élite, its ethnic, religious and class origins and its political affiliations. He then analyses the position occupied by this élite in the institutions which he places beyond the economic system: employers' associations, universities and hospitals, clubs, foundations, government commissions, etc. He concludes from this analysis that the Canadian economic élite is largely anglophone and Protestant, that its members have attended university, that it is drawn from the upper class and that it has few ties with the world of politics. He finds also that this élite is very active in employers' associations and commissions of enquiry, and that it holds numerous "honorific" positions in foundations, universities and hospitals.

Most of the criticisms directed at Porter, such as those compiled and published by Heap, are concerned with the internal coherence of his élite theory, with the definitions (of varying degrees of precision) he gives to his concepts, or with the ideology or implicit ethics of his writings. As far as the question of the internal coherence of his theoretical system is concerned, the criticisms are both valid and substantial. The criticisms directed at his analysis of the economic élite and corporate control, however, are marginal at best. In our opinion, criticism in this area ought to be empirical in nature, based on data invalidating the basic tenets of élite theory. There are four major critiques which may be levelled at Porter's theory of the economic élite.

(1.) One must prove that not all members of the boards of directors of joint-stock companies, whether large or small, have the same degree of power. The "secrecy which operates in all these élite collectivities" is not as complete as it once was and we can increasingly distinguish between the owners and their "organic intellectuals"—their financial, technical, and legal advisers. Porter's theory of the economic élite opposes that of Berle and Means on the issue of managerial control. For the latter, these are only professional advisers, i.e. managers, on the boards of directors; for Porter and Mills, the big shareholders and the chief executives form only one group and together hold power. We shall state, in this chapter, that most boards of directors are composed of major stockholders and their advisers, and that one can and must distinguish between these two types of directors. On this issue, we support Lundberg and Domhoff and we shall introduce data to justify our hypothesis.

(2.) One must also prove that the Canadian economic élite directs the other major institutions of contemporary capitalism—the state, the political parties, the mass media, the universities—and that it therefore deserves to be called the "ruling class". Such proof, of course, would require data from studies which, to our knowledge, have yet to be done in Canada, and furthermore it would lead us considerably afield from the subject of our own research, namely, corporate control. Readers will undoubtedly recall that W. Clement, using data from the report of the Special Senate Committee on Mass Media (1970), showed that the instruments of mass communications are controlled by the principal members of the "economic élite."[27] Also, studies published by the

Committee on Election Expenses in 1966[28] showed that the major federal political parties in Canada, with the exception of the New Democratic Party, have always been financed by big business and wealthy businessmen, a fact which at least partially gives the lie to the supposed autonomy of the economic élite from the political élite. No equivalent study, however, has been done on the relationship between business circles and universities, or between those two circles and the political personnel of the state as such.

(3.) One must examine the abstract and non-historical nature of the economic élite. In Porter, this élite has no history, no more so than the institutional hierarchies whose existence he barely recognizes. Here his study resembles very strongly that of Mills. Porter tells us that economic concentration creates a business élite, as if all large units of production must necessarily be run by a board of directors formed by the large shareholders or named by a parent company. The social process of the capitalist division of labour at both the national and international level is thus skipped over. Moreover, in Porter's world, no conflict cuts across this group of 900-plus people who control the country's major enterprises; no opposition between rival groups of interests, between a Montréal bourgeoisie and a Toronto one, or between Canadian interests and the interests of subsidiaries of American companies.

(4.) Limited by his theoretical framework, Porter sees only "honorific" roles in the massive presence of members of the economic élite in the administration of universities, foundations, hospitals, government commissions and the like. Any empirical criticism of Porter must show that these are not mere prestige roles, but a presence essential to the continuity of the social system. For example, it is known that foundations have had a marked influence on the direction taken by research and university teaching in the United States[29] and that frequently, they have been a legal means of perpetuating family control of huge enterprises, free from public surveillance and taxation.[30] In Canada, foundations based on individual or family donations have much more recently come into being, are fewer in number, and more modest in scale. In a few cases they play an important role in the control of companies: for the Molsons, the Westons and (probably) the Macleans, at least.[31] One would have to do extensive research to discover if, as in the United States, the presence of businessmen in the administration of universities, foundations and the like has more than an "honorific" importance. Digging out such information would certainly be no easy task.

Wallace Clement took important steps to make Porter's economic élite more concrete and more vivid[32]. Unlike Porter, Clement claims that the concepts of social class and élite are complementary approaches and seeks to integrate them. Clement uses a triple hierarchical schema:

(1.) Bourgeoisie/proletariat: defined in Marxist terms by the ownership or lack of ownership of the means of production.

(2.) Upper class/lower class: here we have a simple gradation scheme in which the upper class is defined as the bourgeoisie plus the élites of the other institutional spheres.

(3.) Elites/non-élites: élites being defined as the high-level positions (and the people who occupy them) in every institutional sphere, organized in hierarchical fashion.

Like Porter, Clement defines the economic élite as the positions of power within major companies (and the people who hold these positions). But since his results lead him to conclude that the economic élite and the élite of the mass media are one and the same, he creates the concept of the corporate élite, which encompasses the two.

Clement systematically links his three hierarchical schema:

"Because of their relationships to ownership and control of property, all members of the corporate élite are also members of the bourgeoisie, but all the members of the bourgeoisie are not members of the corporate élite... It will be recalled that the élite is defined as the uppermost positions only within dominant corporations. The corporate élite may then be said to correspond to the big bourgeoisie."[33]

By using these hypotheses about the relationships between his three hierarchical schema, Clement hopes to avoid the criticism levelled at Porter for his vague use of the term "social class", barely juxtaposed with that of "élite". At the same time, Clement adopts Porter's thesis about the internal unity of the economic élite: *all the members of Clement's corporate élite belong to the bourgeoisie.*

In the two historical chapters of his work, the second and the third, Clement tries to compensate for the lack of historicity of the concept of the élite. But his effort fails, because in those chapters, the terms "élite" and "bourgeoisie" or "capitalist class" are synonymous, and one finally begins to wonder about the usefulness of superimposing the élite/non-élite schema on that of class. For example:

"After acquiring large amounts of surplus, merchants evolved into financial capitalists, maintaining the same 'middleman' function as before"[34] "As intended, the National Policy did produce industry within Canada but the ruling financial élite failed to allow its development"[35]

Clement thereby summarizes the history of the Canadian bourgeoisie, but he presents it instead as the history of the economic or corporate élite.

Elsewhere, Clement states that the economic élite was once a ruling class, but that during the 20th century a differentiation arose between the economic and the political élites—though the how and the why of it are never quite explained. He says, referring to the beginning of the 20th century, that "this was an era in Canadian history when it could be said that an economic class ruled politically."[36] He does not explain why the same thing could not be said today.

Within the economic élite, Clement recognizes three different categories: the indigenous, or national, élite, the satellite or comprador

131

élite (which runs the subsidiaries of foreign companies in Canada) and the parasite élite (composed of the directors of parent companies outside Canada). Clement borrows from Marxist theory the concepts forged to characterize the bourgeoisie, such as those of the "national" or "comprador" bourgeoisie, and then applies them to an economic élite. This leads us once again to question the utility of distinguishing between the bourgeoisie and the economic élite.

In the central chapters of his book (the third and fourth), Clement uses the same methods employed by Porter to analyse a list of 113 of the dominant companies of 1971—with the difference that on his list the financial sector is better represented than it was on Porter's list. Clement studies unequal access to the economic élite according to the education level, class origin, region of birth, ethnic group and religious and political affiliations of the members of the boards of directors of the companies which have been defined as dominant. Clement thus confirms Porter's results and adds a few new points. He identifies four types of economic élite: the élite of managers, the wealth élite, the honorific élite (former politicians) and the expertise élite. Throughout, the assumption that he has taken from Porter (that all members of the board of directors have equal power) prevents him from drawing the conclusions of his own distinctions. In fact, he increases his own difficulties by assuming from the beginning that all members of the economic élite belong to the bourgeoisie. The classification of types of economic élite thus loses its usefulness and Clement denies himself the possibility of doing more profound analyses, especially in cases like that of Power Corporation, where he has precise information about the ownership of shares by the different members of the board of directors.

Just like Porter, Clement studies what he calls the "private world of powerful people": the private schools, the private clubs, the philanthropic organizations, etc. He notes the participation of the economic élite in the administration of universities, foundations and other institutions. As Porter however, Clement does not make the link between these "honorific" roles and control of large enterprises. As the title of chapter VI suggests, such activities are for him part of the "private" life of the economic élite.

Clement thus makes an effort to clarify the concepts of social class and their relationship to the concept of an economic élite. He also makes a solid demonstration of the way in which Canadian financial groups have seized control of the mass media. However, he does not manage to endow the concept of élite with any historicity: instead, he simply gives it a history. . . the history of the Canadian capitalist class. His hypothesis, borrowed from Mills and from Porter, of the internal unity and homogeneity of the economic élite is difficult to sustain, as is his claim that all members of the economic élite belong to the bourgeoisie.

How and why does the ownership class (the "corporate rich" of Mills) assimilate non-ownership directors? Porter and Clement, like

Mills, reply that it is done by permitting those directors to buy shares in the companies which they direct. This is not a sufficient explanation because, on the one hand, not all company directors hold large amounts of stock and, on the other, one must still explain how the university graduates (lawyers, technical experts, business-administration specialists) have acquired exactly the very ideology and training that the companies need. It is here that one must introduce the idea of the control of large universities and foundations by the members of the economic élite. It is by directing the most prestigious universities and granting them subsidies through companies and foundations that the ruling class shapes its organic intellectuals. This perspective enables us to escape from the liberal view of the equality of opportunity of access to corporate boards of directors, a view which comes through very clearly in the works of Porter and Clement. This perspective allows us as well to narrow the range of supposed "autonomy" of the economic élite and to destroy the myth of the "private" world of this élite. The presence of the most powerful businessmen on the boards of governors of universities and on the boards of trustees of foundations has nothing to do with "honorifics": it stems from their concern to shape the executive personnel of which they have need and thus to guarantee their own continuity as a class.

Finally, there remains the fact that the partisans of the élite theory have done very inadequate research on the links between the "economic élite" and the other "élites". One of the favourite arguments of the élite theorists is that economics cannot be reduced to politics and culture, and vice-versa. But that is one of the very few hypotheses on which *all* sociological theorists, from the functionalists to the Marxists, are in agreement. The real question is to know if the ownership class dominates the members of the other two spheres. Porter and Clement say not, though Clement does make an exception in the case of the mass media. However, the methods and data which Porter and Clement (like Mills) give themselves prevent them from studying in depth the links between the dominant members of these different "institutional spheres". To understand the links between the "economic élite" and the "political élite", one must take into account:

(a) the financing of political parties, about which considerable data already exist, showing the close dependence of three of the four federal political parties on big business; and

(b) the role of the ruling class, "political intellectuals" *par excellence*—the lawyers, and above all, corporation lawyers.

The Disagregation of the Canadian Economic Elite

A definitive test of the élite theory of Mills, Porter and Clement would involve separate and parallel studies touching on, among other things, the political personnel of the state, control of universities and the politics of investment by "charitable" foundations. It is clear that one cannot cover all these different fields within the framework of a study such as the present one. It is possible, however, to "disagregate" the economic élite. In Mills, Porter and Clement we see this élite as one coherent block. Mills explains this unity by claiming that the corporate rich and the chief executives are, together, only one group. Porter remarks on the collective nature of decision-making within boards of directors and the secrecy which surrounds their inner workings. Clement lumps all the members of the economic élite together in the big bourgeoisie.

However, we have seen that Lundberg, Domhoff and Gramsci identify a variety of functions within the administration of big corporations. These three authors distinguish between the major shareholders, on one hand, and, on the other, the managers and those who are merely legal, fiscal, financial or technical advisers. If one can differentiate between these major types of director, one is in a position to test the theory of the homogeneity and unity of the economic élite. This can best be done by a study of the shares held and the recompense received, by each type.

In the previous chapter, we identified the groups of owners who control 92 of the 136 largest Canadian joint-stock companies. We can now examine the other members of the boards of directors of these same 136 companies, in order to analyze their function and destroy, in part, the "secrecy" to which Porter makes allusion. By separating the owners from their advisers, we hope at the same time to cast some light on the "organic intellectuals" of the ruling class, who so frequently pass from the business world to the political one: corporation lawyers. Finally, this process will allow at least a partial evaluation of the process of assimilation of the managers to the corporate rich, the big shareholders.

We have taken those directors of each company who are not part of the control group and divided them into four categories:

(a) Legal advisers: lawyers sitting on company boards, but whose primary occupation is that of partner in a law firm.

(b) Financial advisers: these are experts working privately, or for a consulting firm, or at the senior-executive level in an investment house. Along with them, though in fewer numbers, we find the accountants and technical experts, who work for companies specialized in accounting or for consulting engineering firms.

(c) The career managers: who have spent their working lives in the company (or other companies) and who are salaried employees.

(d) The owners or managers of other companies.

The primary occupation is that which is placed first by the Financial Post Directory of Directors in their listing of the positions held by each director.

Our hypothesis in the work that follows is that the legal, financial, accounting and technical advisers hold few shares and do not enjoy sufficient remuneration to be assimilated into the world of the major shareholders. Also, the owners or managers of other companies are chosen for their expertise and hold few shares in the companies (other than their own) on whose boards they sit.

Legal Advisers

Contrary to the thesis of Mills, Porter and Clement about the economic élite, we claim that the legal advisers sitting on the boards of major corporations should not be confused with the large shareholders and that their role is purely consultative. They are the kind of expert whom companies like to have at their finger-tips when decisions with legal implications are to be made, and such decisions are frequently made. Every meeting of the board of directors of a company needs advice on matters of fiscal, commercial or labour law. The overwhelming majority (81%) of companies on our list have at least one lawyer, usually a partner in a law firm, on its board. It is worth taking a moment to consider the organization of major law firms in Canada.

The 20th century process of economic concentration in the fields of industry, finance and commerce has had its parallel in the legal profession. The individual lawyer practising on his own has largely given way to the legal firm, in which one finds three categories of lawyers:

(1.) *partners* or members of the firm—lawyers with a minimum of eight to ten years' experience;

(2.) *associates*, or salaried lawyers—frequently young, who are doing their apprenticeship after being called to the bar; some of them will become partners, others will move on to work for other firms or set up their own practise;

(3.) *counsels*—often prestigious members of the bar who have behind them a political or public-service career.

These firms rarely specialize in one field of law alone: they carry on a more general practise, dealing with commercial law, labour law, inheritance, fiduciary, notarial, international, etc. The field least frequently covered is that of criminal law.

The largest law firms in Canada have up to 76 lawyers (partners, associates, counsels). The norm in the major legal firm seems to be one associate per partner. On Wall Street, by contrast, the norm is roughly two associates per partner.[37] There are only a few counsels, four at the most, and then only in some law offices. In each office, certain of the partners and associates take care of the client companies; sometimes these lawyers are invited to join the boards of the companies which they advise.

In the United States, the legal business of most large corporations is carried out by Wall Street lawyers; in Canada, these important offices are to be found in Toronto and Montréal. The table on the following pages gives a run-down, by city, of the largest firms in Canada. Note that they are not necessarily the most important firms, as far as large corporations are concerned, for some very small firms are extremely active in that regard. The Québec City firm of St-Laurent, Monast, Walters and Vallières, for example, has only seven partners, but two of them, Renault St-Laurent and André Monast, hold respectively 12 and 19 Canadian directorships. Monast's list includes the Canadian Imperial Bank of Commerce, Canada Cement Lafargue, Dominion Stores, Confederation Life, Air Canada, Canadian National Railways, IBM Canada, Gaspé Copper Mines and Brunswick Mining & Smelting. The list for Renault St-Laurent includes the Banque Canadienne Nationale, Imperial Life, Home Oil, Reed Paper, IAC Ltd., and Rothmans of Pall Mall Canada. Some firms which have many more lawyers, such as Gowling & Henderson in Ottawa, are much less important in terms of the scale and significance of their links with business.

Only 27 of the companies on our list in the preceding chapter (or 20%) do not have at least one legal adviser on their board. This group includes four subsidiaries in the Canadian Pacific group, four in the Argus Corporation group and a few independent companies of varying size such as Alcan Aluminium, Dofasco, Daon Development Corporation and Moore Corporation. Almost all the other companies have one or two lawyers on their boards who are full partners in their own law firms. Some have many more than one or two: Victoria and Grey Trust has ten lawyers on a 20-man board; Montréal Trust has eight on a 29-man board (see Appendix I at the end of this chapter). The average number of lawyers on a board of one of our dominant companies is 1.6. The following table presents in summary form the information we have concerning the number of lawyers on the boards of directors of major companies.

NUMBER OF LAWYERS ON THE BOARDS OF DIRECTORS OF MAJOR CORPORATIONS (1975)

Number of Lawyers on the Board	Number of Companies (Absolute Numbers)	(%)
0	27	20%
1	53	39%
2	34	25%
3	7	5%
4	9	7%
5 and more	6	4%
	136	100%

Sources: Martindale—Hubbell Law Directory, 1976.
Financial Post Directory of Directors, 1976.

Small companies use the legal services of only one firm; conglomerates call on legal advisers from several firms. The Oshawa Group, for example, wholly-controlled by the Wolfe family, uses the Toronto firm of Shiffrin, White & Spring, and two members of that firm (A. Shiffrin and L.B. White) hold directorships in their company. M. Loeb & Co., jointly controlled by the Loeb and Weston families, uses the firm of Soloway, Wright, Houston, Greenberg, O'Grady and

Morin. Two senior partners from this firm sit on the board of this Ottawa commercial company: Hyman Soloway and M. W. Wright. By contrast, large companies and groups use several firms of legal advisers. Power Corporation (majority-controlled by Paul Desmarais) has four lawyers who belong to four different firms on its board: Wilbrod Bhérer (of Bhérer, Bernier, Côté, Ouellet, Dionne, Houle & Morin, of Québec); Claude Pratte (of Létourneau, Stein, Marseille, Delisle & LaRue, of Québec); Pierre Genest (of Cassells, Brock, of Toronto); and the Honorable John P. Robarts (of Stikeman, Elliott, Robarts & Bowman, of Toronto). Power Corporation subsidiaries use lawyers from a dozen different firms (see Appendix I).

Some conglomerates use a variety of legal firms, yet one lawyer or one firm stands out from the group. Brascan Ltd. uses no less than eight different legal offices, but A.J. MacIntosh, of Blake, Cassels & Graydon (Toronto) holds prime place on the boards of directors of this group controlled by John H. Moore and associates. MacIntosh sits on the board of Brascan Ltd. and its subsidiaries J. Labatt Ltd., Ogilvie Mills (controlled by J. Labatt), Hudson's Bay Co. and Markborough Properties (subsidiaries of Hudson's Bay). The companies controlled by the Bronfman family use lawyers from a dozen different offices, but the Montréal firm of Phillipps & Vineberg holds pride of place. P.F. Vineberg sits on the boards of The Seagram Co., Cadillac-Fairview Corp., Cemp Investments and Edper Investments, which are all key companies in this family empire. The Honorable Lazarus Phillips is director for Cemp Investments and Trizec Corp.; James A. Soden, another partner in this Montréal firm, is chairman of the Trizec board.

Mills, Porter and Clement take for granted that all directors are either major shareholders in the companies on whose boards they sit, or in the process of becoming major shareholders. Yet, as far as legal advisers are concerned, this is far from being the case. *On the contrary, neither the number of shares they hold nor the remuneration they receive as directors permits the legal advisers on the boards of major corporations to be confused with the major shareholders, the family or the group which controls the company.* They are only the experts, the highly-placed specialists, as Lundberg claims. We shall advance five arguments in support of our hypothesis.

(1.) Lawyers who sit on boards of directors hold few shares in the companies which they advise. They frequently hold no more than ten, twenty or a few hundred shares for a total value of $5,000 to $10,000. Sometimes they hold only one share, so as to observe the internal by-laws of companies which rule that all directors be shareholders.

There are some exceptions to this rule. The Jeffery family of London, Ontario, which owns London Life Insurance Company, also has a law firm, Jeffery & Jeffery, in which several of the most prominent members of the family are active. Richard M. Ivey, lawyer with the firm of Ivey & Dowler of London, Ontario, holds (among other interests) 485,000 shares in Prenor Group (29.2% of the vote) through his holding company, Norlac Financial Group. Those shares, in 1975, were worth more than $2,120,000. The most outstanding of these exceptions is the Montréal firm of McMaster, Meighen, Minnion, Patch, Cordeau, Hindman & Legge. Its partners include D.R. McMaster, Theodore Meighen and his son Michael. McMaster holds directorships with numerous companies, including Stelco, Cominco, Dominion Textile and the Bank of Montréal. His shares in Stelco were worth about $1,500,000 in 1975 (his father is a former president of the company), but he has only 25 shares in Cominco and 7,400 in Dominion Textile. Theodore Meighen, son of the former Conservative prime minister of Canada, Arthur Meighen, is the father of Michael Meighen, president of the Progressive-Conservative Party of Canada. He, along with his brother Maxwell, is part owner of the largest closed-end investment company in Canada, Canadian General Investments—founded by Arthur Meighen.

Most lawyers hold few shares in the companies for which they are directors—and that includes former (and future) ministers of Canada, senators, and present and retired lieutenant-governors. They are not on boards of directors as owners nor—as some managerialists insist—as decoration, but purely and simply because they supply precise knowledge about the workings of the judicial apparatus of the state.

(2.) The legal consultants do not accumulate shares: being outside directors, they are not eligible for the stock-purchase options which are open only to company managers.[38] In almost all cases, they are invited to join the board of a company which has long been their client and at that time they purchase, or receive from the company Treasury, a small number of shares. That is frequently their only declaration to the Securities Commissions.

(3.) Legal advisers rarely hold management positions within corporations; they are seldom inside directors. We saw in the previous chapter that the families, individuals or groups of associates which control companies tend to put themselves in key positions on the boards, such as chairman of the board, president of the company, and vice-president. The legal advisers, on the contrary, are to be found among the non-employee directors. Only nine of the lawyers (or 4.7%) for the companies under study held management positions.

There are two types of exceptions. One consists of the few lawyers who remain members of law firms even though they also control a large company. Lawyers such as the Jefferys and John W. McCutcheon (co-owner and president of Canadian General Securities and partner in Shibley, Righton & McCutcheon) fall into this category. The other consists of those lawyers to a group of interests who work as managers for one of the group's subsidiaries. Thus, we have A.J. MacIntosh, lawyer for the Brascan group and delegated governor for Hudson's Bay Co., or M.S. Hannon (of Ogilvy, Cope, Porteous, Montgomery, Renault, Clarke and Kirkpatrick, of Montréal), who is chairman of the executive committee of Montréal Trust, a Power Corp. subsidiary.

(4.)   Lawyers who are outside directors, just like investment consultants or accountants, do not receive large remunerations for their work on the boards of directors. A 1976 study by the Conference Board in Canada gives very precise figures for the remuneration of outside directors. They are defined as follows:

> "An outside director is a non-employee of the firm who sits on the board of directors. He may be an ex-employee, employee of a controlling firm, provide legal or other services, or have no connection with the firm except to sit on the board of directors."[39]

Normally, outside directors are rewarded in two ways: with a yearly retainer, independent of the number of meetings held per year and attendance at those meetings, and with a fee paid for each appearance at a meeting of the board. Those two fees, assuming a perfect attendance record by the director, are the sum total of his annual payment. The Conference Board in Canada study was based on a questionnaire sent out in June 1976 to 400 industrial and non-industrial companies. These companies were of varying sizes, size being calculated on the basis of comapny assets. The study made clear that the potential total remuneration is modest: the average paid by companies with assets of $100 million or more ranged from $3,000 to $8,000 per year, depending on the size of the company. One cannot, therefore, argue (as Mills, Porter, and Clement have done) that outside directors are *de facto* members of the bourgeoisie simply because they sit on the board of directors of a large corporation.

(5.)   Finally, the role of legal adviser has a somewhat higher profile in the case of subsidiaries of foreign companies, whether these companies are under the absolute or the majority control of the parent company. In a small number of cases, the lawyers may hold the position of inside director with the subsidiary, but it is clear that they do not control these subsidiaries.

In sum, one can only adopt the view of Ferdinand Lundberg, expressed in his famous article, "The Law Factories, brains of the status quo":

> "In their capacity as stewards and bailiffs we find lawyers from the leading law firms strewn through the directorates of America's corporate system. . . They are the social overseers for the gentry of the world of business who, unaided, would scarecely be able to cope with these multifarious affairs. Apart from business people, lawyers appear more frequently than any other class of men on boards of directors."[40]

MAJOR CANADIAN LAW FIRMS, BY CITY (1975)

Toronto	Partners	Associates	Counsels	Total
Blake, Cassels & Graydon	38	34	4	76
McCarthy & McCarthy	37	36	3	76
Osler, Hoskin & Harcourt[1]		66	3	69
Fraser & Beatty[1]		58	1	59
McMillan, Binch[2]	36	(?)	—	(?)
Faskell & Calvin	22	25	1	48

Firm				
Lang, Michener, Cranston, Farquharson & Wright	30	14	4	48
Borden & Elliott[1]		46	....	—	46
Tory, Tory, Deslauriers & Binnington[1]		35	....	1	36
Aird, Zimmerman & Berlis	24	5	2	31
Campbell, Godfrey & Lewtas		30	....	—	30
Goodman & Goodman[1]		22	....	—	22

Montréal

Ogilvy, Cope, Porteous, Montgomery, Renault, Clarke et Kirkpatrick[1]		72	....	4	76
Martineau, Walker, Allison, Beaulieu, McKell & Clermont	16	25	3	44
Weldon, Courtois, Clarkson, Parsons & Tétrault[1]		39	....	3	42
Stikeman, Elliott, Tamaki, Mercier & Robb[1]		34	....	—	34
McMaster, Meighen, Minnion, Patch, Cordeau, Hyndman & Legge[2]	23	(?)	2	(?)
De Granpré, Colas, Amyot, Lesage, Deschênes & Godin[1]		26	....	1	27
Phillips & Vineberg[1]		21	....	—	21

Vancouver

Davis & Co	24	20	1	45
Russel & Du Moulin	24	17	3	44
Ladner, Downs	24	18	—	42
Bull, Housser & Tupper	24	15	—	39
Lawson, Lundell, Lawson & McIntosh[1]		29	....	—	29

Winnipeg

Aikins, Macaulay & Thorvaldson[1]		35	....	—	35
Thompson, Dorfman & Sweatman	23	5	1	29
Pitblado & Oskin[1]		24	....	1	25

Calgary

Jones, Black & Co	18	14	1	33
Macleod, Dixon	14	12	—	26
MacKimmie, Matthews	10	14	—	24

Halifax

Stewart, Mackeen & Covert	18	9	1	28
McInnes, Cooper & Robertson	13	11	—	24

Regina

Macpherson, Leslie & Tyerman	11	7	1	19

Ottawa

Gowling & Henderson[1]		42	....	4	46
Soloway, Wright, Houston, Greenberg, O'Grady & Morin	11	8	2	21

Edmonton

Milner & Steer	20	12	—	32

Québec

Létourneau, Stein, Marseille, Delisle & La-Rue[2]	16	(?)	—	(?)
St-Laurent, Monast, Walters & Vallières[2]	7	(?)	—	(?)

Source: Martindale—Hubbell Law Directory, (Annual), New Jersey, Quinn & Boden, 1976.
(1) These law firms have not informed the *Martindale—Hubbell Law Directory* of the number of partners and of associates among the lawyers working in their offices.
(2) These firms did not inform the *Law Directory* either of the names or of the number of lawyers associated with their firms.

Advisers in Financial, Accounting and Technical Matters

This is a much smaller category than the preceding one. It includes several different types of experts. Financial consultants advise on such matters as refinancing, financial methods to adopt for a merger, take-overs and the issuing of stocks and bonds. They are either members of investment houses, associates in a firm of financial consultants, or working as private consultants. One can see in Appendix II to this chapter that 48 companies on our list have a financial, accounting or technical consultant on their boards of directors. Almost all these consultants are financial consultants. Of the 44 companies who do have a financial adviser on the board, 31 have called on people working with a brokerage firm such as Wood, Gundy & Co., Nesbitt Thomson & Co., or Dominion Securities Harris & Partners; 5 have drawn their consultants from specialized offices such as JHC Financial Consultants, Aitken Management Consultants or WDC Mackenzie Consultants; and finally, seven have turned to private consultants such as J.D. Gibson (who sits on seven boards of directors of major Canadian-controlled corporations) or J.N. McMillan.

One finds the same sort of situation with the technical advisers and chartered accountants who, however, are far fewer in number. Some are private consulting engineers, some are private chartered accountants or members of firms which specialize in management consulting, of which the best known is undoubtedly Clarkson, Gordon & Co., which provided the training for the men who now control Canadian Corporate Management and Brascan Ltd.

Companies without financial, accounting and technical advisers are not necessarily any less well-advised. Many career managers have trained in these fields and most, if not all, major corporations have their own financial, accounting and technical departments to guide them.

Though most financial consultants are simply advisers, some investment brokers belong to groups that do control companies: the Burns (father and son) hold more than $13 million worth of shares in Crown Life Insurance; C.F.W. Burns is the chairman of the board of the insurance company, and his son, Herbert Michael, is the vice-chairman. Burns senior has been a broker since 1932 and has controlled the firm of Burns Bros. & Denton since 1939. As well, he holds more than $750,000 worth of shares in Denison Mines. Other investment brokers have inherited large blocks of shares from their forefathers, who acquired them in the golden age of finance capitalism. Charles L. Gundy is a major shareholder in all the companies which he manages. His father, who preceded him as head of Wood, Gundy & Co., sat on the same boards of directors and took an active part in the financial reorganization of such companies as Abitibi Paper, Simpsons Ltd., Canada Cement, Canron and Massey-Ferguson (before 1957, Massey-Harris). Charles L. Gundy holds shares in these companies to the value of $600,000, $10,000,000, $300,000, $150,000 and $1,150,000 respectively—as well as being the principal partner in Wood, Gundy & Co. Arthur D. Nesbitt holds almost $400,000 worth of shares in Power Corporation (of which he was the co-owner); he is also the principal partner in Nesbit Thompson & Co.

Fifty advisers out of 67 hold less than $100,000 worth of stock. Almost all of them are outside directors; only three hold managerial positions—the Burns' in Crown Life Insurance, and Gundy in Simpsons Ltd. The information given in the preceding section about the fees received by outside directors applies equally to the advisers under discussion in this section. Given the modesty both of the shares these advisers hold and the fees they receive, it would be erroneous to class them in the bourgeoisie or the economic élite simply because of their presence on the boards of directors of major enterprises.

Career Managers

The membership of the boards of directors of the largest joint-stock companies consists primarily of the principal owners of the company, the advisers on legal, financial and technical matters, and the career administrators—the managers.

Authors do not agree on the definition of "manager". Some, like Burnham, talk about officials with special technical qualifications; they do not include company directors in this category. Others, like Berle and Means, call company directors, "managers". In what follows, we shall use "manager" to mean those members of boards of directors and of executive committees who have arrived at these positions after a working career within the companies concerned. This definition excludes owner-directors (members of the family or the group which controls the company) and the adviser-directors whose primary occupation lies outside the company.

Usually, a manager only joins the board or the executive committee of a joint-stock company after a long professional career with the company, frequently of twenty or thirty years' duration. Once named to the senior management or the board of his company, the manager may be asked to join the boards of other companies as an outside director. It is still the case that his primary occupation is that of inside director for the company which pays his salary. For example, take the case of Robert C. Scrivener, chairman of the board of Bell Canada, who first entered the company in 1937. He held various positions with Bell over the next 23 years, was elected to the board in 1960 and became president of the company in 1968. He was subsequently chosen as an outside director by Power Corporation, Sidbec and the Canadian Imperial Bank of Commerce.

Mills, Porter and Clement all claim that these career managers assimilate to the ownership class, the corporate rich, the bourgeoisie. They argue that these managers buy shares in the company throughout their career in that company and, consequently, ultimately become major shareholders themselves. Other authors agree. Menshikov [41] considers that because of their salary, their stock portfolios, their expense accounts and their fringe benefits, these top managers must be considered a subordinate part of the monopolist bourgeoisie. He quotes statistics to show that a good number of these managers have gone on to become millionaires after having first become directors of major American corporations.

The question of corporate control, however, is quite a different matter. Do these managers accumulate enough stock in their companies to become comparable to the large shareholders, the corporate rich? The answer to this question, for several reasons, is a categoric *no*:

(1.) The share capital of any large public enterprise is priced beyond the means of any manager, no matter how thrifty he may be, or how well-paid.

(2.) While it may be true that managers buy shares in their companies, it is not always true that they keep them. Many buy shares at preferred prices and sell them again for capital gain.

Menshikov shares this point of view:

"We have analyzed data for over 100 of the biggest U.S. corporations and established that at least in the last ten years there has not been a single case of any of the hired executives advancing to the ranks of their leading stockholders. In smaller companies there were such cases, but even then very rarely. Thus, there are no grounds whatsoever about a radical change in the structure of stock ownership in favour of managers." [42]

We carried out a test similar to that of Menshikov on the dominant companies of our previous chapter. Obviously, we excluded the mutual-insurance companies (which have no share capital) and the wholly-owned subsidiaries (in which managers may not hold voting stock). We then examined the social orgins and professional careers of the inside directors of each company, in order to identify the career managers. We excluded from this category:

(1.) Directors who were lawyers with a law firm but also held the position of inside director—for example, H.B. Rhude, president of Central & Eastern Trust and also a member of the Halifax firm of Stewart, Mackeen & Covert. Such cases were extremely rare.

(2.) Professional consultants who occasionally held the position of inside director with a company—for example, J. Douglas Gibson, private financial consultant and chairman of the board of Consumer's Gas.

(3.) Members of the family or control group of a company—for example, Isin Ivanier, president of Ivaco Industries or John A. McDougald, chairman of the board and president of Argus Corporation.

Finally, we chose the managers who were most highly-placed on the board of each company. When possible, we took the chairman of the board and the president of the company; if these positions did not exist or were occupied by members of the family or control group, we took the principal officer of the board among the managers—the vice-chairman of the board, the vice-president of the company, etc. Then, we calculated the average 1975 value of the shares they held according to the last declaration made by December 1975 to the Ontario and Québec Securities Commissions.

Appendix III to this chapter presents the resulting data. The 145 career administrators are far from poor. One immediately notes at least a dozen millionaires. The average 1975 value of stock held by these managers in the companies they administer was $250,000. One may thus certainly conclude that they are rich men. Not all, however, may be considered part of the ruling class. And not one of them had accumulated enough stock to acquire any control over the company he administered or to dislodge the controlling company or family. Here, for example, are nine millionaire managers and the percentage of the vote they hold in their companies.

Company	Manager	% of vote	Controlling interest
Algoma Steel	D.S. Holbrook	0.7%	C.P.I. (51.1%)
Burns Food	A.J.E. Child	3.8%	R.H. Webster (32-42%)
Cdn. Corp.Management	V.N. Stock	2.7%	W.L. and D.L. Gordon L. Bonnycastle R.R. Rieger (20%)
Cdn. Tire Corp.	J.D. Muncaster	0.08%	Billes family (60.9%)
Consolidated-Bathurst	W.I.J. Turner Jr.	1.2%	Power Corp. (38.1%)
Massey-Ferguson	A.A. Thornbrough	0.3%	Argus Corp. (15.6%)
Moore Corp.	W.H. Browne	0.2%	Managerial
	D.W. Barr	0.1%	Managerial
The Seagram Co.	J. Yogman	0.09%	Bronfman family (32.6%)

We may thus conclude that even the richest managers or those who have amassed the most stock have not, by the end of a long professional career, worked themselves into a position comparable to that of the corporate rich. From Appendix III we may deduce that these managers—holding blocks of shares worth from $5.00 to $4,000,000, for an average value of $250,000—cannot be classified with the groups or families who control large corporations with their blocks of stocks and bonds worth between $20 million and $500 million.

To ask, however, if these managers belong to the bourgeoisie or not, is entirely a different question. Managers have qualifications that are vital and precious to the control groups seeking to preserve their hold on their companies. Thus, career administrators are generously rewarded in salary and through bonuses, profit-sharing schemes, share-purchase options, etc. We do not have information about the 1975 remuneration of the most senior executives in the largest Canadian companies, but American figures are available. In 1975, American manufacturing and non-manufacturing companies with a sales volume of

$300-$500 million and thus assets of slightly more than $100 million (which was the threshold for our own list) were paying the chief executive officer an annual salary of $191,000. This included bonuses, profit-sharing schemes and various forms of compensation, but not the gains realized through purchasing company stock at preferred prices. The largest companies, those with sales of more than $5 billion, paid their chief executive officer an annual salary of $416,000.[43] These figures, of course, do not include dividends paid on investments by the managers in the stocks and bonds of their companies. Even if they do not have legal ownership, these top managers still receive more from their companies than they contribute to them by their own labour. They may thus be classified as belonging to the bourgeoisie, as the élite theorists have done, but only on the understanding that:

(1.) given their status and salary, they are merely a dependent and subordinate fraction of that bourgeoisie;
(2.) they are not in a position to contest the control of the companies by the ruling groups of the bourgeoisie, who hold legal ownership; and
(3.) their position results from a long professional career and not from birth-right; their position, unlike that of the ruling members of the bourgeoisie, will not automatically pass to their descendents.

Owners and Managers of Other Companies

One separate category of advisers is that of the owners and managers of other companies who are invited to sit on the board of a company which neither belongs to them nor pays them a salary. In most cases of this type, the advisers hold few shares in companies other than their own. The example of the board of Power Corp. in Appendix IV shows that the outside directors who are managers or owners of other companies hold few shares in Power. These are A.F. Campo (chairman of the board of Petrofina Canada), W.M. Fuller (of W. & A.P. Fuller), J.-P. Gignac (of Sidbec-Dosco), W.D. McLaughlin (of the Royal Bank) and R.C. Scrivener (of Bell Canada). Their knowledge of business affairs in different sectors of the economy is what makes them good choices as outside directors. *A good part of the exchange of directors, which attracts so much attention from élite theorists, is due to the fact that the ruling capitalists in each company, along with the top managers, are called upon to advise other corporations, just like lawyers, accountants, financial experts and engineering-consultants.*

Conclusion

Evaluating the entirety of élite theory would call for research in many different fields and might well lead us far from the original purpose of this work. We have thus chosen to attack one of the main assumptions, for its analysis of corporate control: this is the assumption about the internal unity and homogeneity of the economic élite.

We have seen that a good many outside directors of major companies are there strictly as advisers on legal, financial, accounting and technical matters. These advisers do not hold many shares (80% of them hold less than $50,000 worth each, according to 1975 figures) and they receive an annual remuneration of between $3,000 and $8,000 for each directorship they hold. It is evident that they do not share in the control of major corporations, as the élite theory would have it, and it is incorrect to classify them as members of the bourgeoisie. In company with Lundberg and Smigel, we can only classify them as advisers, intellectuals in the service of the businessmen.

The few career managers who reach the boards of major companies, usually one to three per company, are large shareholders: in 1975 they held an average of $250,000 worth of stock in the dominant Canadian-controlled companies which publish information on their share capital. Moreover, they receive highly respectable salaries: in the United States, companies the equal of those on our list paid their chief executive between $191,000 and $416,000 a year, not including the benefits received through stock-purchase options. If one adds up their salaries, dividends received from their portfolios and other revenues, one may conclude that they certainly receive surplus value. But they do not have access to the control of these companies and their position is not hereditary. One may classify them as belonging to a subordinate section of the monopolist bourgeoisie, with economic but not legal ownership in the large enterprises.

Elite theorists mistakenly seek to unite all members of boards of directors in one homogenous élite based on ownership. By confusing major shareholders controlling large companies with their advisers, these theorists fall into numerous theoretical and empirical errors, notably a misconception of the role and the formation of the organic intellectuals of the big bourgeoisie. Moreover, if the economic élite may be broken down into two major groups, large shareholders and their advisers, it becomes clear why élite theorists write the history of the bourgeoisie when they refer to the past and/or when they try to render their economic élite somewhat less abstract. In the last analysis, it was this lack of understanding of the composition of boards of directors that led Porter and Clement to see them as homogenous units and to link them, erroneously, with social classes.

NOTE

Among others:
(1) T. Bottomore: *Elites and Society*, C.A. Watts, London, 1964.
(2) C.W. Mills: *The Power Elite*, Oxford University Press, New York, 1956.
(3) T. Bottomore: *Elites and Society*, op. cit., pp. 15-17.
(4) R. Aron: *"Social Structure and the Ruling Class"* in British Journal of Sociology, I(1), March 1950, and I(2) June 1950.
    A. Downs: *An Economic Theory of Democracy*, Harper, New York, 1957.
(5) C.W. Mills: *The Power Elite*, op. cit., p. 9.

(6)   Ibidem., p. 122.

(7)   Ibidem., p. 124.

(8)   Ibidem., p. 17.

(9)   R. Lynd' "Power in the United States" in G.W. Domhoff and H.B. Ballard (eds.) *C.W. Mills and the Power Elite*. Beacon Press, Boston, 1968, p. 110.

(10) F. Lundberg: *The Rich and the Super-rich*; Bantam Books, New York, 1968, p. 543.

(11) Ibidem., pp. 545-546.

(12) P. Sweezy: "Power Elite or Ruling Class" in *Monthly Review*, New York, 1956 (September).

(13) C.W. Mills: *The Power Elite*, op. cit., p. 232.

(14) H. Brawerman: *Labor and Monopoly Capital*, Monthly Review Press, New York, 1974.

(15) R. Miliband: *The State in Capitalist Society*, Wiedenfeld & Nicolson, London, 1969, p. 30.

(16) G.W. Domhoff: *Who Rules America?* Prentice-Hall, New Jersey, 1967. *The Higher Circles*, Vintage Books, New York. 1971. *Fat cats and Democrats*, Prentice-Halls. New Jersey, 1972, "Some friendly answers to Radical Critics," in *The Insurgent Sociologist*, Oregon, Spring 1972, "State and Ruling Class in Corporate America." in *The Insurgent Sociologist*, Oregon, Spring 1974.

(17) G.W. Domhoff: "State and Ruling Class in Corporate America". op. cit., p. 4.

(18) G.W. Domhoff: *Who Rules America?*, op. cit., pp. 50-57.

(19) J. Cammet: "*Antonio Gramsci and the Origins of Italian Communism*". Stanford University Press, 1967, chapter 10, p. 202 (The emphasis, the quote marks and the brackets are those of Gramsci himself.)

(20) J. Porter: "Elite groups: a scheme for the study of power in Canada," in *Canadian Journal of Economics and Political Science*, Vol. XXI. No. 4, 1955.

(21) Ibidem., p. 507.

(22) J. Porter: "Concentration of Economic Power and the Economic Elite in Canada" in *Canadian Journal of Economics and Political Science*, Vol. XXII, No. 2, May 1956.

(23   C.A. Ashley: "Concentration of Economic Power" in *Canadian Journal of Economics and Political Science*, Vol, XXIII, No. 1, February 1957.

(24) J.L. Heap: "Conceptual, Theoretical and Ethical problems in *The Vertical Mosaic*" in J.L. Heap (ed.): *Everybody's Canada*, Burns & MacEachen, Toronto, 1974.

(25) J. Porter: *The Vertical Mosaic*, University of Toronto Press, 1965, p. 245.

(26) Ibidem., p. 252.

(27) W. Clement: *The Canadian Corporate Elite*, McClelland & Stewart, 1975, Chaps. 7 to 9.

(28) Committee on Election Expenses: Report, Queen's Printer, Ottawa, 1966.

(29) D.N. Smith: *Who rules the Universities?*, Monthly Review Press, New York, 1974, pp. 100 and ff.

(30) See R.L. Nelson: *The Investment Policies of Foundations*, Russel Sage, New York, 1967.
      W.A. Nielson: *The Big Foundations*. Columbia University Press, New York, 1972, F. Lundberg: *The Rich and the Super-rich*, op. cit., pp. 476-8.

(31) The W. Garfield Weston Foundation, administered by members of the Weston family, holds 84% of the shares of Wittington Investments, which in turn holds 49.7% of the shares of G. Weston Ltd. The Molson Foundation, administered by members of the Molson family, holds 15% of the shares of Molson Companies. According to P.C. Newman, the MacLean family controls Canada Packers through the MacLean Foundation. See A. Arlett: *A Canadian Directory to Foundations*, A.U.C.C., Ottawa 1973; and P.C. Newman: *The Canadian Establishment*, McClelland and Stewart, 1975, p. 296.

(32) W. Clement: *The Canadian Corporate Elite*, op. cit.

(33) Ibidem., pp. 5 & 6.

(34) Ibidem., p. 49.

(35) Ibidem., p. 67.

(36) Ibidem., p. 64.

(37) E.D. Smigel: *The Wall Street Lawyer*, Indiana University Press, Bloomington, 1969, p. 203.

(38) The Conference Board in Canada: *Stock options plans*, Ottawa, 1973.

(39) The Conference Board in Canada: *Canadian Directorship Practices: compensation 1976*, Ottawa, 1976, p. IX.

(40) F. Lundberg: "The Law Factories: brains of the status quo" in *Harpers' Magazine*, New York, 1939, No. 179, p. 190.

(41) See also M. Meyer: "The Wall Street Lawyers" *Harpers' Magazine*, New York, 1956, No. 212, pp. 31-37 and 50-56.

(41) S. Men'shikov: *Millionaires and Managers*, Progress Publishers, Moscow, 1969, Chap. III.

(42) Ibidem., p. 111.

(43) A. Young & Co: *Top Management Compensation*, New York, 1976, p. 15.

APPENDIX I

LAWYER-MEMBERS OF BOARDS OF DIRECTORS OF DOMINANT COMPANIES UNDER CANADIAN CONTROL

A. Companies which are not part of groups

Abitibi Paper:
John A. Tory: — Tory, Tory, Deslauriers & Binnington (Tor.)

John P. Robarts: — Stikeman, Elliott, Robarts & Browman (Tor.)

Price Co. (subsidiary of Abitibi Paper):
Roger Létourneau: — Létourneau, Stein, Marseille, Délisle & LaRue (Qué.)

F.J. Ryan: — Sterling, Ryan & Goodridge (St-John, Nfld)

E.D. Wilkinson: — Russel & Du Moulin (Vancouver)

Acklands Ltd: — none

Alberta Trunk Line:
P.L.P. Macdonnell: — Milner & Steer (Edmonton)

Alcan Aluminium Ltd: — none

Allarco Developments: — none

Block Bros Industries:
M. Koffman: — Freeman & Co. (Vancouver)

Bombardier Ltd: — none

Bow Valley Industries:
W.A. Howard: — Howard, Dixon, Forsyth (Calgary)

Bramalea Consolidated Dev:
R.T. Clarkson: — Weldon, Courtois, Clarkson, Parsons & Tétreault (Mtl.)

Burns Food:
John P. Robarts: — Stikeman, Elliott, Robarts & Bowman (Tor.)

J. Sedwick: — Seed, Long, Howard & Cook (Tor.)

Cadillac Fairview Corp.:
P.F. Vineberg: — Phillips & Vineberg (Mtl.)
E.A. Goodman: — Goodman & Goodman (Tor.)

Calgary Power:
R.J. Pitt: — Jones, Black & Co (Calgary)
D.D. Duncan: — Duncan & Craig (Edmonton)
R.G. Black: — Jones, Black & Co (Calgary)

Campeau Corp.:
F. Mercier: — Stikeman, Elliott, Tamaki, Mercier & Robb (Mtl.)

R.W. Macaulay: — Macaulay & Perry (Tor.)

148

Canada Packers:
D.R. Harvey: McCarthy & McCarthy (Tor.)

Canada Permanent Mortgage Corp.:
R.D. Wilson: Faskell & Calvin (Tor.)
C.M. Strathy: Strathy, Archibald, Seagram & Cole (Tor.)
J.F. Perrett: Robertson, Lane, Perrett, Frankish & Estey (Tor.)
Hon W.S. Owen (Lieutenant Governor
  of British Columbia):   Owen, Bird (Vancouver)
G.F. Maclaren: Maclaren, Corlett & Tanner (Ottawa, Ont.)
T.E. Ladner: Ladner, Downs (Vancouver)
W.H. Jost: Burchell, Jost, MacAdam & Gayman (Halifax)
J.H.C. Clarry: Mc Carthy & Mc Carthy (Tor.)
C.F.H. Carson: Tilley, Carson & Findlay (Tor.)
R.L. Beaulieu: Martineau, Walker, Allison, Beaulieu, Mackell & Clermont (Mtl.)

Canadian Corporate Management:
A.J. Mac Intosh: Blake, Cassels & Graydon (Tor.)

Canadian Tire Corporation:
R. Law: Blackwell, Law, Treadgold & Armstrong (Tor.)

Canron Ltd:
J.G. Kirkpatrick: Ogilvy, Cope, Porteous, Montgomery, Renault, Clarke & Kirkpatrick (Mtl.)

Central & Eastern Trust:
M.A. Savoie: Yeoman, Savoie, LeBlanc & DeWitt (Moncton)
G.B. Robertson: McInnes, Cooper & Robertson (Halifax)
I.C. Pink: I.C. Pink & Assoc. (Yarmouth, Nova Scotia)
L.O. Clarke: Patterson, Smith, Matthews & Grant (Truro, Nova Scotia)
G.C. Bingham: lawyer (Moncton)
H.B. Rhude: Stewart, McKeen & Covert (Halifax)
J.E. Murphy: Murphy & Mollins (Moncton)

City Savings & Trust Co:
M. Koffman: Freeman & Co (Vancouver)
J. Shoctor: Shortreed, Shoctor, Enright, Stevenson-Guille & Binder (Toronto)

Consumers' Gas:
W.H. Zimmerman et R.S. Paddon: Aird, Zimmerman & Berlis (Toronto)
D.E.B. Low: Low, Murchison, Burns, Thomas & Haydon (Ottawa)
R.H. Carley: Carley, Lech & Lightbody (Peterborough, Ontario)

Crown Life:
D. McK. Brown: Russell & Du Moulin (Vancouver)

149

Crown Trust:
M. Bruce: Manning, Bruce, Macdonald & McIntosh (Toronto)

Daon Development Corp.: none

Deltan Corp.:
D.A. Berlis: Aird, Zimmerman & Berlis (Toronto)

Denison Mines:
J.S. Elder et J.A. Mullin: Fraser & Beatty (Toronto)

Dominion Foundries & Steel Corp.: none

Dominion Textile:
D.R. McMaster: McMaster, Meighen, Minnion, Patch, Cordeau, Hyndman & Legge (Montreal)

Federal Industries:
J. B. Macaulay: Aikins, Macaulay & Thorvaldson (Winnipeg)

Finning Tractor & Equipment:
T.E. Ladner: Ladner, Downs (Vancouver)

First City Financial Corp:
M. Koffman: Freeman & Co. (Vancouver)
J. Schoctor: Shortreed, Shoctor, Enright, Stevenson-Guille & Binder (Toronto)

Home Oil:
W.H. Zimmerman: Aird, Zimmerman & Berlis (Toronto)
R. St-Laurent: St-Laurent, Monast, Walters & Vallières (Quebec)
P.L.P. Macdonnell: Milner & Steer (Edmonton)
W.F. James: James & Buffam (Toronto)

I.A.C. Ltd:
R. St-Laurent: St-Laurent, Monast, Walters & Vallières (Quebec)
F.M. Covert: Stewart, Mackeen & Covert (Halifax)
E.J. Courtois: Weldon, Courtois, Clarkson, Parsons & Tétreault (Montreal)

Inco Ltd:
R.W. Bonner: Bonner & Fouks (Vancouver)

Ivaco Industries:
H.B. McNally: Byers, Casgrain & Stewart (Montreal)

Jannock Corp:
L.Y. Fortier: Ogilvy, Cope, Porteous, Montgomery, Renault, Clarke & Kirkpatrick (Mtl.)

M. Loeb & Co:
H. Soloway and M. Wright: Soloway, Wright, Houston, Greenberg, O'Grady & Morin (Ottawa)

Maclaren Power & Paper:
G.F. Maclaren: Maclaren, Corlett & Tanner (Ottawa)

MacLean Hunter Ltd: none

S.B. McLaughlin Assoc.:
James D. Tory: Tory, Tory, Deslauriers & Binnington
                                    (Toronto)

Molson Companies:
R. Létourneau: Létourneau, Stein, Marseille, Delisle &
                                    LaRue (Quebec)
T.E. Ladner: Ladner, Downs (Vancouver)
F.M. Covert: Stewart, Mackeen & Covert (Halifax)
J.B. Aird: Zimmerman & Berlis (Toronto)

Moore Corp: none

National Trust Co:
H.A. Martin: Martin & Martin (Hamilton)
R.T. Clarkson: Weldon, Courtois, Clarkson, Parsons &
                                    Tétreault (Montreal)

Neonex International:
M.D. Eastern: Harper Grey, Eastern & Co. (Vancouver)

Newfoundland Light & Power:
D.C. Hunt: Halley, Hickman, Hunt, Adams, Steele,
                                    Carter, Martin, Whelan & Heemebury
                                    (St. John's, Nfld)

Norcen Energy Resources:
R.B. Love: Mcleod, Dixon (Calgary)
F.A.M. Huycke: Osler, Hoskin & Harcourt (Toronto)
E.J. Courtois: Weldon, Courtois, Clarkson, Parsons &
                                    Tétreault (Montreal)

Gaz Métropolitain (subsidiary of Norcen Energy Resources):
E.J. Courtois: Weldon, Courtois, Clakson, Parsons &
                                    Tétreault (Montreal)
W. Bhérer: Bhérer, Bernier, Côté, Ouellett, Dionne,
                                    Houle & Morin (Quebec)

Nu-West Development Corp:
H. Field: Field, Owen (Edmonton)

Carma Developers (subsidiary of Nu-West Development Corp.)
S.H. Wood: Mackimmie, Matthews (Calgary)

Oshawa Group:
A. Shiffrin et L.B. White: Shiffrin, White & Spring (Toronto)

Orlando Corp:
A. Page and A. Magerman: Magerman & Page (Downsview, Ontario)

Oxford Development Group: none

Prenor Group:
R.M. Ivey: Ivey & Dowler (London, Ontario)
J. Tétreault: Weldon, Courtois, Clarkson, Parsons &
                                    Tétreault (Montreal)

Royal Trust:
Hon. M. Riel (senator):   Riel, Vermette, Ryan, Dunton & Graccia
                                    (Montreal)

Hon. C. Marler:	McLean, Marler, Tees, Watson, Poitevin, Javet & Roberge (Montreal)
F.M. Fell:	Faskell & Calvin (Tor.)
D.N. Byers:	Byers, Casgrain & Stewart (Mtl.)
R.J. Balfour (M.P.):	Balfour, Moss, Milliken, Laschuk, Kyle, Vancisse & Camiron (Regina)

H. Russell Ltd:

J.D. Reilly:	Hill, Friend & Reilly (Tor.)

The Seagram Co.:

Hon. L. Gélinas (senator):	Geoffrion, Robert & Gélinas (Mtl.)
P.F. Vineberg:	Phillips & Vineberg (Mtl.)

Simpson's Ltd:

James M. Tory:	Tory, Tory, Deslauriers & Binnington (Tor.)

Simpsons-Sears Ltd (subsidiary of *Simpson's Ltd*):

James M. Tory:	Tory, Tory, Deslauriers & Binnington (Tor.)

Southam Press:

G. Pouliot:	Pouliot, Dion & Guilbault (Mtl.)
B.B. Osler:	Blake, Cassels & Graydon (Tor.)
G.L. Crawford:	McLaws & Co (Calgary)

Stelco:

D.R. McMaster:	McMaster, Meighen, Minnion, Patch, Cordeau, Hyndman & Legge (Mtl.)
A.J. McIntosh:	Blake, Cassels & Graydon (Tor.)

Steinberg's Ltd:

L. Phillips:	Phillips & Vineberg (Mtl.)

Trust Général du Canada:

Hon. Edouard Asselin:	lawyer (Mtl.)
L. Sirois:	Sirois & Tremblay (Que.)
I.C. Pollack:	Létourneau, Stein, Marseille, Delisle & LaRue (Que.)
M. Piché:	Blain, Piché, Godbout, Emery & Blain (Mtl.)
D.O. Doheny:	Doheny, Mackenzie, Grivaker, Gervais & Lemoyne (Mtl.)

Unicorp Financial Corp:	none

Union Gas:

D.J. Wright:	Lang, Michener, Cranston, Farquharson & Wright (Toronto)

United Grain:	none

United Trust:

B. Shinder:	Goldbert, Shinder, Shmelzer, Gardner & Kronick (Ottawa)
H. Solway et E.A. Goodman:	Goodman & Goodman (Toronto)

Hiram Walker—Gooderham & Worts:

J. Jeffery:	Jeffery & Jeffery (London, Ontario)
F.C. Cope:	Ogilvy, Cope, Porteous, Montgomery, Renault, Clarke & Kirkpatrick (Mtl.)

Westburne International Industries:
F.R. Matthews: Mackimmie, Matthews (Calgary)

United Westburne Industries (subsidiary of *Westburne Int. Industries):*
F.R. Matthews: Mackimmie, Matthews (Calgary)

G. Weston Ltd: none

Kelly, Douglas & Co. (subsidiary of *G. Weston Co.*)
C.N. Wills: Farris, Vaughan, Wills & Murphy (Vancouver)

Woodward Stores:
R.A. White: lawyer (Vancouver)

B. Companies Belonging to Groups

Power Corp:
W. Bhérer: Bhérer, Bernier, Côté, Ouellett, Dionne, Houle & Morin (Quebec)
P. Genest: Cassels, Brock (Toronto)
C. Pratte: Létourneau, Stein, Marseille, Delisle, LaRue (Quebec)
Hon. J.P. Robarts: Stikeman, Elliott, Robarts & Bowman (Toronto)

Consolidated—Bathurst (subsidiary of *Power Corp.*):
Hon. J.B. Aird: Aird, Zimmerman & Berlis (Toronto)
R.E. Morrow: Ogilvy, Cope, Porteous, Montgomery, Renault, Clarke & Kirkpatrick (Mtl.)

Dominion Glass Co. (subsidiary of *Consolidated-Bathurst*):
Hon. J.B. Aird: Aird, Zimmerman & Berlis (Toronto)

Canada Steamship Lines (subsidiary of *Power Corp*):
W. Bhérer: Bhérer, Bernier, Côté, Ouellett, Dionne, Houle & Morin (Que.)
Hon. J.P. Robarts: Stikeman, Elliott, Robarts & Bowman (Tor.)

Imperial Life Ass. (subsidiary of *Power Corp.*):
J.G. Porteous: Ogilvy, Cope, Porteous, Montgomery, Renault, Clarke & Kirkpatrick (Mtl.)
R. St Laurent: St Laurent, Monast, Walters & Vallières (Que.)

Laurentide Financial Corp (subsidiary of *Power Corp.*): none

Investors Group (subsidiary of *Power Corp.*): none

Montreal Trust (subsidiary of *Investors Group*):
M.S. Hannon: Ogilvy, Cope, Porteous, Montgomery, Renault, Clarke & Kirkpatrick (Mt.)
D.A. Berlis: Aird, Zimmerman & Berlis (Tor.)
K.H. Brown: Lafleur & Brown (Mtl.)
Hon. J.M. Godfrey: Campbell, Godfrey & Lewtas (Tor.)
Hon. J. Lesage: Howard, Mc Dougall, Ewasew, Graham & Stocks (Mtl.)
R. de W. Mackay: Duquet, Mackay, Weldon & Bronstetter (Mtl.)

153

J.W.E. Mingo:	Stewart, Mackeen & Covert (Halifax)
A.E. Shepherd:	Shepherd, Mackenzie, Plaxton, Little & Jenkins (London, Ont.)
Hon. W. Owen:	Owen, Bird, (Vancouver)

Great West Life Ass. (subsidiary of *Investors Group):*
| J.B. Macaulay: | Aikins, Macaulay & Thorvaldson (Winnipeg) |

Argus Corporation:
| D.A. Mc Intosh: | Fraser & Beatty (Tor.) |

B.C. Forest Products (subsidiary of *Argus Corp.* and of *Noranda Mines):*
| D.C. Davenport: | Bourne, Lyall, Davenport & Spencer (Vancouver) |
| O.F. Lundell: | Lawson, Lundell, Lawson & McIntosh (Vancouver) |

Hollinger Mines (subsidiary of *Argus Corp.):*
| Hon. Edouard Asselin: | lawyer (Mtl.) |

Noranda Mines (subsidiary of *Hollinger Mines):*
| A. Monast: | St Laurent, Monast, Walters & Vallières (Que.) |

Placer Development (subsidiary of *Noranda Mines):* none

Brunswick Mining & Smelting (subsidiary of *Noranda Mines):*
| A. Monast: | St Laurent, Monast, Walters & Vallières (Que.) |

Mattagami Lake Mines (subsidiary of *Noranda Mines* and of *Placer Dev.):*
| R. Létourneau: | Létourneau, Stein, Marseille, Delisle & LaRue (Que.) |

Fraser Companies (subsidiary of *Noranda Mines):* none

Domtar Ltd (subsidiary of *Argus Corp.):*
| R. Létourneau: | Létourneau, Stein, Marseille, Delisle & LaRue (Que.) |
| J.G. Kirkpatrick: | Ogilvy, Cope, Porteous, Montgomery, Renault, Clarke & Kirkpatrick (Mtl.) |

Dominion Stores (subsidiary of *Argus Corp.):*
| A. Monast: | St Laurent, Monast, Walters & Vallières (Que.) |

Massey Ferguson Ltd (subsidiary of *Argus Corp.):* none

Gaspé Copper Mines (subsidiary of *Noranda Mines):*
| A. Monast: | St Laurent, Monast, Walters & Vallières (Que.) |

Brascan Ltd:
| A.J. MacIntosh: | Blake, Cassels & Graydon (Tor.) |
| B. Matthews: | Mc Carthy & Mc Carthy (Tor.) |

Commerce Capital Corp. (subsidiary of *Brascan Ltd):*
| R.H.E. Walker: | Martineau, Walker, Allison, Beaulieu, Mackell & Clermont (Mtl.) |
| R.B. Love: | Macleod, Dixon (Calgary) |

154

Farmers & Merchants Trust (subsidiary of *Commerce Capital Corp.*):
D.P. Hays and R.B. Love: Macleod, Dixon (Calgary)

J. Labatt (subsidiary of *Brascan Ltd.*):
A.J. MacIntosh: Blake, Cassels & Graydon (Tor.)
J.D. Harrison: Harrison, Elmwood (London, Ont.)
E.A. Goodman: Goodman & Goodman (Tor.)

Hudson's Bay Co. (subsidiary of *Brascan Ltd.*):
A.J. MacIntosh: Blake, Cassels & Graydon (Tor.)
G.R. Hunter: Pitblado & Oskin (Winnipeg)

Ogilvie Mills (subsidiary of *J. Labatt*):
E.A. Goodman: Goodman & Goodman (Tor.)

Markborough Properties (subsidiary of *Hudson's Bay Co.*):
A.J. MacIntosh: Blake, Cassels & Graydon (Tor.)

E.-L. Financial Corp.:
Hon. R. Michener: Lang, Michener, Cranston, Farquharson & Wright (Tor.)

Victoria & Grey Trust (subsidiary of *E.-L. Financial Corp.*):
G.E. Wallace: Wallace & Carr (North Bay, Ont.)
J.F. Reesor: Mewburn, Marshall & Reesor (Hamilton, Ont.)
D.J. Murphy: Domelly & Murphy (Goderich, Ont.)
R.N. McLaughlin et R.H. Soward: McLaughlin, May, Soward, Morden & Bales (Tor.)
W.A. Macdonald: McMillan, Binch (Tor.)
Hon. W.E. Harris: Harris & Dunlop (Markdale, Ont.)
W.C. Hamilton: Kearns, McKinnon, Gifford, Hamilton & Bean (Guelph, Ont.)
J.W. Graham: Payton, Biggs & Graham (Tor.)
J.R. Anderson: Anderson, Neilson, Bell, Dilks, Misener, Skinner & Anderson (Stratford, Ont.)

Canadian General Investments:
T.R. Meighen: McMaster, Meighen, Minnion, Patch, Cordeau, Hindman & Legge (Mtl.)

Huron & Erie Mortgage Corp. (subsidiary of *Can. General Investments*):
J.D. Harrison: Harrison, Elmwood (London, Ont.)

Canadian Pacific Ltd:
C. Pratte: Létourneau, Stein, Marseille, Delisle & LaRue (Que.)
A. Findlay: Tilley, Carson & Findlay (Tor.)

C.P. Investments (subsidiary of *C.P. Ltd*): none

C.P. Air (subsidiary of *C.P. Ltd*):
J.B. Hamilton: Hamilton, Torrance, Stinson, Campbell, Nobbs & Woods (Tor.)

Trans-Canada Pipelines (subsidiary of *C.P. Ltd.*):
B. Matthews: McCarthy & McCarthy (Tor.)
J.R. Tolmie: Herridge, Tolmie, Gray, Coyne & Blair (Ottawa)

Cominco (subsidiary of *C.P. Investments*):
D.R. McMaster: McMaster, Meighen, Minnion, Patch, Cordeau, Hyndman & Legge (Mtl.)

R.A. Mackimmie: Mackimmie, Matthews (Calgary)

Great Lakes Paper (subsidiary of *C.P.I.*): none
Algoma Steel Corp. (subsidiary of *C.P.I.*):
R. Dunn: McMillan, Binch (Tor.)

Dominion Bridge (subsidiary of *Algoma Steel*):
J. Angus Ogilvy: Ogilvy, Cope, Porteous, Montgomery, Renault, Clarke & Kirkpatrick (Mtl.)

Pan Canadian Petroleum (subsidiary of *C.P.I.*): none

MacMillan Bloedell (subsidiary of *C.P.I*): none

Bell Canada:
Hon. J.P. Robarts: Stikeman, Elliott, Robarts & Bowman (Tor.)

D. McInnes: McInnes, Cooper & Robertson (Halifax)

E.N. Mckelvey: Mckelvey, Macaulay, Machum & Fairweather (St John, N.B.)

Northern Electric (subsidiary of *Bell Canada*):
J.A. Ogilvy: Ogilvy, Cope, Porteous, Montgomery, Renault, Clarke & Kirkpatrick (Mtl.)

G. de L. Demers: Lesage, Demers, Lesage & Brochu (Que.)

New Brunswick Telephone (subsidiary of *Bell Canada*):
A.R. Landry: Landry, Brisson & Leblanc (Moncton)

Maritime Telegraph & Telephone (subsidiary of *Bell Canada*):
G.C. Piercey: Daley, Black, Moreira & Piercey (Halifax)

Newfoundland Telephone Co. (subsidiary of *Bell Canada*):
F.A. O'Dea: O'Dea, Greene, Neary & Puddester (St John, Nfld)

Trader's Group (subsidiary of *Cdn. General Securities*):
D.A. McIntosh: Fraser & Beatty (Tor.)
J.W. McCutcheon: Shibley, Righton & McCutcheon (Tor.)

Guaranty Trust (subsidiary of *Traders Group*):
A.F. Sheppard: Martin, Sheppard, Clark, Mckay & Denouden (Niagara Falls, Ont.)

W.J. Shea: Shea, Weaver & Simmons (Sudbury, Ont.)

J.W. McCutcheon: Shibley, Righton & McCutcheon (Tor.)

J.P. Bassel: Bassel, Sullivan, Lawson & Leake (Tor.)

C. Private Companies and Companies without share Capital

Canada Life Assurance:
E.J. Courtois: Weldon, Courtois, Clarkson, Parsons, Tétreault (Montréal)

B. Matthews: McCarthy & McCarthy (Toronto)

Confederation Life:	
T.E. Ladner:	Ladner, Downs (Vancouver)
D.A. McIntosh:	Fraser & Beatty (Tor.)
HCF Mockridge:	Osler, Hoskin & Harcourt (Tor.)
A. Monast:	St-Laurent, Monast, Walters & Vallières (Que.)
T. Eaton Acceptance Co.:	no lawyer
T. Eaton Co.:	no lawyer
T. Eaton Realty:	no lawyer
F.P. Publications Ltd:	
J. Sedwick:	Seed, Long, Howard, Cook & Caswell (Tor.)
Irving Oil:	no lawyer
Kruger Pulp & Paper:	no lawyer
London Life Insurance Co.:	
J. Jeffery, G.D. Jeffery, A.H. Jeffery:	Jeffery & Jeffery (London, Ont.)
Manufacture Life Insurance Co.:	
L.Y. Fortier:	Ogilvy, Cope, Porteous, Mongomery, Renault, Clarke & Kirkpatrick (Mtl.)
CFH Carson:	Tilley, Carson & Findlay (Tor.)
Mutual Life Assurance Co.:	
E. Fiset:	Fiset, Miller (Mtl.)
North American Life Assurance Co.:	
P.L.P. Macdonnell:	Milner & Steer (Edmonton)
Sun Life Assurance Co. of Canada:	
John A. Tory:	Tory, Tory, Deslauriers & Binnington (Tor.)
F.M. Covert:	Stewart, Mckeen & Covert (Halifax)
Wood, Gundy & Co.:	no lawyer

Sources: F.P. *Directory of Directors,* 1967
  Martindale Hubbell Law Directory, 1967

APPENDIX II

FINANCIAL, ACCOUNTING AND TECHNICAL CONSULTANTS ON THE BOARD OF MAJOR COMPANIES

Companies	Consultant	Consulting, Brokerage or other Firm
Abitibi Paper	N.J. MacMillan	Private Consultant
Acklands Ltd.	D.E. Boxer	Burns Bros. & Denton
Algoma Steel	J.B. Barrington	Consulting engineer
Bell Canada	J.D. Gibson	Financial consultant
Bombardier Ltd.	J.N. Cole	Vice-ch. of board, Wood, Gundy & Co.
Bow Valley Ind.	D.L. Sinclair	Financial consultant
Brascan Ltd.	J.H. A'Court	Financial consultant
Brunswick M.S.	J.A. McMurray	Partner, Richardson Securities
Calgary Power	A.S. Gordon	Consultant, Merrill Lynch Royal Sec.
	J.H. Coleman	JHC Financial Consultants
Canada Perm. Mortgage	G.L. Jennison	Financial consultant, Wills, Bickle & Co.
	H.H. Mackay	Pitfield, Mackay, Ross & Co.
	C.F.W. Burns	Burns Bros & Denton
Cdn. Gral Investments	J.B. Barrington	Consulting mining engineer
C.P. Investments	S.E. Nixon	Financial consultant, Dom. Sec. Corp. Harris & Partners
Canron Ltd.	C.L. Gundy	Wood, Gundy & Co.
	J.S. Dinnick	Hon. ch. of board, McLeod, Young Weir & Co. Ltd.
Central & Eastern Tr.	W.W. Blackie	Consultant
Cominco	S.E. Nixon	Financial consultant, Dominion Sec.
Consol.-Bathurst	A.D. Nesbitt	Nesbitt Thomson & Co.
Consumers' Gas	D.B. Mansur	Private consultant
	J.D. Gibson	Private financial consultant
Crown Life	C.F.W. Burns	
	H.M. Burns	Burns Bros & Denton
Daon Dev. Corp.	W.J. Corcoran	Exec. V.P., McLeod, Young, Weir & Co.
Denison Mines	C.F.W. Burns	Burns Bros & Denton
Dofasco	H.N. Bawden	Dir., Dominion Sec. Corp. Harris
E.-L. Financial Corp.	Hon. L.P. Beaulieu	Lévesque, Beaulieu Inc.
Federal Industries	G. Aitken	*Aitken Management Consultants Ltd*
Finning Tractor	J.R. LeMesurier	Vice-pres.: *Wood, Gundy & Co.*
Fraser Comp.	D.J. Hennigar	*Burns Bros & Denton*
Great West Life	J.H. Coleman	*J.H.C. Financial Consultants*
Guaranty Trust	D.I. Webb	Financial Consultant
Home Oil	J.D. Gibson	Financial Consultant
Hudson' Bay Co.	W.D.C. Mackenzie	*W.D.C. Mackenzie Consultants Ltd.*
I.A.C. Ltd.	P. Kilburn	Ch. of the Board, *Greenshields Inc.*

Imperial Life	J.D. Gibson	Financial Consultant
Ivaco Industries	A.S. Gordon	Financial Consultant
Laurentide Financial Corp.	W.Y. Soper	*Pitfield, Mackay, Ross & Co.*
S.B. McLaughlin Ass.	J.G. Davies	*A.C. Ames & Co.*
Maritime Telegraph & Telephone	P.J. Smith	Financial Consultant
Massey-Ferguson	C.L. Gundy	*Wood, Gundy & Co.*
Moore Corp.	J.D. Gibson	Financial Consultant
National Trust	J.K. Godin	Consulting Engineer
	J.D. Gibson	Financial Consultant
	J.R. Beattie	Economic & Financial consultant
	J.D. Barrington	Consulting engineer
Newfoundland Light & Power	A.S. Gordon	Financial consultant
Norcen Energy Resources	J.I. Crookston	Ch. of the Board: *Nesbitt Thomson & Co.*
Northern Electric	J.D. Gibson	Financial Consultant
Ogilvie Mills	P. Bienvenu	Financial Consultant
Orlando Corp.	R.M. Hanbury	Financial Consultant
Placer Development	H.R. Whitthall	Deputy manager partner: *Richardson Securities of Canada*
Power Corp.	A.D. Nesbitt	Nesbitt Thomson & Co.
Prenor Group	G.H. Garneau	Dir: *Burns Bros & Denton*
Price Co.	A.S. Gordon	Financial consultant
	N.J. McMillan	Private consultant
The Seagram Co.	C.E. Medland	Pres.: *Wood, Gundy & Co. Ltd.*
Simpsons Ltd.	J.M.G. Scott	*Wood, Gundy & Co. Ltd.*
Stelco	J.D. Gibson	Financial consultant
Steinbergs Ltd.	A. Charron	*Lévesque, Beaulieu, Inc.*
Traders Group	D.I. Webb	Financial consultant
Trans-Canada Pipelines	J.H. Coleman	*J.H.C. Financial Consultants*
United Westburne Industries	D.N. Stoker	Vice-pres.: *Nesbitt Thomson & Co.*
Westburne International Industries	D.N. Stoker	Vice-pres.: *Nesbitt Thomson & Co. Ltd.*
	J.H. Coleman	*J.H.C. Financial Consultants*

Source: Financial Post Directory of Directors, 1976.

APPENDIX III

CAREER MANAGERS
AMONG THE MAJOR INSIDE DIRECTORS
OF DOMINANT COMPANIES

Company	Director	Position	
Abitibi Paper	T.S. Bell	Ch. of board	$ 281,875
	C.H. Rosier	Pres.	$ 148,975
Acklands Ltd.	G. Forzley	Vice-pres.	$ 386,856

Alberta Gas Trunk	H. J. Pearson	Ch. of board	$ 50,198
	S.R. Blair	Pres.	$ 80,500
Alcan Aluminium	P. Leman	Pres.	$ 174,675
Algoma Steel	D.S. Holbrook	Ch. of board	$2,183,342
	J.B. Barber	Vice-ch. of board	$ 466,052
Allarco Developments	M. Klimove	Vice-pres.	$ 381,710
Argus Corp.	J.N. Swinden	Gen. Manager	$ 12,645
Bell Canada	R.C. Scrivener	Ch. of board	$ 140,745
	A.J. de Grandpré	Pres.	$ 80,965
Block Bros. Ind.	N.E. Sawatzky	Vice-pres.	$ 140,202
Bombardier Ltd.	J.C. Hébert	Ch. of board	$ 770,430
Bow Valley Ind.	H.H. Binney	Sr. V.P.	$ 76,642
Bramalea Cons. Dev.	M.I. Speigal	V.P.	$ 460,688
Brascan Ltd.	E.C. Freeman Atwoo(	Exec. V.P.	$ 165,510
B.C. Forest Products	A. Powis	Ch. of board	$ 28,533
	I. A. Barclay	Pres.	$ 70,625
Brunswick M & S	W. G. Brissenden	Ch. of board	$ 74,322
	M.E. Taschereau	Pres.	$ 32,450
Burns Food	A.J.E. Child	Pres.	$1,046,240
Cadillac Fairview Corp.	N.R. Wood	Pres.	$ 11,699
Calgary Power	A.W. Howard	Ch. of board	$ 274,075
	M.M. Williams	Pres.	$ 8,973
Campeau Corp.	R.B. McCartney	Pres.	$ 342,990
Canada Packers	G.H. Dickson	Exec. V.P.	$ 80,219
Can. Perm. Mortgage Corp.	D.G. Neelands	Ch. of board	$ 78,210
	E.J. Brown	Pres.	$ 4,345
Cdn. Corp. Management	V.N. Stock	Pres.	$1,182,000
Cdn. Gral Investment	A.E. Barron	Pres.	$ 380,000
C.P. Investments	I.D. Sinclair	Ch. of board	$ 442,350
	W. Moodie	Pres.	$ 14,688
C.P. Ltd.	I.D. Sinclair	Ch. of board	$ 122,444
	F.S. Burbidge	Pres.	$ 77,324
Cdn. Tire Corp.	A.E. Barron	Ch. of board	$ 708,345
	J.O. Muncaster	Pres.	$1,681,059
Canron Ltd.	H.S. Lang	Ch. of board	$ 437,310
	C.S. Malone	Pres.	$ 25,200
Carma Developers	R.J. Wilson	Ch. of board	$ 57,023
Central & Eastern Trust	H.P. Connor	Ch. of board	
City Savings & Trust	F.E. Burnett	Ch. of board	$ 38,807
Cominco	G.H.D. Hobbs	Pres.	$ 51,763
	J.B. Whitely	Pres.	$ 354,454
Commerce Capital Corp.	T.L. Charne	V.P.	$ 37,200
	R.A. Irwin	Ch. of board	$ 155,354
Consol. Bathurst	W.I.M. Turner Jr.	Pres.	$3,520,266
	J.C. McCarthy	Vice-ch. of board	$ 71,355
Consumers' Gas	G.E. Creber	Pres.	$ 15,466
	A.F. Williams	Vice-ch. of board	$ 308,409
Crown Life Ins.	R.C. Dowsett	Pres.	$ 55,248
Crown Trust	H.F. Kerrigan	Pres.	$ 4,250
Daon Development Corp.	N.E. Cressey	V.P.	$ 300,100
Deltan Corp.	K.A. Mackenzie	Pres.	$ 28

Denison Mines	J. Kostiuk	Pres.	$	196,659
Dofasco	R.R. Craig	Exec. V.P.	$	32,064
Dominion Bridge	M. McMurray	Ch. of board	$	425,220
	K.S. Barclay	Pres.	$	313,320
Dominion Glass	W.I.M. Turner Jr.	Ch. of board	$	12
	E.A. Thompson	Pres.	$	12
Dominion Stores	T.G. Bolton	Pres.	$	59,116
Dominion Textile	R.H. Perowne	Ch. of board	$	71,505
	T.R. Bell	Pres.	$	45,034
Domtar	A.D. Hamilton	Pres.	$	84,980
E-L. Financial Corp.	K.G. Hutchisson	Pres.	$	840
Farmers & Merchants Trust	J.B. Whitely	Ch. of board	$	20,520
	D.A. Ross	Pres.	$	27,353
Federal Industries				
Finning Tractor	R.E. Lane	Pres.	$	272,636
First City Financial Corp.				
Fraser Companies	A.H. Zimmerman	Ch. of board	$	3,680
	C.R. Recor	Pres.	$	102,719
Gaspé Copper Mines[1]	W.G. Brissenden	Pres.		
Gaz Métropolitain	A.E. Sharp	Pres.	$	1,197
Great Lakes Paper	P.M. Fox	Ch. of board	$	395,000
	C.J. Carter	Pres.	$	14,813
Great West Life Ass.	P.P. Curry	Ch. of board	$	97,963
	J.W. Burns	Pres.	$	10,430
Guaranty Trust	A.R. Marchment	Pres.	$	109,152
Hollinger Mines	A.L. Fairley	Pres.	$	20,286
Home Oil	A.G.S. Griffin	Ch of board	$	40,976
	R.F. Phillips	Pres.	$	181,033
Hudson Bay Co.	D.S. McGiverin	Pres.	$	328,391
Huron & Erie Mortgage Corp.	A.H. Mingay	Pres.	$	1,789
I.A.C. Ltd.	K.H. Macdonald	Ch. of board	$	225,639
	J.S. Land	Pres.	$	42,539
Imperial Life Ass.	A.R. Poyntz	Ch. of board	$	27,000
	G.K. Fox	Pres.	$	6,750
Inco Ltd.	L.E. Grubb	Ch. of board	$	283,250
	J.E. Carter	Pres.	$	142,269
Investors Group	P.D. Curry	Ch. of board	$	132,709
	R.H. Jones	Pres.	$	328,000
Ivaco Industries				
Jannock Corp.				
Kelly Douglas & Co.	R.J. Addington	Pres.	—	
J. Labatt Ltd.	P.N.T. Widdrington	Pres.	$	24,924
Laurentide Financial Corp.	P.O. Curry	Ch. of board	$	36,550
	E.M. Lindberg	Pres.		
M. Loeb Co.	F. Warnock	Pres.	$	303
Maclaren Power & Paper	J.S. Hermon	Pres.	$	28,703
MacMillan-Bloedell	G.B. Currie	Ch. of board	$	71,719
	D.W. Timmis	Pres.	$	111,563
Maclean Hunter	D.G. Campbell	Pres.	$	892,328
Maritime Tel & Tel	A.G. Archibald	Ch. of board	$	34,513
Markborough Properties Ltd.	B.R.B. Magee	Ch. of board	$	473,000

Massey-Ferguson	A.A. Thornbrough	Pres.	$1,033,712
Mattagami Lake Mines	W.S. Row	Ch. of board	$ 291,200
	J.A. Hall	Pres.	$ 45,136
S.B. McLaughlin Assoc.	E.A. Kirk	V.P. of finance	$ 27,930
Molson Companies	J.T. Black	Pres.	$ 85,075 (2)
Montreal Trust	P.B. Paine	Ch. of board	$ 19,688
Moore Corp.	W.H. Browne	Ch. of board	$2,532,760
	D.W. Barr	Pres.	$1,265,000
National Trust	J.G. Hungerford	Ch. of board	$ 130,000
	J.L.A. Colhoun	Pres.	$ 60,450
Neonex International	F.W. Vanstone	Vice-pres. of finance	$ 45,450
New Brunswick Tele- phone	K.V. Cox	Pres.	$ 59,423
Nfld Light & Power	D. Stairs	Ch. of board	$ 348,338
	A. Bailey	Pres.	$ 25,245
Nfld Telephone	L.H.M. Ayre	Ch. of board	$ 153
	A.A. Brait	Pres.	$ 2,388
Noranda Mines	W.S. Row	Ch. of board	$ 360,525
	A. Powis	Pres.	$ 464,025
Norcen Energy Res- ources	E.C. Bovey	Ch. of board	$ 176,400 (3)
	E.G. Battle	Pres.	$ 181,053
Northern Electric	J.C. Lobb	Ch. of board	$ 28,572
	W.F. Light	Pres.	$ 47,715
Nu West Development Corp.	M.R. Gerla	V.P.	$ 29,445 (4)
Ogilvie Mills	J.W. Tait	Pres.	
Orlando Corp.	S. Craig	Exec. V.P.	$ 3,383
Oshawa Group	W.L. Atkinsons	Exec. V.P.	$ 26,875
Oxford Dev. Group			
Pan Canadian Petro- leum	R.W. Campbell	Ch. of board	$ 1,043
	J.M. Taylor	Pres.	$ 10
Placer Development	T.H. McClelland	Ch. of board	$ 301,148
	R.G. Duthie	Pres.	$ 41,170
Power Corp.	P.D. Curry	Pres.	$ 91,250
Prenor Group	S. Rocheleau	Exec. V.P.	$ 66,719
Price Co.	T.R. Moore	Ch. of board	$ 5,188
	C.R. Tittemore	Pres.	$ 1,563
Royal Trust	C.F. Harrington	Ch. of board	$ 290,030
	D.A. White	Pres.	$ 202,441
Hugh Russel Ltd.	J.P. Foster	Pres.	$ 167,873
The Seagram Co.	J. Yogman	Exec. V.P.	$1,012,556
Simpson's Ltd.	C.B. Stewart	Pres.	$ 546,700
Southam Press	R. Munro	V.P.	$ 100,000
Stelco	H.M. Griffith	Ch. of board	$2,862,500
	J.P. Gordon	Pres.	$ 148,850
Steinberg's Ltd.			
Traders Group	H.E. Dynes	Pres.	$ 84,078
Trans-Canada Pipe- lines	J.W. Kerr	Ch. of board	$ 74,987
	G.W. Woods	Pres.	$ 38,440
Trust Général du Ca- nada	R. Jussaume	Pres.	$ 42,779
Unicorp Financial Corp.			
Union Gas Co.			

United Trust Co.	V.E. Daughney	Pres.	$ 3,157
United Westburne Ind.	L. Cornez	Pres.	$ 18,150
Victoria and Grey Trust	C.F. Fleming	Vice-ch. of board	$ 893,597
Hiram Walker-Gooderham & Worts	P.G. Kidd	Sr. V.P.	$ 227,966
Westburne Int. Industries	W.S. Zaruby	Pres.	$ 179,900
G. Weston	M. Hoffman	Sr. V.P.	$ 202,725
Woodward Stores	C.R. Clarridge	Pres.	$ 118,900

(1) Gaspé Copper Mines: its shares are not quoted on the Exchange
(2) According to the 1974 quotation
(3) According to the *Northern Central Gas Corp,* quotation of 1975.

Sources: Ontario Securties Commission *Monthly Bulletin*
Commission des Valeurs Mobilières du Québec: *Rapport hebdomadaire* Financial Post Survey of Industrials F.P. Survey of Oils, F. P. Survey Mines et Moody's Bank & Finance Manual, all for 1976 (1975 figures)
F.P. Directory of Directors, 1976
Canadian Who's who, 1974-75
Who's who in Canada, 1975-76
National Reference Book, 1967-1968.

APPENDIX IV

POWER CORPORATION OF CANADA
EXCERPT FROM PROXY MANAGEMENT CIRCULAR*

Director—Name and Principal Occupation	Company	Approx. No. of Shares
W. Bhérer: Ch. of board, Cdn. Vickers Ltd. (Partner: Bherer, Bernier, Côté, Ouellet, Houle & Morin, Lawyers)	Power Power	1,000 pref. conv. 1,500 common
A.F. Campo: Ch of board, Petrofina Canada	Power Investors Mtl. Trust	1,100 common 1,000 common 2,000 common
P.D. Curry: Pres. & chief op. officer Power Corp., Ch. of board Great West Life, Investors and Laurentide Financial Corp.	Power Gr West Investors Laurentide Mtl. Trust	10,000 common 1,700 common 20,000 common 5,000 common 2,000 common
L.R. Desmarais: Dpty ch. of board, Power Corp; Ch. of board, Canada Steamship Lines	Power Power	25,800 pref. conv. 60,000 common
W.M. Fuller: Partner, W.A.P. Fuller	Power	4,500 common
P. Genest: Partner, Cassels & Brock lawyers	Power	100 common
J.-P. Gignac: Pres., Sidbec-Dosco	Power	200 common
R.H. Jones: Pres. and Chief of officer, Investors Group	Power Gr West Investors	100 common 500 common 5,125 common "B" 44,875 common "C"

163

W.E. McLaughlin: Ch. of board and pres., Royal Bank	Power	2,000 common
	Mtl. Trust	500 common
A.D. Nesbitt: and Chief op. officer, Nesbitt Thomson & Co.	Power	21,000 pref. conv.
	Power	21,100 common
P.D. Paine: Pres. and Ch. of board, Montreal Trust	Power	52,500 common
	Gr West	500 common
	Investors	1,001 common
C. Pratte: lawyer (partner: Létourneau Stein, Marseille, Delisle & LaRue, lawyers)	Laurentide	1,500 common
	Mtl Trust	1,500 common
	Power	5,065 pref. conv.
	Imp. Life	310 common
Hon. J.P. Robarts: partner, Stikeman, Elliott, Robarts & Bowman	Power	100 common
W.E.M. Turner Jr: Pres. and Chief op. officer, Consolidated-Bathurst, Ch. of board, Dominion Glass Ltd.)	Power	43,100 common
	Investors	101 common
	Laurentide	100 common
	(Dom. Glass)	(1 common)
R.C. Scrivener: Ch. of board and Chief op. officer, Bell Canada	Power	100 common
P. Desmarais[1]: Ch. of board and Chief op. officer, Power Corp; V.P., Imperial Life	Power	100 common
	Imp Life	100 common
	Investors	1 common
	Mtl. Trust	500 common
P.N. Thompson[2]: Dpty Ch. of board, Power Corp.	Power	82,505 common
	Mtl. Trust	500 common

* Dated 31 March 1976. The information in parentheses has been added by the author.
(1) Gelco Enterprises Ltd. and its associated companies hold 53.1% of the 28,536,873 voices represented by the preferred shares having a right to vote in Power Corp. Nordex Ltd. controls Gelco. Nordex Ltd. is controlled by Paul Desmarais, in that he owns 56.7% of its voting shares.
(2) Companies controlled by Mr. Thompson hold 375,000 of the preferred convertible stock in Power Corp., and 24,000 common shares.
Sources: Power Corp., Proxy Management Circular, 31 March 1976
Ontario Securities Commission, Monthly Bulletin.

CONCLUSION

In the preceeding three chapters, we have examined the major theories about the control of large corporations, we have seen how different authors have applied them to the Canadian context and we have introduced statistics which tend to invalidate much of the usefulness of these theories as a description of corporate control in Canada. We may now summarize the main results of our research.

The Theory of Finance Capital

In the initial theoretical discussion of the theory of finance capital, we showed that there are two different understandings of this theory in historical materialism. First, there is the classical version, that of Hilferding and Lenin, stated in terms of bank control or, at least, the coalescence of banks with industry. We showed that this version corresponds to the continental model of bank-industry relations found from 1870 to 1914 primarily in Germany, Belgium, Czarist Russia and Italy. This model, which inspired Hilferding and Lenin, is characterized by multifunctional banks active in the foundation, reorganization, financing and control of industrial companies. This classic version is less applicable to France and to the United States, which have different types of banks, only some of which (business banks in France, brokerage houses in the United States) carry on the activities which could give them power over industry. The Hilferding-Lenin version does not apply to England, where the differentiation of the financial system is even more marked and where no type of bank seeks industrial control.

The second version of the theory of finance capital is that of Chevalier, Menshikov and Fitch and Oppenheimer. It was formulated strictly for the United States of today. It holds that since World War II commercial banks, through the accumulation of shares in their trust departments, have been gaining control over industry. According to this version, banks gain this power, not by mergers, founding companies or issuing stocks and bonds, but rather by using the pension funds which they administer to purchase shares on the market.

The theory of finance capital has both its critics and its supporters within the school of historical materialism. Sweezy has demonstrated the decline of investment banks in the United States since the Great Depression, due to the slump in stock markets from 1930 to 1945, the growth of working capital held by industrial companies, legislation affecting securities, various inquiries and injunctions against the Wall Street "money trust" and, finally, the complete separation of commercial banks from investment firms brought about by the 1933 Glass-Seagall Act. Herman, Sweezy and O'Connor have attacked the "modern" version of the theory of finance capital. According to them, even if the trust departments of commercial banks do amass stocks through their pension funds, the banks are not exercising control on the companies in which they are shareholders. They are more interested in the benefits they receive as investors than in the benefits that might accrue to them as company administrators.

In the first chapter, we tested both versions in the Canadian context. We concluded that chartered banks do not control non-financial institutions in Canada. They own little stock and have never seemed interested in industrial control. They did not play any direct role in the reorganization of companies that occurred in the great wave of mergers of 1909-1913 and of 1925-30; they do not now administer pension funds and they do not handle the first floatings of company stocks or debentures. In the past, certain investment brokers, such as James H. Gundy (of Wood, Gundy & Co.), A.J. Nesbitt and P.A. Thomson (of Nesbitt Thomson) and Lord Beaverbrook and then I.W. Killam (of Royal Securities), have accumulated major blocks of shares in companies through their instrumental role in share offerings and company mergers. These blocks meant directorships for them in the companies and, sometimes, a stable and permanent position of control. The situation, however, has turned against the investment bankers. The growth of institutional investors, the collapse of the stock market from 1930 to 1945 and its subsequently feeble recovery, the establishment of working capital by many industrial companies—these are the factors which largely explain the decline of Canadian investment houses. These days, three types of private financial institutions accumulate shares: trust companies (major generators of pension funds), life-insurance companies and mutual-fund companies. They seem, however, to act strictly as investors and not to "delegate" their own people to the boards of the companies in which they are shareholders.

The Theory of Internal Control

According to the most wide-spread theory in academic social-science departments, the dispersal of shares in industrial companies which took place in the 20th century has left control of these companies in the hands of their own managers and senior executives. That is theory of Berle and Means, Galbraith or Larner in the United States, of Dahrendorf in the Federal Republic of Germany, and others. According to these authors, the dispersal of stocks and bonds is such that even minority blocks will soon disappear.

Kolko, Burch, Zeitlin and Chevalier insist that large blocks of shares do still exist, that share-dispersal has only dispossessed the *small* shareholders from positions of control (by strengthening the power of the big shareholders) and that the unequal distribution of shares has not changed in the last three-quarters of a century.

In order to test this theory in the Canadian context, and with the introduction of supplementary data to illuminate the theory of finance capital, we drew up a nearly-exhaustive list of the dominant companies under Canadian control. We excluded companies under foreign control because neither the finance-control theory nor the managerial-control theory is applicable to such cases—at least not without expanding our study to include parent companies. We established a threshold of $100 million worth in assets, which gave us a list of 146 companies; we obtained data on share-ownership in 136 of them (there being no official or private sources of information concerning ownership of stock in chartered banks and thus no way of knowing the ultimate control of the subsidiaries of those banks). Of the 136 companies for which we possess information, 68% are controlled by individuals, groups of associates or by families. The other 32% *seem* to be in the hands of senior management, but in many of these cases more complete or more trust-worthy sources of information might have shown a situation of majority control by a small group of shareholders. The companies which we found to be apparently under managerial control include many of the largest in the country, for example, Canadian Pacific, Norcen Energy Resources, Alcan Aluminium, Inco Ltd., Royal Trust and Bell Canada. Contrary to the theory of Berle and Means, Galbraith and Larner, these "management controlled" companies did not go through successive stages in which blocks of shares became increasingly dispersed. Moreover, the process of share-dispersal has been reversed and there now tend to be *fewer* shareholders in the largest companies. Here are a few examples:

NUMBER OF SHAREHOLDERS (1970 AND 1975)

Company	1970	1975	% of Variation
Stelco	49,985	37,864	−24.3%
Trans-Canada Pipelines	29,420	24,244	−17.6%
Inco Ltd.	84,320	84,369	+0.05%
Moore Corp.	23,636	20,198	−14.6%
Massey-Ferguson	45,744	35,844	−22.7%
Alcan Aluminium	76,000	47,000	−38.2%
Bell Canada	241,971	217,227	−10.3%
Noranda Mines	33,991[1]	31,610	− 7.1%
MacMillan-Bloedell	21,575	16,654	−22.9%
Imperial Oil	52,934	44,672	−15.6%

Source: *La Presse*, Economic and Financial Section, 23 Sept. 76, page B 5.
(1) This is the 1971 figure, the 1970 figure being unavailable.

The drop in the number of shareholders in major corporations coincides with the growth of institutional investors, the development of conglomerates and the lack of public interest in holding stock. Contrary to the assumptions of the managerialists, we found that individual, associated group or family control is not an archaic form of control in large corporations. On the contrary, it is to be found in all stages of Canadian capitalism. Individuals like Paul Desmarais, Lorne C. Webster, Kenneth C. Irving and Robert Campeau can still climb to the rank of multi-millionaire and control huge enterprises, even conglomerates. Families like the Eatons, the Westons, the Richardsons, the Meighens, the Molsons, the Siftons and the Russels are still today at the head of the companies founded by their ancestors several generations ago. Companies said to be under "management control" are often either companies with "hidden control" or companies whose main stockholders do not sit on the boards and prefer to leave the direction of their companies to the managers and consultants.

The Elite Theory

With C. Wright Mills and his *The Power Elite*, a radical interpretation of corporate control was born. He claimed that power in large corporations belongs to the board of directors as a whole, a board which consists of a homogenous economic élite (corporate rich and managers being the major shareholders). This economic élite has progressively separated itself from the ruling American class of the 19th century; today, it no longer runs the state and no longer dominates the military. These two institutional spheres have developed their own élites, each of which is relatively independent of the economic élite.

There have been two main critiques of this theory. One has tried to show the intermingling of these three supposedly autonomous élites, dominated by the ownership class. The other, put forward by F. Lundberg among others, has questioned the internal unity of this economic élite and insisted that big capitalists are not to be confused with their salaried advisers and technicians. In the third chapter, we tested this theory along with the criticisms directed at its view of the internal unity of the élite (any test of the first major criticism would have led us too far from our study of corporate control). We therefore analysed the shares held by the directors of the Canadian companies which had been studied in the previous chapter. We concluded that the major shareholders (the "corporate rich" of C. Wright Mills) are definitely to be found on the boards of directors of joint-stock companies. But, contrary to the assumptions of the élite theorists, not all members of the boards are large stockholders. Outside directors, especially legal and financial advisers, hold few stocks and receive annual remuneration of between $3,000 and $8,000 a year; they do not participate in stock-purchase plans and do not receive the fringe benefits given to the managers. It is incorrect to put them in the same category as the large stockholders, as did Mills and Porter, or to assimilate them to the bourgeoisie, as did Clement. One can therefore question the validity of the very concept of an economic élite, since this "élite" consists, in fact, of three distinct groups: the large stockholders (the controlling group), the salaried managers and various types of advisers. Each of these three groups is in a very different position of stock ownership and of remuneration from the large corporation. Moreover, the economic élite has no history of its own but, rather, a history borrowed by Mills and Clement from the bourgeoisie. We can conclude that the economic élite is nothing more than the big bourgeoisie, poorly delineated and just as poorly conceptualized.

The Canadian Ruling Class

To the opening question—who controls Canadian big business?—one is led to reply, the Canadian ruling class. This ruling class, whose group unity is assured by its economic and social organizations, its marriage ties and its interlocking directorships, consists of two major groups: a dominant inner circle of families and individuals (the corporate rich of Mills, the "millionnaires" of Menshikov) and a subordinate group of salaried senior executives. This latter group only joins the rulint class for one generation, since its appropriation of surplus the ruling class for one generation rather than from legal ownership. A few of them, however, manage to win themselves a permanent position and thus assure not just their own assimilation with "the better elements of the subordinate classes" of the big bourgeoisie, but, as well, a broader base for the continuity of the ruling class.

This conclusion agrees with that of Sweezy concerning the American ruling class:

> "It would be a mistake to think of a class as perfectly homogeneous internally and sharply marked off from other classes. . . We must therefore think of a class as being made up of a core surrounded by fringes which are in varying degrees attached to the core. A fringe may be more or less stable and have a well-defined function in relation to the class as a whole, or it may be temporary and accidental. Moreover, we must not think of all the class members (in either the family or the individual sense) as playing the same role in the class: some are active, some passive; some leaders, some followers; and so on. . . The core of the ruling class is made up of big capitalists (or, more generally, big property owners, though the distinction is not very important since most large aggregates of property have the form of capital in this country today). There are numerous fringes to the ruling class, including smaller property owners, government and business executives (in so far as they are not big owners in their own right), professionals and so on."[1]

The Canadian ruling class may be characterized by a number of distinctive traits. First, it is largely concentrated in Toronto and

Montréal, although it is pan-Canadian in several regards. For one thing, it has representation in almost every large city; for another, large Canadian companies are active from coast to coast. The distribution of headquarters and effective control (parent companies of the conglomerates), by province and by city, bears out this interpretation.

There is a discrepancy between the two columns, "Headquarters" and "Effective Control". This is because the parent companies of three large conglomerates (Bell Canada, C.P. Ltd. and Power Corp.) are headquartered in Montréal and four others (Argus Corp., E-L Financial Corp., Canadian General Investments and Canadian General Securities) in Toronto.

MAJOR CANADIAN COMPANIES

Distribution of Headquarters, by city and by province			Effective Control	
	H.Q.	(%)		
Ontario	65	(48%)	75	(55%)
Toronto	48		61	
Québec	30	(22%)	37	(27%)
Montréal	27		34	
Alberta	14	(10%)	11	(8%)
Calgary	11		9	
British Columbia	13	(10%)	7	(5%)
Vancouver	12		7	
Manitoba	6	(4%)	4	(3%)
New Brunswick	4	(3%)	1	(1%)
Nova Scotia	2	(1%)	—	—
Newfoundland	2	(1%)	1	(1%)
	136	100%	136	100%

The permanent and dominant inner circle consists of families who have controlled major Canadian enterprises for generations: the Molsons, the Maclarens, the Eatons, the Richardsons, the Meighens, the Gundys, the Russels, the Jefferys, the Websters, etc. The dependent nature of the Canadian economy has consequences even for the continuity of the local bourgeoisie: a number of its most representative members have emigrated to England (e.g. Lord Strathcona, Lord Beaverbrook, Lord Thomson of Fleet) or to the United States (James T. Hill) and integrated themselves with the ruling classes of those countries. The original Anglo-Saxon inner circle, the oldest circle, has been joined by other elements, in particular, by a Jewish bourgeoisie which began to appear around the time of World War I (e.g. Bronfmans, Steinbergs, Loebs, Wolfes, Belzbergs, Wolinskys) and a French-Canadian bourgeoisie (the Desmarais, the Bombardier, etc.). Most of the companies controlled by French-Canadians are too small to appear on our list; however, they are growing quickly and a few of them have already reached quite respectable proportions—for example, the Simard family's group of companies, the Sodarcan group (of the Parizeau family), the Québecor group (of Pierre Péladeau) and Provigo. In another article, we deal separately with French-Canadian capitalism and its control. [2]

Ethnic origin is a factor of major importance within the ruling class, and in a variety of ways. First, there is a most unequal representation of the major Canadian population groups. According to Porter or Clement, there is a clear over-representation of Anglo-Saxons and assimilated ethnic groups, which control 80% of the companies on our list. The Jewish group, which owns 10% of the companies, is also over-represented. The French-Canadian group, with only thirteen companies (including Power Corp. and its eight subsidiaries) on our list, controls barely 10% of the total: sufficient to say that this group is markedly *under*-represented. Anglo-Saxons dominate the oldest sectors of activity, such as banks, insurance companies, mortage companies and industry. The Jewish group is much less important in industry: only three major industrial companies out of fifty (6%) are controlled by Jewish businessmen, namely. The Seagram Co., Ivaco Industries and Kruger Pulp & Paper. This group, however, is much more prominent in the various branches of finance, commerce and real estate. Only four independent companies on our list (Power Corp., Trust Général du Canada, Bombardier Corp. and Campeau Corp.) are owned by French-Canadian businessmen. To this short list one must, of course, add the two French-Canadian chartered banks, one of which (Banque Provinciale du Canada) is under the control of the Québec Federation of the Caisses Populaires Desjardins. We cannot identify the locus of control for the other one, the Banque Canadienne Nationale.

This unequal ethnic representation is accompanied by a tendency for holders of control to recruit their advisers from their own ethnic group. Appendix I, for example, shows that almost all the lawyers who sit on the boards of French-Canadian companies are themselves French-Canadian. One finds the same phenomenon in companies controlled by Anglo-Saxon or Jewish businessmen.

A third indication of the importance of this ethnic division is that very few companies are under the joint control of two different ethnic groups. In the rare exceptions to this general rule—for example, M. Loeb Co. or Jannock Corp.—it is always an association between Anglo-Saxon businessmen and other non-French Canadians. This can probably be explained by the very small numerical size of the French-Canadian bourgeoisie.

The Canadian ruling class exercises its control through a variety of institutions, most frequently, through private holding companies. In at least 20 independent companies, this is the intermediary used by the controlling families, individuals or groups of associates. Here are a few examples.

Company Under Control	Private Holding Company
Argus Corporation	Ravelston Corporation
Deltan Corporation	Prudel Ltd.
Crown Life Insurance	Scotia Investments; Kingfield Investments
Power Corporation	Gelco Enterprises
Bombardier Ltée	Les Entreprises J.A. Bombardier Ltée
Bramalea Consolidated Deve.	Braminuest Corporation
First City Financial Corporation	Bel Alta Holdings, Bel Cal Holdings Bel Fran Holdings
Maclaren Power & Paper	MacRoy Investments, MacBar Investments C.H. Maclaren Trust Co.
T. Eaton Co.	Eaton's of Canada Ltd.
Prenor Group	Gilbert Securities

In other cases, the controlling interests use charitable foundations for the same purposes as a private holding company. Representative examples of this phenomenon are the Molson Foundation, the George Weston Foundation and the Fondation Jean-Louis Lévesque.

Sometimes a mixed formula for control is preferred, using a variety of intermediaries. IAC Ltd., for example, is controlled by Edward and Peter Bronfman, through the following pyramidal structure:

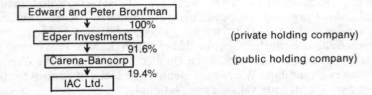

The private holding companies, the foundations and the private trusts perform several different control functions. They hold together the shares of a group of associates (as in Ravelston Corp.) or of a family (like Cemp Investments and Edper Investments, belonging respectively to the children of Samuel and of Allan Bronfman). They thus prevent the dispersal of securities and the eventual loss of control that such a dispersal could engender. Furthermore, these intermediaries serve to transmit shares, and thus control, from one generation to the next. They also insure maximum secrecy and confidentiality, and provide ways around both income and succession taxes. These companies are therefore an essential part in the reproduction and continuity of the ruling class.

Public holding companies, on the other hand, serve to centralize control of companies which one cannot or does not wish to merge. Controlling groups prefer holding companies to outright mergers when they wish to (or must) preserve a provincial incorporation of subsidiary companies, when they find themselves faced with a minority group of shareholders firmly opposed to total absorption, or when the very diversity of the subsidiaries' activites makes merger difficult. Public holding companies are nothing more than a type of concentration; they cannot possibly be seen as examples of "finance capital".

This book has separated out a few of the characteristics of the Canadian bourgeoisie, a bourgeoisie which one would have trouble calling "national" or "nationalist", but which may be called "local" or "internal." What connections does this ruling class have with the subsidiaries of American companies established in Canada? Data presented in preceding chapters suggest that there are few instances of association or joint control, with Alcan Aluminium and Inco being the exceptions. For each of the major companies incorporated in Canada, one can identify the national locus of control. From this, one can claim that the Canadian bourgeoisie does exist and that it has its own social boundaries: neither economically nor socially does it dissolve into or mingle with an American bourgeoisie. However, Canadian capitalism has a complementary relationship with American (dominant) capitalism in Canada: Canadian companies are strongest in finance, utilities, transportation and communications, real estate and traditional industry (with the exception of steel and agricultural machinery). In sum, Canadian capitalism and its bourgeoisie are strong in the simpler technological fields or the more traditional ones. And that is one of the distinctive traits of Canada's dependence on the United States: to the extent that most modern sectors of industry are technologically off-limits to this bourgeoisie, it is imprisoned in the sectors which it already occupies, and "nationalist" legislation at the federal or provincial level is primarily a defensive action to prevent even banks, insurance companies and communications from being absorbed by American companies. This is not to deny that a number of Canadian companies—such as chartered banks, insurance companies, transportation companies, utilities, and even a few industrial companies—have become sizeable multinationals. But we insist—and here we are in agreement with Tom Naylor—that the essential trait of the Canadian bourgeoisie is its non-industrial and dependent character.

The theoretical and empirical conclusions presented above should be followed by a few methodological remarks which will help to explain both our own use of data and that of the authors criticized in these pages. First, a word about sources. The Parks believed in banking and financial control of industry, or the banking-industry "merger", largely because of their theoretical orientation, but at least partly because of the incomplete nature of their sources. Their work, originally published in 1962, could not take advantage of "Inter-Corporate Ownership", which first appeared in 1965. It would have shown them that the banking and financial control theory and the "bank-industry merger" theory were invalid, at least as far as stock ownership is concerned. Porter and Clement believed that all directors of major corporations belonged to an undifferentiated economic élite of ownership. Obviously, they were inspired by the élite theory of C. Wright Mills, but it is also the fact that they did not examine the most complete possible sources for information concerning ownership of shares by directors and senior corporate executives, namely, the Monthly Bulletins of the Securities Commissions of Ontario (which began to appear in June 1967) and of Québec (which began in March 1974). In each case, the results obtained were the consequences not only of a theoretical choice by the authors but also of the availability (or selection) of sources with which to work.

One can make the same remarks about our own material. If we tend to reject the most recent version of the theory of finance capital (that of Chevalier and Menshikov), it is partly because we believe Sweezy, O'Connor and Herman present more solid arguments, but also because we do not have access to the statistics which would allow us to cross-check Chevalier's or Menshikov's position on the new forms of control by financial institutions. The fact is that there are no complete public statistics on the stock portfolios of the pension funds directed by these trust companies or on the shares held by the life-insurance companies. We have figures and precise data only on the shares held by the mutual funds. We had, therefore, to depend on more qualitative and aggregate figures to reach our conclusions which negate Chevalier's position. In other words, more complete statistics might have led to a partial modification of our results.

Lacking data about ownership of shares, Porter, Clement and the Parks committed the error of drawing numerous conclusions from available information on interlocking directorships. However, we now know that one person may sit on several boards because he is the major shareholder in the companies concerned, or because he is lawyer or financial adviser to the companies, without those enterprises having any connection with each other. It is methodologically incorrect to confuse the two types of "interlocking directorships" and one runs the risk of drawing theoretically false conclusions. For example, Park and Park believed they saw in the exchange of directors between chartered banks and major non-financial companies a proof of control by the banks and other financial institutions over industry or, at least, a proof of "fusion". But this is not at all the case: the banks just as frequently invite senior executives and major shareholders of industrial companies to sit on their boards as they send their managers to the boards of their industrial and commercial clients. Moreover, as we saw in the charts I—VII in this book, the various conglomerates or financial groups similarly exchange directors between the parent company and the subsidiaries, and there is no direct relationship between the degree of control and the number of directors the two companies have in common. It is therefore dangerous to employ this criterion without reference to the more solid and more determining link of stock ownership.

Porter and Clement could now abandon their theory of the internal unity of boards of directors. Not all voices in senior management of companies have the same weight. Paul Desmarais certainly has more authority than any of the four lawyers who sit on the boards of his Montréal holding company. If one breaks the boards down into owners, managers and advisers, one can assuredly draw more sophisticated conclusions than those drawn by the partisans of the élite theory. On these boards, one generally finds major shareholders, career managers as a subordinate and dependent fraction of the ownership class and, finally, advisers who generally do not belong to the bourgeoisie since they have neither enough stock nor huge remuneration for their efforts. Moreover, as Domhoff has already pointed out, not all the bourgeoisie is engaged in running companies any more than it is in running the State. Some major shareholders leave the running of the large enterprises to salaried managers and consultants, satisfied to watch them from the exterior—becoming, in the words of Marx, "capitalist money-lenders". In such cases, the company in question looks like it is under managerial control; the relationships between the active (managers) and the passive capitalists (non-directing shareholders) are often well hidden, but they exist.

This situation is strikingly illustrated by several companies which, in chapter II, we classified as being under managerial control but which might very well turn out to be still under the control of the founding families (the Davises in Alcan Aluminium, the Hatches in Hiram Walker-Gooderham & Worts, the Macleans in Canada Packers, etc.) or, in other cases, under the control of individuals or groups of associates who do not sit on the boards. Let us recall that ever since the Ontario Securities Act of 1966 and the Québec Securities Act of July 1973 (chapter 67 of the Laws of Québec, 1973), only the directors and the senior management of companies quoted on the stock exchange are required to declare to the respective Commissions all transactions carried out affecting all capital securities of the companies with which they are associated. All associates of these directors or senior executives must do likewise. By "associate", the laws mean every member of their family who has the same home, every trust or estate in which the directors and senior executives have substantial beneficial interest and all companies in which they own directly or indirectly equity shares carrying more than 10% of the voting rights. As well, every company or individual holding more than 10% of the voting stock in a company must declare it. All this means that a family with several members each holding 9.5% of the voting rights in a company, but who leave the running of the company to their managers and advisers, need not declare anything to the Commission and nothing will appear in the Monthly Bulletins of transactions. Similarly, if in a family whose members do *not* live under the same roof, only one or a few of them sit on the board of a family company, then only that one or few of them must declare holdings. One can fill in some of these information gaps by studying the financial and daily papers and the annual publications of Moody's and the Financial Post. But precise identification of the groups and of their real level of control would require additional information which is not available to the public.

(1) P. Sweezy: *The Present as History*, Monthly Review Press, New York 1953, pp. 124-125 and 128.

(2) J. Niosi: "La nouvelle bourgeoisie canadienne-française" in *Cahiers du Socialisme* N° 1, Montréal, Spring 1978.

BIBLIOGRAPHY

General and Comparative Theory

Books

D.J. Baum and N.B. Stiles: *The Silent Partners: Institutional Investors and Corporate Control,* Syracuse Univ. Press, New York, 1965.
H. Baverman: *Labor and Monopoly Capital,* Monthly Review Press, New York, 1974.
A.A. Berle Jr: *Power Without Property,* Harcourt, Brace & Co, New York, 1959.
A.A. Berle Jr. and G. Means: *The Modern Corporation and Private Property,* (1932), Harcourt, Brace & World, 1968.
J.M. Blair: *Economic Concentration,* World, Brace & Jovanovitch, New York, 1972.
J.C. Bonbright and G. Means: *The Holding Company* (1932), A.M. Kelley, New York, 1969.
T. Bottomore: *Elites and Society,* C.A. Watts, London, 1964.
J. Bouvier: *Un siècle de banque française,* Hachette, Paris, 1973.
P.H. Burch: *The Managerial Revolution Reassessed,* Health & Co. Lexington, Mass., 1972.
J. Burnham: *The Managerial Revolution* (1942), Penguin, London, 1962.
R. Cameron (ed.): *Banking in the Early Stages of Industrialization,* Oxford University Press, New York, 1967.
R. Cameron (ed.): *Banking and Economic Development,* Oxford University Press, New York, 1972.
V.P. Carosso: *Investment Banking in America,* Harvard Univ. Press, 1970.
J.-M. Chevalier: *La structure financière de l'industrie américaine,* Cujas, Paris, 1969.
R. Dahrendorf: *Classes et conflits de classes dans les sociétés industrielles* (1957), Mouton, Paris, 1972.
G.W. Domhoff: *C.W. Mills and the Power Elite,* Beacon Press, Boston, 1968.
G.W. Domhoff: *Fat Cats and Democrats,* Prentice Hall, New Jersey, 1972.
G.W. Domhoff: *The Higher Circles,* Vintage Books, New York, 1971.
G.W. Domhoff: *Who rules America?,* New Jersey, 1967.
A. Downs: *An Economic Theory of Democracy,* Harper, New York, 1957.
J.K. Galbraith: *American Capitalism,* Houghton, Miffllin Co, Boston, 1952.
J.K. Galbraith: *The New Industrial State,* Houghton, Mifflin Co, Boston, 1967.
A. Gerschenkron: *Economic Backwardness in Historical Perspective,* Praeger, New York, 1965.
A. Gramsci: *Oeuvres Choisies,* Ed. Sociales, Paris, 1959.
A.T.K. Grant: *A study of the capital market in Britain from 1919 to 1936,* (2nd ed.), A.M. Kelley, New York, 1967.
R. Hilferding: *Le Capital Financier* (1910), Ed. de Minuit, Paris, 1970.
J. Houssiaux: *Le Pouvoir de Monopole,* Sirey, Paris, 1958.
G. Kolko: *Wealth and Power in America,* Praeger Publishers, New York, 1962.
R. Larner: *Management Control and the Large Corporation,* Dunellen, New York, 1970.
V.I. Lénine: *Cahiers de l'Impérialisme,* O.C., Tome 39, Ed. Sociales, Paris, 1970.
F. Lundberg: *The Rich and the Super-Rich,* Bantam Books, New York, 1968.
H. Magdoff: *The Age of Imperialism,* Monthly Review Press, New York, 1967.
S. Menshikov: *Millionaires and Managers,* Progress, Moscow, 1969.
R. Miliband: *The State in Capitalist Society,* Wiedenfeld and Nicholson, London, 1969.
C.W. Mills: *The Power Elite,* Oxford Univ. Press, New York, 1956.
F. Morin: *La structure financière du capitalisme français,* Paris, Calman-Lévy, 1975.
B.D. Nash: *Investment Banking in England,* A. Shaw & Co, Chicago and New York, 1924.
R.L. Nelson: *The Investment Policies of Foundations,* Russell Sage, New York, 1967.
W.A. Nielson: *The Big Foundations,* Columbia University Press, New York, 1972.
V. Perlo: *The Empire of High Finance,* International Publishers, New York, 1961.
A. Rochester: *Rulers of America: A study of finance capital,* F. White Publishers, Toronto, 1936.
P. Sargant Florence: *Ownership, control and success of large companies,* London, 1961.
E.O. Smigel: *The Wall Street Lawyer,* Indiana University Press, Bloomington, 1969.
D.N. Smith: *Who rules the Universities?* Monthly Review Press, New York, 1970.
S. Schwarzchild & E.A. Zubay: *Principles of Life Insurance,* R.C. Irwin & Co., Illinois, 1964, 2 volumes.
P. Sweezy: *The Present as History,* Monthly Review Press, New York, 1953.
P. Sweezy: *The Theory of Capitalist Development* (1942), Dobson, New York, 1967.
P. Sweezy: and P. Baran: *Monopoly Capital,* Monthly Review Press, New York, 1966.
J.S. Warner and C. Russell Doane: *Investment Trusts & Funds,* Boston, 1955.
F.B. Whale: *Joint stock banking in Germany,* McMillan & Co., London, 1930.

Articles

R. Aron: "Social Structure and the Ruling Class", in *British Journal of Sociology,* I[1], March 1950 and I[2] June 1950.
J.O'Connor: "Finance capital or corporate capital" in *Monthly Review,* New York, Dec. 1968.
G.W. Domhoff: "Some friendly answers to radical critics" in *The Insurgent Sociologist,* Oregon, Spring 1972.
G.W. Domhoff: "State and Ruling Class in Corporate America" in *The Insurgent Sociologist,* Oregon, Spring 1972.
R. Fitch: "Reply", in *Socialist Revolution,* (vol. 2, No. 7) Jan-Feb. 1971.
R. Fitch: "Sweezy and Corporate Fetishism" in *Socialist Revolution,* (Vol. 2, No. 12), Dec. 1972.

R. Fitch and M. Oppenheimer: "Who rules the Corporations?" in *Socialist Revolution*, (Vol. 1, Nos. 4, 5, 6), San Francisco, July-Dec. 1970.

E. Herman: "Do bankers control corporations?" in *Monthly Review*, New York, June 1973.

R.J. Larner: "Ownership and control in the 200 largest non-financial corporations, 1929 and 1963", in *American Economic Review*, Sept. 1966.

F. Lundberg: "The Law Factories: brains of the Status Quo", in *Harper's Magazine*, New York, 1939, No. 190.

E.S. Mason: "The Apologetics of Managerialism" in *The Journal of Business of the University of Chicago*, Vol. XXXI, Jan. 1958.

M. Meyer: "The Wall Street Lawyers" in *Harper's Magazine*, New York, 1956, No. 212.

V. Perlo: "People's Capitalism and stock ownership", in *American Economic Review*, June 1958.

P. Sweezy: "The Resurgence of Financial Control: Fact or Fancy?" in *Socialist Revolution*, (Vol. 2, No. 8), Mar-April 1972 and in *Monthly Review*, Nov. 1971.

D. Villajero: "Stock ownership and the Control of Corporations", in *New University Thought*, Autumn 1961, Winter 1972.

M. Zeitlin: "Corporate ownership and control: the large corporation and the Capitalist Class" in *American Journal of Sociology*, Vol. 79, No. 5.

Canada

Books and Theses

H. Aitken: *American Capital and Canadian Resources,* Harvard Univ. Press, Toronto, 1961.

C.A. Ashley and J.C. Smyth: *Corporation Finance in Canada,* MacMillan, Toronto, 1956.

D.J. Baum: *The Investment Function of Canadian Financial Institutions,* Praeger, New York, 1973.

H. Bullock: *The Story of Investment Companies,* New York, Columbia Univ. Press, 1959.

R. Chodos: *The C.P.R.: A Century of Corporate Welfare,* J. Lorimer & Co., Toronto, 1973.

W. Clement: *The Canadian Corporate Elite,* McClelland & Stewart, Carleton Library, Toronto, 1975.

A.E. Epp: *Cooperation among Capitalists: the Canadian Merger Movement, 1909-1913,* Ph. D. Thesis, The Johns Hopkins University, Baltimore, Maryland, 1973.

R.C. Fetherstonhaugh: *Charles F. Sise,* Gazette Printing Co., Montreal, 1944.

J.L. Heap (ed): *Everybody's Canada,* Burns & MacEachen, Toronto, 1974.

L.S. Keoch: *Restrictive Trades Practices in Canada,* McClelland & Stewart, Toronto, 1966.

K. Levitt: *Silent Surrender,* Macmillan, Toronto, 1970.

O.W. Main: *The Canadian Nickel Industry,* Univ. of Toronto Press, Toronto, 1955.

F. Marshall et al: *Canadian American Industry (1936),* McClelland & Stewart, Carleton Library, 1976.

J.L. McDougall: *Canadian Pacific,* McGill University Press, 1968.

T. Naylor: *The History of Canadian Business 1867-1914,* (2 vol.), J. Lorimer & Co., Toronto, 1975.

E.P. Neufeld: *A Global Corporation: A History of the International Development of Massey-Ferguson,* Univ. of Toronto Press, 1969.

E.P. Neufeld: *The Financial system of Canada,* Macmillan of Canada, Toronto, 1972.

P.C. Newman: *Flame of Power,* McClelland and Stewart, Toronto, 1959.

P.C. Newman: *The Canadian Establishment,* Vol. 1, McClelland and Stewart, Toronto, 1975.

F. and L. Park: *Anatomy of Big Business* (1962), James Lewis & Samuel, Toronto, 1973.

J. Porter: *The Vertical Mosaic,* Univ. of Toronto Press, Toronto, 1965.

G. Rosenbluth: *Concentration in Canadian Manufacturing Industries,* Princeton University Press, 1957.

J. Schull: *The Century of the Sun,* Macmillan of Canada, Toronto, 1971.

H.G. Stapells: *The Recent Consolidation Movement in Canadian Industry,* M.A. Thesis, Univ. of Toronto, 1922.

A.J.P. Taylor: *Beaverbrook,* Penguin Books, London, 1974.

D.H. Wallace: *Market Control in the Aluminium Industry,* Cambridge, Harvard Univ. Press, 1937.

J.P. Williamson: *Securities Regulation in Canada,* Univ. of Toronto Press, 1960.

Articles

C.A. Ashley: "Concentration of Economic Power" in *Canadian Journal of Economics and Political Science,* Vol. XXIII, No. 1, Feb. 1957.

"Brokers, the Battle for Survival" in *Montreal Star,* 26/10/74, page G-1. "La Bourse perd du terrain au profit des banques" in *La Presse,* 23/9/76, p. B-5.

J. Porter: "Concentration of Economic Power and the Economic Elite in Canada" in *Canadian Journal of Economics and Political Science,* Vol. XXII, No. 2, May 1956.

J. Porter: "Elite groups: a Scheme for the Study of Power in Canada" in *Canadian Journal of Economics and Political Science,* Vol. XXI, No. 4, 1955.

G. Rosenbluth: "Concentration and Monopoly in the Canadian Economy", in M. Oliver (ed): *Social Purpose for Canada,* University of Toronto Press, 1961.

J. Weldon: "Consolidations in Canadian Industry 1900-1948", in L. Skeoch: *Restrictive Trade Practices in Canada,* McClelland & Stewart, Toronto, 1976.

Government Documents and Sources

House of Commons: *Standing Committee on Banking & Finance*, 1928 session, "Sur le Perfectionnement du régime bancaire au Canada"
House of Commons: Standing Committee on Banking and Finance, 1934 session.
Committee on Election Expenses: *Studies in Canadian Party Finance*, Queen's Printer, Ottawa 1966.
Committee on Election Expenses: *Report*, Queen's Printer, Ottawa, 1966.
Quebec Securities Commission: Monthly Bulletin, Montreal, 1972-76.
Royal Commission on Price Spreads, *Report* and *Appendices*, King's Printer, Ottawa 1935.
Royal Commission on Banking and Finance: *Report*, Queen's Printer, Ottawa 1966.
Ontario Legislature: *Report of the Nickel Commission*, Sessional Papers, Toronto 1917.
Ontario Securities Commission: *Bulletin* (monthly), Toronto, 1967-76.
Gray Report: *Foreign Direct Investment in Canada*, Information Canada, 1972.
Statistics Canada: *Inter-Corporate Ownership*, 1965, 1967, 1969, 1972, Information Canada, Ottawa.

Privately-Published

A.E. Ames & Co: *A.E. Ames & Co., 1899-1949*, Toronto, 1950.
A. Arlett: *A Canadian Directory to Foundations*, Association of Universities and Colleges of Canada, Ottawa, 1973.
Houston Publishing Co: *Annual Financial Review*, Toronto, (Annual), 1901-1960.
International Press Ltd: *Who's who in Canada*, (Annual), Toronto, 1912-1976.
Martindale—Hubbell Law Directory (Annual), Quinn & Boder, New Jersey, 1976.
MacLean-Hunter Ltd: *Financial Post* (weekly), Toronto, 1910-1976.
MacLean-Hunter Ltd: *Financial Post Corporation Services* (Annual), Toronto, 1976.
MacLean-Hunter Ltd: *Financial Post Directory of Directors*, (Annual), Toronto, 1931-1976.
MacLean-Hunter Ltd: *Financial Post Survey of Corporate Securities* (Annual), Toronto, 1927-1948.
MacLean-Hunter Ltd: *Financial Post Survey of Funds* (Annual), Toronto, 1962-1976.
MacLean-Hunter Ltd: *Financial Post Survey of Industrials* (Annual), Toronto, 1949-1976.
MacLean-Hunter Ltd: *Financial Post Survey of Mines* (Annual), Toronto, 1926-1976.
MacLean-Hunter Ltd: *Financial Post Survey of Oils* (Annual), Toronto, 1936-1976.
Moody's Investor Service Inc: *Moody's Bank & Finance Manual*, (Annual), New York, 1928-1976.
Moody's Investor Service Inc: *Moody's Bond Survey*, (Annual), New York, 1909-1976.
Moody's Investor Service Inc: *Moody's Industrial Manual*, (Annual), New York, 1914-1976.
Moody's Investor Service Inc: *Moody's Transportation Manual*, (Annual), New York, 1928-1976.
Moody's Investor Service Inc: *Moody's Utility Manual*, (Annual), New York, 1920-1976.
Standard & Poor's Corp.: *Standard & Poor's Register of Corporations, Directors & Executives* (Annual), New York, 1928-1976.
The Conference Board in Canada: *Canadian Directorship Practices: Compensation 1976*, Ottawa, 1976.
The Conference Board in Canada: *Stock options plans*, Ottawa, 1973.
The Globe Publishing Co: *Commercial Register of Canada*, London, 1930.
Who's Who Canadian Publications: *The Canadian Who's Who*, (Irregular), 1912-1976.
A. Young & Co: *Top Management Compensation*, New York, 1976.

IS THE CANADIAN ECONOMY CLOSING DOWN?

edited by Fred Caloren

Two economists and a sociologist carefully examine the Canadian economy and some of its basic problems. Professor Michel Chossudosky of the Department of Economics, University of Ottawa looks at the structural problems built into the economy, while Professor Paul Gingrich who teaches statistics and demography at the University of Regina surveys the nature and extent of unemployment by studing critically among other factors the role of *Statistics Canada*. Professor Gingrich shows that unemployment statistics are incomplete and misleading. Professor Fred Caloren of the Department of Sociology, University of Ottawa contributes a major study on the implications of layoffs and plant shutdowns, the results of an investigation which took several years to complete.

Prof. Caloren introduces the collection by situating these outstanding economic issues. The book is written lucidly and will be useful to a large readership.

200 pages/Hardcover $16.95/Paperback $5.95
ISBN: 0-919618-81-2/ISBN: 0-919618-80-4

Contains: Canadian Shared Cataloguing in Publication Data

BLACK ROSE BOOKS No. H43

THE CITY AND RADICAL SOCIAL CHANGE

edited by Dimitrios Roussopoulos

What is the role of the city in determining the evolution of society as a whole? What perspective do people who fight to improve public transportation, housing, public health and related issues have? What are the results of the community-organising movement in cities like Montréal? How have the concepts of participatory democracy, decentralisation, and the creation of neighbourhood councils evolved?

With a focus on Montréal, the book examines through a collection of essays the dynamics of the community-organising movement and its impact on urban politics. The contributors follow the emergence of various municipal political parties including the Front d'Action Politique and the Montréal Citizens Movement (MCM). The major controversies surrounding the MCM are included, after it became the official opposition political party to the Drapeau dominated City Council. The internal developments of the MCM are analyzed, its strategies, its tactics, its overall impact on neighbourhoods as well as the evolution of its programme. Most of the articles are drawn from the journal *OUR GENERATION*. Additional material on the MCM is drawn from various documents and published reports. An evaluation of the MCM and the municipal elections during the fall of 1978 is included.

280 pages Hardcover $16.95/Paperback $5.95
ISBN: 0-919618-83-9/ISBN: 0-919618-82-0

Contains: Canadian Shared Cataloguing in Publication Data

BLACK ROSE BOOKS No. H44

NATIONALISM AND THE NATIONAL QUESTION

by Jacques Dofny and Nicole Arnaud

translated by Penelope Williams

This book is a dialogue between two sociologists. It is a comparison based on personal experience and study of nationalism and of the national question as it has evolved in Québec and Occitanie (at present a region of France).

What are the dynamics of nationalism in Québec in comparison to Occitanie, which also has a distinct culture, history and geographical area within France? The Nation-states of Europe and North America, have many smaller nations and cultures within them struggling for one form of self-determination or another — Wales, Scotland, Basque, Catalonia, Dene, Blacks and many others. What should be the essential elements of a radical analysis of the national question, given this reality? National or cultural self-determination has not vanished in advanced industrial societies, why? With an emphasis on the Québec and Occitanian situation, the book concludes with a major chapter evaluating the first eight months of the Parti Québécois government and the new Québec.

The two authors are Jacques Dofny, professor of sociology at the Université de Montréal and president of the Institut de recherche appliquée sur le travail, and Professor Nicole Arnaud who teaches at the Université Laval.

200 pages / Hardcover $16.95 / Paperback $5.95
ISBN: 0-919618-46-4/ISBN: 0-919618-45-6

Contains: Canadian Shared Cataloguing in Publication Data

BLACK ROSE BOOKS No. G 38

THE POLITICS OF URBAN LIBERATION

by Stephen Schecter

A broad-ranging study which covers the political economy of the urban question and the importance of the city in the history of social revolution. Prof. Schecter provides the reader with an original evaluation of libertarian insurgency during this century in various countries and urban struggles. The importance of movements from below dealing with housing, transportation and other issues of daily life are contrasted to classical upheavals.

The city is also examined as a focal point of social control for authoritarian societies. The case of Montréal is carefully examined and an evaluation of the radical potential of the Montréal Citizens Movement (MCM) is offered.

Professor Schecter studied at McGill University and received his Ph.D., from the London School of Economics and Political Science. Dr. Schecter teaches sociology at l'Université du Québec à Montréal and is an activist in the MCM.

"This book not only offers an important body of analysis with which to look at the city and the urban question but also offers the most important social and political perspective to date with which to build a revolutionary movement in an advanced industrial/technological society".

Dimitrios Roussopoulos

240 pages/Hardcover $16.95/Paperback $5.95
ISBN: 0-919618-79-0/ISBN: 0-919618-78-2

Contains: Canadian Shared Cataloguing in Publication Data

BLACK ROSE BOOKS No. H42

BETWEEN LABOR AND CAPITAL
BY PAT WALKER

What are the functions and class alliances of those between labour and capital: technicians, scientists, managers, administrators, professionals, teachers, service workers, cultural and media producers? Is their purpose to manage the working class and society for the capitalists, or does their vision of a rationally planned society truly represent the middle class' own interests and attempts to supercede the class struggle? Do these middle strata constitute a new third class, "The Professional and Managerial Class," or will different sectors tend to ally with either the working class or the capitalists, or does the emergence of the middle strata require a whole new conception of the dynamics of social change? This book takes off from a controversial piece written by John and Barbara Ehrenreich and proceeds with a series of extensions and critiques of their approach by Ann Ferguson, Erik Olin Wright, Al Syzmmansky, David Noble, Stanley Aronowitz, Jean Cohen and Dick Howard, and others, *Between Labor and Capital* represents a major step forward towards understanding the class structure of North America.

049/200 pages/Hardcover $16.95/Paperback $6.95

THE INDUSTRIAL SYNDICALIST
WITH AN INTRODUCTION BY GEOFF BROWN

The seeding of the syndicalist upheaval, which had a profound effect on many workers, and could be said to have transformed whole sections of the British Trade Union Movement, can all be traced back to the modest publication which is reproduced here. This collection has an authoritative introduction by Brown, the biographer of Tom Mann, which admirably explains the context in which Mann was operating.

034 / Paperback $5.25 / Hardcover $11.00

Printed by
the workers of
Editions Marquis, Montmagny, Québec
for
Black Rose Books Ltd.